My Participation in the National War of Liberation 1984 - 2005

§

Jurkuch Barach Jurkuch

The ideas and opinions in this book are ultimately those of the author. Their authenticity is the responsibility of the author, not Africa World Books.

The publisher wishes to acknowledge and thank Dr. Douglas H. Johnson for his invaluable help and support for Africa World Books and its mission of preserving and promoting African cultural and literary traditions and history. Dr. Johnson and fellow historians have been instrumental in ensuring that African people remain connected to their past and their identity. Africa World Books is proud to carry on this mission.

© Jurkuch Barach Jurkuch, 2022, All rights reserved.

ISBN: 9780645522914

No part of this publication may be reproduced, stored in a retrieval system, or transmitted, in any form, or by any means, electronic, mechanical, photocopying, recording or otherwise, without the prior permission of the publishers.

This book is sold subject to the conditions that it shall not, by way of trade or otherwise, be lent, re-sold, hired out or otherwise circulated without the publisher's prior consent in any form of binding or cover other than in which it is published and without a similar condition including the condition being imposed on the subsequent purchaser.

Cover design, typesetting and layout : Africa World Books

Acknowledgements

Metaphorically, I would like to appreciate the Staff of the Africa World Book Centre for great role and the updated job they have made for the book to be accomplished. My heartfelt gratitude to Brother Peter Lual Reech Deng, and his colleagues for making this historic event for me and my Family.

Again, my sincere appreciation goes to my intimate and honest brother Chol Akoi (Lothdit) de Jurkuch Yaak for financial contribution for the book production. Without your Grant delivery Mr. Chol, this work would have not been materialised. This is the dedication from the bottom of my heart Mr. Chol. I hope you will do more.

My appreciation also goes to my brother and friend Atem Garang Deng de Kuek, for his splendid contribution. Mr. de Kuek participated thoroughly in the revision and betterment of the book. My thanks and regards to you Mr. Atem Garang.

I also recognized contribution of Brothers General Pieng Deng Kuol, Koang Dawnhier, Dr. Majak da Agoot Atem, Abel Manyok Ajak Cheng, Abuoi Arok Deng, Dau (Jerus) Akoi Jurkuch, Maduk Dau Koach, Marshall Stephen Babaanen, James Hoth Mai, Malony Akau Nai, Atem Zachariah Duot Atem, Gier Chung Aluong, Riak Jeroboam Machuor Kulang Abrham Gieth Dau Koach and for their worthily support.

Finally, I would appreciate my lovely wives, Achol Juach diing, Nyibol Nathan Riak Anyuon and the kids for their moral encouragement and relentless stand by my side during the long and exhaustive writing process.

Prologue

Thank you, dear reader, for showing an interest in the history of South Sudan. It has endured a long and difficult struggle for independence, hoping to improve the lives of its people. I've been proud to represent my country and contribute to this change.

To share a little about my background. I was born in Twic East County, Nyuak Payam at a place called Ajuong da Ayual in 1950 to the family of Barach-dit de Jurkuch de Barach de Jurkuch de Yaak, Sub-section Panwiir of Ayuaal Clan.

I attended Kongor Elementary School in 1960 and achieved my elementary certificate from Thoura Elementary School in Malakal and then joined Jongulei Intermediate School in 1969.

When President Jaafer Mohamed Nimeiri ceased power overnight in May 1969, the system of education was changed by el Ustaz Mohidin Sabir. I therefore had to sit exams for senior secondary school in 1974 and was admitted to Malakal Senior Secondary School. In 1977, I completed senior secondary school and got accepted at Zagazig University in Egypt at the faculty of commerce. I obtained a Bachelor of Commerce in 1981 and became an Establishment Officer for the Ministry of Public Service and Human Resource Development in Sudan.

In 1983 I came to Malakal, the capital city of the Upper Nile region, after the division of the southern administration. The rebellion of southern elements within the Sudanese Army then occurred in Bor on May 16, 1983.

A liberation movement named Sudan People's Liberation Movement and Sudan People's Liberation Army (SPLM/A) was formed under the leadership of Dr John Garang de Mabior, which I joined on March 6, 1984.

This is where my story begins.

My Journey to the Bush From Malakal Town To Join The SPLM/A On March 6, 1984

I was joined by my dear Uncle Kuoreng Akoi Yaak Jurkuch, who attended elementary school in Pawel with me in 1960, and another dear friend, Mr. Atem Bul Gak, along with many others. Our journey commenced at 9:00am via lorry, heading to the nearby town of Bailiet. The move was not easy, because all vehicles travelling that route were subjected to thorough searches by security and military personnel, since the final departure point was near the Malakal Army Barracks. Our belongings were thoroughly checked. Personal searches were also conducted, to ensure no recruits were at risk of joining the newly established rebel movement, The Sudan People's Liberation Movement/Army (SPLM/A.)

The security situation in the town was extremely tense. The newly formed Movement SPLM/A, had trained and sent a battalion to South Sudan, which was sighted near town by security. On the 8th February 1984, coordinated attacks were launched on a small nearby Sudan army in the garrison town of Canal Mouth in the Upper Nile Province. They also launched an attack on Ayod and Poktap in Jongulei province, followed by another attack at Wathkei town on February 12, 1984. The Wathkei town attack was launched on a White Nile passenger steamer, leaving Malakal town and moving southwards to Bor and Juba. Both sides suffered losses, which is common during a battle between two armed forces. However, the concern of the Malakal town inhabitants was their own safety from government security agencies, since they were unable to differentiate between a rebel and an ordinary citizen. A few days following the incident, the rebels dispersed a large government army convoy, to stop the rebels advancing. These attempts by the government were futile however, and on February 22 the rebels penetrated and bombarded the town. I was awoken at midnight by mortar bomb shells, falling near my home. It was a terrible sign that the rebels meant business.

After the military check, there was nothing of value found on the travelling passengers, giving them no reason to obstruct our journey. The driver asked us to climb onto the lorry. We were relieved to start our journey, as we were concerned our intentions would be questioned. We headed towards Mohamed Ajak and once we arrived we caught up with the military convoy that left Malakal town, and were heading in the same direction. This convoy avoided the road, preferring to move in the bush, fearing the rebels had planted landmines. This fear was due to the skirmishes that occurred in the same location, five days prior. Our lorry driver had used this road the day prior to our travel commencing. The army convoy took a sigh of relief, watching us travel safely down the road. We took a brief stop at Nakdiar village to fetch some drinking water, then resumed our journey to Bailiet. The convoy following us had to leave, and they continued their travel to Nasir town.

In Bailiet, we received a warm welcome from local youths who were highly charged by their moral obligation towards their fellow Southern Sudanese who were visiting their town. They may have suspected we were intending to join the rebel movement and liberate the aggrieved southern people. The youths took us to different residential places. They were quick to provide services, without enquiring on our identity, intention and the destination we were travelling to. I had assumed at that time, all southern people were rebels including government officials. An example of this, was when we were taken to the residence of the Assistant Commissioner Mr Hussein Ajuong Deng, who received us warmly at his place. It was the first time we had the opportunity to meet Mr Ajuong in person. He was an affable gentleman with whom you could share your matters of concern. We chatted briefly and informed our intention. Mr Ajuong then ordered the youths to round up some canoes to ferry us across the Sobat river. We were advised to take turns. I was in the second group to cross the river and we all converged on the other side at 3:00 pm.

It was then we felt the real journey to the bush to join the SPLM/A Movement had begun. Reflecting on the whole process starting from Malakal to Bailiet, we questioned why those young men from Ngok of Padaang committed themselves to serve us. Was this treatment being rendered to every person passing through this community? What motivated them to carry out this dangerous business, which could result in loss of life? Along with these men from Bailiet town, were also the youths operating in and around Malakal who hailed from the same area. We discovered the elders of the community, were the master minds of their youth. Dr. James Thuch Arial along with others, were netting like a spider to assist Movement of those wishing to join the Movement. His pharmacy was a daily meeting point for the potential SPLM/A recruits to plan their escape through Bailiet town.

As the group started to move from the southern side of the Sobat River, the sons of the area were leading us to safer places. We were heading east and had to walk along the Sobat River. We continued receiving good advice from the citizens of the area, as we passed by. One lady advised to distant yourself from the riverbank, because the Arabs in Adong town would bombard you with mortar shells if you were too close to town. We immediately complied to the call of the woman, by entering the nearby forest to use as cover. We very much relied on the youths in the area in every aspect. Among them was Mr. Maduk Dau Koach, whose father did not hesitate to slaughter a ram for us when we arrived at his house at Awiir Village. His son had unexpectedly surprised him by dropping in with 10 to 12 guests. The family meal was finished, but either way it would have been too great to share, with the large number of guests. Being a Dinka man from a native home, he wanted to display his generosity to the friends of his son. Family members stayed up late to prepare food for the guests. After we were served a meal, we slept for two to three hours, then woke up ready to continue our journey. We thanked Uncle Dau de Koach and the members of his family for their generous welcoming and services rendered to us. We farewelled them too, for we were embarking on an indefinite journey with an uncertain mission. None of us were sure if we would meet again. Uncle Dau provided some important advice on our way to Abwong village. The village had come under attack from government forces the day prior and no one was certain if risk remained. We were advised to detour for our safety, which was exactly what we did.

After the surreptitious detour of Abwong village, around Abwong we encountered some remaining soldiers from the Jamus (Buffalo) Battalion, who lost the main body in one of the battles near Nakdiar village. Those Soldiers directed our group to continue with the journey to Gakyuom village where we arrived at 10:00am. It was an assembly point for the recruits who had been tracking the route at night under the control of the Jamus Battalion soldiers. Upon arrival, we were received and organised into military formation after being served with light food and boiled sorghum (belilla).

Bush life had commenced and I was immediately assigned on cooking duty for my group, composed of 51 platoon members. Twelve members were assigned cooking duty for the group. We received food rations in the form of grains and meat donated by the local community. Some of us were required to fetch water from the nearby Sobat River and firewood.

Others were given the job of pounding grains and the last group had to carry out the cooking. Commander of the Jamus remnants, SGT Major Dhieu (Kachlech) Luach Chotjak whom we departed with at Abwong village, dropped in with instructions that the whole group would start around 3:00pm to Wunthou village. After the cooking duties were finished, the group was served with food. As declared, we began to move at exactly 3:00pm but this time in accordance with a military marching order. The group was divided into four platoons, of which our platoon was number one and therefore we were in the lead according to military order. At 7:30pm we arrived at Wunthou, and we joined 400 recruits, both men and women. Wives and children of those who had already joined the Movement were among them. The two day experience in the bush, helped us gain experience in military drills, cooking and walking for continuous long distances. Upon arrival, the group was informed they will start moving to Chuei village in the Nasir District at dawn. As mentioned, there were families present of those who had joined the Movement. Some of those family members were vulnerable and as a result they needed support from the recruits by either carrying their children or luggage. This demonstrated the strong level of comradeship and patriotic support to those families. The following morning, I was selected by one of the Jamus force soldiers to be among those who would help the families. I accepted without hesitation. But I then wondered why that soldier opted to single me out from the rest of my colleagues? I was a government official who had worked for three years and a university graduate from three years ago. This is unlike Uncle Kuoreng, who had graduated only a few months ago and from Atem Bul who was currently teaching, in addition to students with us in the group. I undoubtedly concluded it was a question of height and weight, as I did not match up to the rest when considering the African way of rating people in their communities.

We commenced at dawn, and the soldiers had to make sure bulls were collected from the cattle camps for food along the way. It was a huge responsibility to ensure there was enough food for almost 600 plus recruits. At 11:00am we stopped to rest and prepare breakfast, when a colleague we left Malakal town with two days prior, caught up with us. Learning of our departure, Mr. Malou da Ajak da Aguer, decided to track the road to Bailiet alone, hoping to catch up with us along the way. Back home, we hailed from the same village of Wangkulei. When he saw us, he could not believe his eyes! Happily, he hugged us one after the other. We warmly welcomed him into our group and it was clear the journey must continue. At 3:00pm, we moved until we arrived at Chuei village at 8:00pm. We arranged to sleep in military order. We organised our sleeping materials and laid down to sleep, when one of the guards leading the group suddenly fired his AKM rifle towards us. Another guard then fired from the other side, and a third from a different direction. The shooting continued for five minutes, despite the fact their Commander SGT. Major Dhieu (Kachlech) attempted to distract the shooter. Although the group remained in position, they were forced to run to safety, fearing for their lives. We ran away from the scene with bare feet, leaving our bags behind. The commander finally managed to stop the shooting. Luckily we didn't run far, and quickly returned to our positions. A casualty of the shooting was our newly arrived colleague Mr. Malou da Ajak da Aguer, who sustained an injury to his leg. It was unfortunate he had joined us that morning and became a casualty on the first day he arrived. Another man from Jamus force who was guarding us, suffered an injury to the thigh. The situation in the camp was tense, as people who we trusted to guide us safely to our last destination of Bilpam, began to behave in this manner.

§

We now had three major issues to contend with. Firstly, we had no medical supplies to treat the patients. Secondly, the new recruits had the burden of carrying two wounded people. Thirdly, we had come to the dangerous area of Anyanya 11, who wouldn't allow people to proceed who weren't interested in joining their forces. This was concerning as we were approaching the Anyanya 11 Headquarters, in the Nyandieng forest.

The situation in the camp returned to normal. However, our group was speculating on what could potentially occur the next day. Could we start moving at dawn, to cover a good distance before breakfast? Or should we delay and perform a reconnaissance (Recce) to examine the safety of the route? Did the shooting in Chuei expose us to the enemies along the route who could plan an ambush? If we can't make our way to Bilpam, could we return to Malakal or any other government held town?

These questions and many others were lingering on everyone's mind. Tomorrow was the 4th day since the group left Malakal on the March 6, 1984, but there were still no signs of our journey continuing. We had to wait to find out the security situation ahead and prepare stretches to carry the injured people. We remained in Chuei Village until 3:00pm, before we could resume our journey. We only managed to walk for three hours until stopping for the night.

The general feeling of the group was enigmatic. We first came to an area close to Nyandieng, the headquarters of Anyanya 11. This was a pivotal point. Either we safely cross this tributary stream then proceed to our target of Bilpam, or we could be dispersed by Anyanya 11 members resulting in a failed mission. This meant a lot to those who considered South Sudan to be an independent nation, achieved through their own merits and standing among other world nations. It used to be a nagging expectation that South Sudan at this point in time, must be liberated by the youth. We naively thought as youths, that we were well educated people from different fields of specialisation. University graduates, Master

Degree and PhD holders are among us. We have qualified army officers in the national armed forces, police, prisons and wildlife services. There is a strong and unwavering determination amongst the youth to complete the unfinished jobs that our grandfathers, fathers and the generations before us, didn't have the chance to accomplish. That is why the youths of Padaang, as mentioned earlier, opted to serve whole heartedly, those passing through their areas.

We spent the night speculating how to address the challenges we faced. The first challenge was how to carry the wounded comrades. Those who were assigned to carry the two wounded comrades, did not convince the group they were committed to the assignment. As relatives of comrade Malou da Ajak, we offered to carry him for the rest of the journey to ensure he wasn't neglected, even though there was just a few of us. This move was also in anticipation of a dangerous security situation, potentially waiting for us near Nyandieng village. The following day we decided not to depart until evening, so the darkness could assist us crossing the river and trying our best to evade Anyanya 11 forces that may be hovering. We cautiously started to move in the evening towards Nyandieng, an area manned by Anyanya 11 groups and many local cattle camps. We were charged with the responsibility of carrying Mr. Malou da Ajak da Aguer. It might seem like a simple job, but it's quite a burden to carry a 90kg person through bushy areas. Sometimes there were only two of us in the bushy area, while other times there were four in the areas which were less dense.

We came to the Nyandieng crossing at 10:00pm expecting to be shot at any time. But to our surprise nothing occurred. We only heard the moans of cows from the nearby cattle camps. We started to gain confidence in ourselves as we moved along. Finally, we received information that all Anyanya 11 elements had left the area for Bilpam a few days prior. It was a huge relief to hear. We then continued our journey, until we reached another obstacle. We received an alert from our leaders to be quiet and calm, as we were about to approach the Sudanese Army Garrison town of Wutlang. This wasn't a major issue, since it was situated on the northern left hand side of the Sobat River. We took every piece of advice and information very seriously. We complied as we walked carrying the wounded people. It was a hectic leg, walking 12 hours nonstop. We stopped at 8:00am at Nyarkueth village to rest and cook, and we were relieved we had bypassed the bottle neck. We bathed in the river and washed our clothes.

Walking non-stop through the night, couldn't go without injury. I had a serious pain in my leg, which could end my journey to Bilpam and make me the most vulnerable in the group. This was causing considerable alarm at this particular point. We had no relatives around to rely on, and no nearby hospital. The situation was a nightmare, in the middle of nowhere. Though we are people of one nation, the community we lived in was subjected to unfair policies, turning them against those willing to join the Movement (SPLM/A). The fear of the unknown danger that could occur to anyone at any time, was highly speculated. I consulted with friends and colleagues on my injury, and was provided with an ointment to rub on the swollen part of my leg. I applied this immediately and the pain slowly started to disappear. In the evening, we started our journey to Kurenge village where we camped for the night. Thankfully I didn't experience much leg pain on the walk to Kurenge. During the night I was fully relieved of pain.

As usual, we began our journey at dawn to cover a good distance before the tropical heat was upon us. We travelled for 6kms arriving at Tolor village which is opposite Nasir town and across the Sobat River. We then commenced our routine of preparing meals. This was done by those on duty, while those off duty, including our wounded comrades, were made to rest. Orders to move to the next camping area in Dualdahab village were issued. We then commenced the next leg of our journey at 3:00pm in a military formation. We arrived at Dualdahab at 9:00pm, then needed to find somewhere to sleep. In the morning, our leaders decided we should remain in this area for the day, as we were unsure of the security situation ahead. The Sudanese government was deploying troops along the Akobo River to deny free access to the returning battalions of Jamus 104 and 105 to Ethiopia. From this point, it was around 20 – 25kms to walk across the border to Ethiopia. Bukteng Village, which is the springboard to cross, was suspected to be manned by Sudanese government troops. Later that day, it was confirmed no enemy troops were in the area.

The camp breathed a sigh of relief, and we prepared to move at 3:00pm. Though we were confident of no enemy presence ahead of us, the thought still played on our mind. Very cautiously and carefully we walked to Bukteng village. We were instructed to speak quietly while walking, otherwise we would be reprimanded. We avoided passing through Bukteng village and reached the river crossing point safely. The small group of leaders had to proceed to the riverside and secure it. There was an advanced team of two from Dualdahab, who secured two canoes at the riverside for our crossing. Women, children and wounded people were to be ferried across first. Those who were good swimmers were able to cross unassisted. When the crossing was successfully completed, we celebrated by gathering together and our leaders fired rounds of live ammunition from their AKM machine guns. While this was happening, we songs which boosted the morale and spirit of the Jamus battalion.

Now we were on the Ethiopian side of the border, we were safe from the government's army as they cannot pursue people on the other side. The Sudanese government could not justify following rebels into Ethiopian territory, so we were extremely happy to be evading the enemy danger inside the Sudan. We began to move to Kuanylou village in a confident and relaxed manner, where we spent the night. The following morning, orders were issued by the commander of the group to prepare food early, as he was travelling to the Ethiopian town of Burbiege to contact the Jamus battalion's main body via radio. He failed to locate exactly where the battalions' main body was. We therefore had to spend another day in the same area, and the commander went back to Burbiege for the same purpose. This time he succeeded in locating the Jamus battalion's headquarters.

Jamus and the 104/105 battalions were ordered back to Bilpam (the headquarter of the Movement SPLM/A) for reasons I was unable to explain. This occurred even though they had conducted a successful operation around the Malakal and Jonglei areas in February. They had also carried out operations around the town of Akobo close to the Ethiopian border when our commander was doing his best to locate them. The Khartoum Government got wind of information that southerners were defecting en masse to join the SPLM/A Movement. It was clear beyond doubt they were tracking their route through the Akobo area. As a preventative measure, the enemy in Akobo dispatched some of their units to try and end the situation.

The commanders of battalions Jamus and 104/105, CDR Kerbino Kuanyin Bol and CDR William Nyuon Bany, found this challenge ahead. It was disruptive to the flow of recruits, and therefore must be brought to an end. Two of the government's newly established outposts, Dengjok and Kir, were dealt with by the two battalions. They continued their journey to (Bahr Alual) where we caught up with them, then proceeded to Adura (Thiajak) town where the force was assembled. Immediately, the two wounded people were airlifted to the Itang Refugee Centre for further medical treatment. In Adura (Thiajak), all recruits were welcomed, praised and encouraged by the two CDRs Kerbino and William in a military rally. We were provided with different food options as soon as we arrived. We had an enjoyable three days in Adura (Thiajak) intermingling with brothers and friends who had left us more than a year ago. The role of SGT Major Dhieu Kachlech as commander of our group, ended when we met with the remaining force. We were grateful and thanked them for their guidance, as our journey without them would have been difficult.

As mentioned earlier, we left Adura for the Itang Refugee Camp after three days. Since we no longer had to carry the two wounded comrades, we had fewer rest stops which made the walk feel longer. The number of recruits had grown from 600 to more than 2000. They were partly made up of recruits coming from Bor and other areas of Southern Sudan. Due to the long and treacherous walk, seven of us continued, leaving the new recruits behind. We came to Mangok Village which is adjacent to Jokau town around 11:00am, after walking for a good eight hours. Those on duty began preparing us food. We ate and rested for four hours, then started for Majak village where we planned to spend the night. We left at 4:00am arriving at Makuach village at 10:00am. This village is opposite Bilpam, the historical Anyanya 11 and SPLM/A Headquarters. According to the information gathered at Itang, the distance was estimated to be 18km which should take 3 hours to complete. At 3:00pm, we crossed the Baro River at Makuach village, which is on the lefthand side of the river. All of a sudden, we encountered two lorries carrying SPLA soldiers and coming from the direction we were heading. They stopped and promised the lorries would return shortly, so we should wait for them. We thought it was wise to continue walking since it would make little difference. The Ural Lorries returned and caught up with us along the road as promised. What luck, they finally brought us to Itang, the final destination, on the March 26, 20 days since our journey began from Malakal on March 6.

Let me rewind a little to explain the enigmatic circumstance which occurred on the way to Nyandieng village. This area was reported to be used by Anyanya 11 forces as their headquarters. When crossing the tributary in this area, there was no presence of Anyanya 11 forces as reported, and we were surprised they were nowhere to be seen. What had happened to Anyanya 11 forces? We were extremely happy to cross the small tributary at Nyandieng safely. However, we were still curious why there were no forces in that area. We were concerned and couldn't find a valid reason from either ourselves, our leaders or the inhabitants of the area.

When we arrived at Adura (Thiajak), all the forces of the SPLM/A came together. Another puzzling question, was why the whole SPLA/M force was ordered back to Ethiopia leaving behind the known enemy in Sudan? In Adura (Thiajak) itself, they were airlifting SPLA/M forces by helicopters to unknown destinations. What was the reason behind that? Another bizarre situation was when we left Adura (Thiajak) we encountered South Sudanese people around Marial village advancing to where we had come from. Those people were in a different mood altogether, which raised questions on our side. Being new people in a strange area, we failed to reach a reasonable conclusion but time would reveal they were important and relevant observations.

Itang is a small town situated on northern side of the Baro River. It has a local government administration made up of town council, police and local chiefs. It is a part of the Illubabor region, which is known as Western Ethiopia. Itang harboured thousands of South Sudanese refugees in the 1960's and early 1970's until the Addis Ababa Peace Agreement was signed on March 3, 1972. Those refugees returned to Sudan following the agreement. Itang became a fall back position for the people of South Sudan. They returned to the same town with the same refugee status when war broke out in the southern part of the country in May, 1983. At Itang, we were organised into a military battalion composing of 1,225 people. There were more than 10,000 people with refugee status, when they were in fact SPLA/M recruits waiting for training opportunities to avail.

I previously mentioned some observations from our journey to Itang. The two Ural Lorries who brought us to Itang from Makuach, were transporting SPLA/M troops. The Anyanya 11 rebels who were in hot pursuit by the SPLA/M troops, came to Itang in anticipation of meeting the newly graduated battalions of Tiger and Crocodile (Timsah). The reason was most of the trainees from the two battalions hailed from the Nuer tribe. Therefore, the commanders of Anyanya 11 were desperately trying to persuade them to join their movement, rather than the SPLA/M who trained and armed them. This plan wasn't received well, as they were detected and hence quickly moved back to South Sudan before being caught by the SPLA/M armed forces. Those Anyanya 11 forces were the ones we encountered at Marial village in the morning of March 24, 1984, on our way to Itang from Adura (Thiajak). According to their appearance, we could tell these forces were in a different mood. Learning of their departure, the SPLA/M hurriedly sent a force to catch up with them before they caused any damage to the SPLA/M units along the route. Unfortunately, attempts to curve their movements were unsuccessful as Anyanya 11 attacked and overran Adura (Thiajak) on March 26, 1984, the day we arrived at Itang. The town was badly devastated. They pillaged important war materials, especially anti-aircraft missiles and radios used for communication. However, the SPLA/M forces regained the town afterwards. The battle of Adura (Thiajak) was a great loss to the Movement, but equally it was a gain to the SPLM/A since the Anyanya 11 senior commander was eliminated in the battle. General Samuel Gai Tut was ambushed and killed by the SPLA/M forces, as they were advancing towards the town.

General Tut who hailed from Lou Nuer, was a respected and beloved personality in the south. His contributions in the first southern struggle were commendable. He joined the Sudanese armed forces as Lt Colonel, when a peace agreement was signed between Anya-nya one and the Sudanese Government in the Ethiopian capital city of Addis Ababa on March 3, 1972. He later differed with his former commander, General Joseph Lagu, over southern politics that forced him to resign from the Sudanese army and he later lived in the local community after working shortly with government as a local Administrator. He then served briefly as minister in the caretaking government of General Gismallah Abdallah Resas from 1981-1982, before he defected and joined the Anyanya 11 Movement in 1983.

If the loss of General Gai Tut was branded a success to the SPLM/A, it was a devastating setback for the Anyanya 11 Movement. When a top military leader of his calibre is lost, the group is like a ship in the sea without a captain to navigate. Indeed, the Anyanya 11 Movement didn't have the confidence in themselves to choose a better leader amongst so many. They came out clearly to support the enemy, which was a compelling reason for them and others to rebel. In a war situation such as this, the contribution of each South Sudanese was dearly needed to defeat the common enemy. Therefore the loss of General Gai Tut, was a serious setback for all southern people.

Life at The Itang Refugee Camp in 1984

More than 10,000 South Sudanese lived in Itang as refugees. Who was feeding this huge population in the camp? The main body in charge was the United Nations High Commissioner for Refugees (UNHCR). Upon arrival, military parades were part of the daily routine. The 10,000 people considered as refugees, were SPLA/M recruits. They were disguised as refugees but were actually waiting for an opportunity for military training. The camp was in the early stages of establishment, and services were scarce and limited to those registered by the camp's administration. The amount of recruits flocking to the camp was overwhelming in every aspect. Everything had to be supplied by the UNHCR, including all food and non-food items (e.g. kitchen equipment, water containers, tents and blankets). Despite the insufficiency of so many items, the camp managers did their best to ensure the services reached everyone.

Although we were considered refugees, we were a full military organisation. Our battalion was the 6th group of recruits to arrive at the camp. We received daily provisions of essential food rations, despite the fact some critical food items were missing. Pounding grains was a challenge to us. Traditionally, men in Africa didn't perform such duties as dura pounding, cooking, collecting firewood and collecting water from the river. Such tasks were completed by women. Most of the recruits at the Itang refugee camp were men and therefore they found it difficult to carry out cooking duties. UNHCR ration distribution included maize, oil, salt and sugar. These rations did little to satisfy the needs and expectations of the refugees in the camp. Many refugees resorted to using fishing spears in the small Baro River tributaries, which contained many species of fish. They caught enough fish to satisfy their hunger, then sold the remaining for cash to meet other needs.

It had been one month since we arrived at Itang. Chairman of the SPLM and Commander in Chief of the SPLA, Dr. John Garang de Mabior, together with Major Salva Kiir Mayardit and Major Arok Thon Arok (both Members of Politico-Military High Command), visited the camp and addressed the refugees at a rally, attended by most, if not all. Many promises were made including military training which would commence in the coming days. Nothing pleased the recruits more than attending military training in Bonga. His speech was eloquent and made life in the camp joyful. A week following the visit from the Movement's leader, Dr. John Garang de Mabior, Itang received another visit from the most senior man of the land, the President of the Republic of Ethiopia, His Excellency Colonel Mengistu Hailemariam. He was visiting Western Ethiopia to confirm reports he'd received of an influx of Sudanese refugees to his country. He delivered a powerful speech which enabled us as recruits to assess our future. To quote His Excellency, "You are highly welcomed to Ethiopia, your second home or country". He continued with, "You will stay here in this country and if there is nothing to feed on, you can share half a loaf of bread with your brothers in this country". Calling Ethiopia a second country to the Sudanese refugees was comforting to hear and sharing bread with the nationals, was an exciting thought.

To us the recruits, we fell short of the contribution Ethiopia made towards the Movement's survival, from the time of inception some months ago. The two battalions that terrorized Sudan (namely Jamus and 104/105) were trained, fully armed, and equipped by the government of Ethiopia. When those who fought the battle of Bor against the Sudanese government in May 1983 fled to Ethiopia, they were well received by their Ethiopian counterparts and also protected from their enemies of Anyanya 11 forces. It's no secret the areas of Bilpam, Itang, Makuach, Mangok and Thiajak (Adura) were completely under Anyanya 11 administration. This meant anyone coming to those areas without their approval or recognition, were considered hostile and therefore must be dealt with. Commanders of Anyanya 11, including Gordon Kong Chol, were in charge of Bilpam and Garjiek Wei (nick-named as Lothkol) was in charge of Itang, to mention a few. The latter unfortunately met his fate along with others on board a buffalo aircraft which was shot down by SPLA forces. This occurred around Akobo town, when he desperately wanted to travel to Malakal in early 1985. These commanders had managed to sign a peace agreement with the SPLM/A in 1988. Their management in those areas ended when the current SPLM/A and those who became Anyanya 11, had a dispute over the leadership of the southern movement. This was a setback to the southern people who needed unity, purposely and spiritly to overcome the mighty force of the oppressors in Khartoum. Uncle Akuot da Atem de Mayen and General Samuel Gai Tut along with their group, fled the area and headed back to Sudan. They left behind the group led by Dr. John Garang de Mabior and hence was the formation of the SPLM/A Movement.

Movement of Locust Division to Bonga Training Camp

The order to move to the Bonga training facility, finally came to the disguised recruits in May 1984. The group comprised of 12,000 people, so it was not possible to commence the journey in one trip considering the limited transport available. Trucks arrived at the Itang Refugee Camp to commence the transportation process. This operation was to be completed in seven days. On the first run, 4000 recruits were transported to the training facility, leaving 6000 plus behind at the camp. Those who remained in Itang, were disappointed to be detached from the rest of the group. The Bonga Training Centre had four accommodation facilities, enough to host only 4000 people. My group and I were not amongst the lucky ones who were selected for training in Bonga. The policy and intention of the Movement was to train the recruits as early as possible, enabling them to launch efficient and effective military operations against government positions in the southern part of the country. With that in mind, the Movement leaders asked for more recruits to be transported to Bonga, not to train but to construct camp facilities for the remaining 6000 recruits. That became the mission for our platoon, as we were selected to construct four more camp sites. There were four hundred recruits designated to the assignment. We were immediately rushed to the Bonga Training Camp, thinking we were about to join those who had commenced training. However, we were shocked to find the real reason we were brought to Bonga. Secrecy in the army always reigned. We were not informed of the actual duties we were expected to undertake, but nonetheless, orders were to be respected and implemented.

Construction commenced during the second week of May 1984. Local materials were in abundance, so the assignment was completed within three weeks. Considering the short completion time and our lack of experience, it was a rough job. Back home, local engineers would perform activities such as grass thatching on roofs and huts, and unfortunately the recruits were not experienced in this area. However, we were happy that we completed the assignment in the shortest possible time required. Once the leaders were informed that the construction was complete, the remaining recruits were immediately sent to the Bonga Training Centre. This time, there was no transport available and they had to cover the distance to Bonga by foot. Bonga who normally hosted between 1000–2000 recruits, was now unexpectantly overwhelmed with over 10,000 people.

Hosting all recruits in Bonga, was considered by the Movement's leaders as a major achievement and this was celebrated by gathering all the recruits for a parade. The morale of the recruits skyrocketed with the arrival of Dr. John Garang. Songs praising Dr. John and the Movement were sung with gusto! Songs disgracing Arabs and President Nimeiry were equally performed. Extreme levels of euphoria would erupt when Dr. John spoke. He delivered an exemplary speech, explaining the Movement's objectives, where we were, where we are now, challenges and achievements made so far.

He also spent a considerable amount of time explaining the real meaning of the Sudan People's Liberation Movement/Army (SPLM/A), for it was elusive and unclear in the minds of many South Sudanese illiterates, as well as the educated. Many South Sudanese considered liberating the south, but not the whole country. The reason was the oppressors were in the northern part of the country and should therefore be left alone where they belong. It was an open policy being advocated for by the Sudanese elites to Arabicize and Islamicize non Arabs, who make up more than 70% of the population. They had also attempted to Islamicize southern Christians, which had resulted in the first struggle from 1955—1972, when General Nimeiri reached a settlement with the Anya-nya one Movement. This was replicated in 1983, when General Nimeiri abolished the Addis Ababa Agreement which he himself had initialled with the Anya-nya one Movement, giving birth to the present struggle (SPLM/A). The Arab elites were very welcoming of Sudan to the Arab world. There was no shame in calling Southern Sudanese and other Africans in the Sudan, as fellow Arab countrymen when they are in fact, true African people. Dr. Mohamed el Nowehi, who was a Khartoum University lecturer and an Egyptian Arab by origin, denies existence of Arab's blood in any of the Sudanese societies. I will quote his statement later in the book.

Following the rally, we dispersed and returned to our quarters according to military formation. Our battalion was given the name of "Bilpam", which is an historical place that hosted members of Anya-nya 11 before the establishment of the SPLM/A in 1983. Other battalions were given different names. Tough as it was, the military training commenced. I was given the temporary rank of Regimental Sergeant Major (RSM) of the battalion, to run the daily affairs of more than 1,300 recruits. Comrade Dengtiel Ayuen Kur was a Battalion Commander and Comrade Kuol Manyang Juuk who later became the most senior among us when we were commissioned into military ranking in January 1985, was the Commander of the 1st Company (COY). Other COYs were assigned to different capable recruits.

Finding yourself in a new and unknown position can be quite daunting. Being responsible of the 1,300 recruits at the military training centre, was not a simple task. Some duties commenced as early as 3:00am. I had to blow a whistle to wake up the recruits for morning drills, with some not wanting to comply. I also had to enter every room to get people ready, even when it was raining outside. I was bombarded with verbal abuse directed towards myself and my parents, which greatly upset me as I was only trying to assist the recruits and achieve our purpose in Bonga. I managed to put those insults behind me, as I was committed and focused on our assignment.

Before we commenced our morning training session, we had to adhere to a break for breakfast. At midday we had a lunch break, and our training session concluded at 5:00pm when we ensured all recruits had returned to camp and any necessary disciplinary action was taken. The Ethiopian trainers would retire to their barracks and spend the night promising to join us the following morning. The evenings were spent doing personal activities such as washing clothes and bathing in the nearby Bonga river, before our dinner would commence. At 7:00pm, the SPLM Political Commissioners would conduct a political lesson. Following that, we could sleep until 3:00am, when the drills commenced for the new training day.

We followed this routine consistently for three months, until the first batch of Koryom Locust, graduated to their relief. The remainder of the group was in continuous doubt as to when they would have the opportunity to graduate. The first locust division was pleasantly surprised when they received their armaments and military uniforms. Songs praising the Movement and it's leaders were passionately sung by the graduating group. We in the second division, were disheartened by the event, cursing our misfortune at having to remain in Bonga.

In the graduating ceremony of the first division, two comrades, Lokurnyang Lado and Doctor Juach, were formerly sentenced to death by the Movement's Court Martial, and executed in front of the group.

They were accused of practicing subversive activities against the Movement which I, personally could not affirm whether the conviction was true. The third comrade, engineer Manyang Diu, unfortunately had to undergo a tough security interrogation before reaching that stage.

Military training had officially and effectively ended within three months. The reason the second division had to remain for another three more months was due to the lack of armament. To fully arm more than 12,000 recruits with donated weapons or equipment, would require more time. The recruits were obsessed with receiving their armament, but could not understand the difficulty encountered by the leaders in search of weapons. Any blame could be considered as an abuse or an insult to the Movement's leaders, if we questioned why they fell short in the provision of arms.

Whilst in Bonga, we were busy moving around looking for anything that would be beneficial to us. Having to spend three more months at the Bonga Training Centre was an unimaginable hell. A contributing factor was the trainee's poor diet. Usually when military training is conducted in other countries to build up an army, food resources are given full attention. A variety of food must be available in decent quantities, to ensure recruits have enough sustenance to undertake the difficulties and challenges of their training regime. That is the norm in worldwide military establishments, but is unlikely to occur in the Guerrilla military setup, where everything is based on voluntarily contributions from friends and well-wishers.

When training started in Bonga, the Movement did not have a well prepared and articulated budget that was to meet the training requirements. Food items supplied to the trainees were rice, maize flour, oil, sugar and salt, all in insufficient quantities. From the items mentioned above, you can conclude the health condition of the recruits had become very poor. Many of them became emaciated to the extent that some were unable to attend the early morning drills. As a result, many were evacuated back to the Itang Refugee Camp for medical attention. The majority had come from rural areas, where food such as milk, fish, meat and different types of grains, were plentiful. Whilst at the Bonga training camp, the recruits were shocked with the basic range of food, which had to last from morning to evening. The weak health of the trainees in Bonga, was a result of the poor diet along with the difficulty of the training itself.

This was creating great discomfort to the recruits in Bonga, and no one wished to remain for a day, let alone three months. However, since the objective which brought us to Bonga had not yet been achieved, we had to carry on no matter how challenging it felt. Life in Bonga started to change a little for the better. Training was cut back, and recruits were relieved from the early morning whistle, which was also a relief to me being the one who had to blow the whistle and the insults that came with it. Training came to an official end with a graduation ceremony for Division One members. It took place on the September 4, 1984 and was attended by Dr. John Garang de Mabior, CDR Salva Kiir Mayardit, current President of the Republic of South Sudan, Ethiopian friends and many others.

The long-awaited provision of AKM rifles and magazines, pistols, hand grenades, military uniforms including hats, boots and socks, bayonets and water containers were made available to the lucky graduating members of the First Division. Military ranks from 2nd Lieutenants to Majors, were given to those deserving. Marching order was determined according to the battalion's seniority from first to fourth. The military equipment mentioned above, was handed over to those departing. It took four days to transport Division One to the nearest departure point at the south of the country, taking one battalion each day. It was the middle of the rainy season when riverbanks were overflown with water.

This hindered a smooth movement of the troops to the field. It was a challenge for the soldiers on this journey to cross high-level rivers with their heavy load, which consisted of personal belongings, AKM Rifles, types of ammos and food items. However, this challenge was nothing compared to the living conditions of those who remained at the Bonga Training Centre.

Training activities had drastically reduced, except for the morning and evening parades and some ad hoc duties. Recruits began to look for ways they could diversify their food supplies, by using any available material they could cleverly utilise. Nylon sack fibres were transformed into fishing nets to catch fish in the Baro River and Bonga tributary stream. Hunting in and around the forest for small wild animals, became order of the day among the trainees. One day, they managed to catch an antelope close to camp, and the recruits tore apart the animal with their bare hands, without using knives or sharp materials. This illustrates the magnitude of the recruits desire for meat, which I termed 'Wolves Style'. Meat in Bonga was a rare commodity, and since arriving six months ago, none had been available. Given their rural life back home, it would be considered a nightmare by the South Sudanese, to spend a day without having meat or fish once, if not twice, a day. Now this staple had returned to their diet through freedom of movement, their life in Bonga started to relax.

A second event that relaxed life a little more, was when the Radio SPLA opened in October 1984. In one of the rallies conducted at Bonga, the Chairman and Commander in Chief Dr. John Garang said, "We are going to bring a gun with a big muzzle, if we fire it, it will reach every corner of the Sudan". The opening of Radio SPLA was a major and significant achievement, not only to the Movement but also to the entire Sudanese people. News of the SPLA operations in the field started to be heard all over the country, by those interested. The Movement's objectives were clearly articulated and were heard in every Sudanese public area or house. Speeches from the SPLM/A leaders were openly played without any hindrance, unlike the situation in 1983 when news on the Movement could only be obtained from the international media. Radio SPLA would be on air from 1:00pm – 2:00pm in local languages, and 3:00pm - 4:00pm in Arabic and English Languages. This would occur daily with music and slogans from the station. Listeners would look forward to tuning in, and acquainting themselves with the daily developments of the SPLA/M.

News of the newly graduated First Division of Locust, had begun to emerge from the field. Cobra Battalion successfully stopped a river transport steamer, heading to Malakal near Bor town. There were hostages on board, including foreigners, who were eventually released. Zendia Battalion, from the same division, dispersed a convoy of paratroopers heading to Bor from Juba on December 24, 1984. Juba residents were in disbelief when they received news of the paratroopers being dispersed by the newly established SPLA/M forces. There wasn't much else to hear, aside from the SPLA/M victories in the field. Those who remained at Bonga, including myself, were eager for the armaments to arrive, so we could join the front line and be part of the impending victory. There was a feeling amongst us that the war of liberation could end any day. The vehicles of the paratrooper's convoy were still standing until 2007, when they were finally taken away by the road works on Juba Bor Road.

Following Zendia battalion's victory, they were instructed by the Movement's top leaders to advance to Eastern Equatoria and begin recruiting. Equatoria lagged behind in their contribution of manpower within the SPLA/M. In the minds of Equatorians, the new Movement (SPLM/A) was a Dinka Movement who fought them after the southern administration had split into three regions, Equatoria, Bahr El Gazal and Upper Nile. They were therefore not to be trusted, as they weren't part of their national movement. Southern politics became very sour during this time, prompting Equatorians to support their own region. This policy was unpopular in both the Bahr el Gazal and Upper Nile regions, and even amongst the real Equatorial nationalists who believed in unity of the southern people. President Jaafer Mohamed Nimeiri declared division of the south in June 1983, against the opinion of the southern majority. This disregarded the Addis Ababa Agreement, when the President was quoted as saying, "Addis Ababa Agreement was neither Qoran nor Holy Bible to remain". It was a policy devised by northern oppressors, to divide and destroy southern unity.

Following their previous battle, Zendia Battalion prepared to move to Eastern Equatoria under the instructions of the High Command Member, CDR Arok Thon Arok and the battalions direct commander, Captain Peter Panhom Thenypieny. They fought successfully in Eastern Equatoria, capturing towns and dispersing convoys as they moved along the area. The main objective for this area, was to recruit among their community. News of Zendia's successful operation reached the public through Radio SPLA. This motivated not only us at the Bonga Training Centre but also the entire southern people. The Zendia Mission in all aspects was deemed a success, especially to the thousands of recruits in Jonglei about to commence training in Ethiopia. We will discuss this mission in more detail, in the pages to come.

Three months at the training centre passed quickly, following the graduation of the First Division. We meanwhile sensed our graduation must be soon, with rumours filtering through from reliable sources. At the end of December, Dr. John and CDR Salva Kiir came to Bonga and started to interview senior recruits within the ranks of battalion's trainees. In our Battalion (Bilpam), brother Kuol Manyang Juuk became the most senior among us with the rank of Major and was assigned Deputy Commander of the Battalion, followed by Dengtil Ayuen Kur with the rank of Captain. I was ranked 1st Lieutenant among many comrades.

Some recruits were commissioned as 2nd Lieutenants. My assignment in the battalion was to control logistics. This would be challenging due to the meagre and poor resources.

The final graduation of the Second Division of Locust, occurred on January 10, 1985. This was marked with a special celebration bringing many leaders and other dignitaries from the Itang Refugee Camp. Senior representatives from the host country also attended the ceremony. Speeches delivered by senior members, including Martin Majier Gai Ayuel and Joseph Oduho among others, were exemplary. Comrade Yusuf Kowa Maki, who was currently untrained, delivered an elaborate and eloquent speech, still vivid in my memory.

Comrade said, "At the time of Sudan independence, you people (Southerners) were honoured with political and administrative positions in the Sudan's new administration, yet you rebelled on August 18, 1955 against the system complaining of marginalisation. You struggled then until you signed the peace agreement with President Jaafer Mohamed Nimeiri on March 3, 1972, known as the Addis Ababa Agreement. That resulted in a comprehensive government in the south. Then, you again, were not satisfied prompting another rebellion on May 16, 1983. Can I ask you southerners, at the time of the independence, which and how many administrative and political positions were given to the Nuba people? Nothing. This time around you have decided to pick up arms and fight against the government leaving behind your own regional administration in Juba, can I again ask you - what do Nuba people have back home as we speak? Nothing, except implementing un-noble and unrespectable jobs, and we are still loyal to that system. This time around, we will surely be together with you, no matter how long it takes and what is demanded from us, until we the Nuba people get what we deserve from that cake called Sudan".

After his speech was delivered, we all went wild clapping hands, singing morale songs and there was an outpouring of emotion from the female battalion. Southerners did not take Commander Yusuf seriously, as Nuba people are considered part of North Sudan and he might therefore not be willing to aid the southern struggle. But he proved himself as time went by. Nuba People joined the Movement in great numbers. They fought and died together with their comrades from the south, in every corner of the war.

Ethiopian government representative, General Maspin, spoke in praise of the Movement leaders recent military victories across different war fronts. He also praised the establishment of Radio SPLA, urging division two to be vigilant in the field and focused on achieving more victories. Locust Female and red army battalions came from Itang with Mr. Ring Akuei, who punctuated speeches with admirable songs in praise of the Movement's leadership, battalions and divisions. We received AKM rifles (minus the ammunition) to raise in the air whenever songs of morale were sung. You can imagine the impressive sight this created. More than 4000 recruits armed with automatic machine guns, was a formidable force for anyone to encounter.

The last to speak, was the Chairman of the Movement and Commander in Chief of the SPLA. In his filibuster speech, he congratulated the graduating group and apologised for their delay in graduating. His speech was well articulated and thorough, full of military news around the south. He assured us that we will soon be deployed, which was received by singing and shouts of joy. The objectives of the Movement were made very clear. Liberating the whole country was a must and called on Sudanese people around the country to follow the advice of Yusuf Kowa Maki. He urged Sudanese to join the Movement and liberate themselves. Having sufficient artillery would be no issue, as long as the manpower was available. This was proven when military equipment was sent at short notice, to more than 10,000 recruits.

During the speeches, the two Commanders, Kerbino Kuanyin and William Nyuon outlined military activities using newly acquired military mounted vehicles (Jeeps) mounted with 106 heavy artillery guns. They were extremely excited about the new equipment, their first since the inception of the Movement two years ago. Both Kerbino and William had just returned from the war front, where they faced an enemy with superior weapons. The Movement now had weapons to match, justifying their excitement. They also had the rare opportunity to show our graduating class, some real military tactics that will soon be applied in the field. Of course, they will be their commanders in the days to come.

Overall, our day ended smoothly when Dr. John Garang concluded the ceremony. Our songs of morale flared up from different battalions as they moved back to their respective residential camps for night. The following day, the first battalion to receive an order to move to the field, was Lion. Lion battalion wouldn't have been the first to receive an order, if Iron battalion hadn't already been dispatched in November 1984. Nonetheless, Lion prepared to leave Bonga for South Sudan having to stop at Makuach, on the Ethiopian side, on January 11, 1985.

Lion battalion was heading to Boma town in the Pibor district, when an urgent situation emerged prompting a change of plan. Bandits, or local Nuer citizens of Gajak, had mobilised themselves and were planning to attack and capture the Bilpam military base, the Movement's HQ. If they didn't counteract within the next two days, the route of Lion battalion would be diverted to Makuach. Thankfully, when the attack occurred on January 13, 1985, Lion battalion successfully averted the situation which would have caused a major setback. They defeated the bandits after a furious battle, which left behind many casualties on both sides. Following this, Bilpam was guarded by more than 1,000 men.

According to military order, the next group to follow suit was Agareb (Scorpion) battalion, which occurred on the 12th of January 1985. Due the attack on Bilpam, this battalion would head towards Boma which they later attacked and captured on April 1, 1985. The last two battalions that departed Bonga Training Centre, on January 13 and 14, 1985 were Bilpam and Elephant (El Fiil).

The recruits' morale was sky rocketing. The recruits had just spent 8 long months at Bonga, where they trained hard with little sustenance. They were starting to achieve their objectives and were eager to win the war of liberation in the shortest possible timeframe.

They were extremely happy and proud to graduate. The fact we were eager to face war, surprised our Ethiopian trainer friends. They wondered why we were comfortable risking our lives by facing our enemies on the battlefield. The trainers questioned whether we understood the real risks of heading to the war front, and if we did, what was the reason for the excitement? Our friends and trainers all shared the same concerns. However, there was a big difference in thinking between the Ethiopians who have an independent country and the South Sudanese who have no country of their own. We came to Bonga to expand our military knowledge and capacity, so we can fight in the war of liberation. We were now ready and equipped to face our oppressors no matter what the outcome. But for our Ethiopian friends, their objective in life was to work for a better future for themselves and their families, since they already have their independent nation.

The Movement's allies would transport us to a certain point in the field, usually in the afternoon. The walk from this departure point to the assembly area, would normally take six hours. However it was taking us 16-17 hours, due to our poor condition of health. We were completely exhausted and emaciated due the difficult and lengthy training period. Also, the heavy load we were carrying had increased. Personal luggage, AKM rifle, magazines loaded with 120 rounds, hand grenades and water containers, increased this weight. We also hadn't received any food within the last 24 hours, which was also contributing to our level of exhaustion. I still remember when I arrived at Makuach village, and was greeted by members of the Lion battalion who served me with boiled meat and soup. I managed to swallow the first two bites, but the third wouldn't make its way through the oesophagus and down to my stomach. I had never had this issue before, and I'm still unsure why it happened. For some of us, it took three days for our normal digestion to resume.

It was late in the evening when we received food rations from the Commander Chagai Atem de Biar, for bulls, rice and a small quantity of salt. This was a welcome relief, as we hadn't eaten for the last 24 hours. These food rations contained protein, which hadn't been provided at the Bonga Training Centre over the last eight months. The rations were immediately distributed to the platoons and squads. They quickly rushed to slaughter the six bulls, one for each company (coy). Once this was done, they were cooking and feasting together!

The final battalion to arrive at the assembling area in Makuach, were El Fiil (Elephant) battalion on January 15, 1985. They received the same positive reception as those who preceded them. The SPLA general headquarters had to supply them with daily rations equal to what had previously been provided to the other battalions. The two former battalions (Lion and Bilpam), embraced the latest arrivals. They would prove to be a formidable force, as they would face the mission together and were committed to the operation.

There was an incident that occurred the night Elephant battalion came to Makuach, which really stuck in my mind. Captain Michael Makol Deng Kuol, shot himself to the surprise of everyone in the camp. He was a first (Coy) commander of the Elephant battalion. We learnt of his death early the following morning. Many were in shock and disbelief at what had occurred. Speculation on why he shot himself was abundant. Some people believed the reason he shot himself was due to the death of his brother, Captain Bolbek Deng Kuol, two days prior by the bandits at Makuach village. Others say he shot himself because of the low military rank given to him by the SPLM/A leadership. People of this opinion said, Michael Makol was formerly holding a rank of Major General commanding Anya-nya 11 forces. He then expected to have been commissioned much higher above his Anya-nya 11 former colleagues.

To analyse the two speculations mentioned above;

Firstly, let's suppose he shot himself because his dear brother was killed by bandits opposed to the Movements' leadership. This was not a wise way to deal with the loss of his dear brother. Instead of denying the Movement his services by ending his life, he should have continued with the struggle by working on strategies to defeat the enemy. Captain Makol, together with his compatriots, could have participated effectively in the long war to come. This would have been the best way to avenge the life of his beloved brother. Captain Makol like the rest of his compatriots, should have been psychologically prepared for the outcomes of war, knowing they joined the Movement to either kill or be killed by the enemy.

Secondly, if he shot himself due to his low military rank, this was also unjustifiable. All the Anya-nya 11 Commanders who held the rank of Major General, who joined the Movement together with him were also commissioned as Captains. There were nine of them altogether; Luka Lual Riiny, Paul Malong Awan, Anthony Bol Madut, Ring Madut, Daniel Deng Ajuong, himself Mickael Makol Deng, Wieu Kuol, Akol Kuol and Chol Morwel. In the Movement, the highest rank was the Colonel held by the Movement's leader and Commander in Chief, Dr. John Garang de Mabior. Next to follow were the members of Politico-Military High Command; Lt Colonel Kerbino Kuanyin Bol and Lt Colonel William Nyuon Bany Machar, followed by Major Salva Kiir Mayardit and Major Arok Thon Arok. It seems the Movement's leadership may not have allocated ranking due to previous positions, but rather in accordance with the numbers the Movement acquired. It was rare to sight a major in the Movement's rank and file. For the Anya-nya 11 members absorbed into the SPLA, it was a policy that major generals and brigadier generals were commissioned as captains, colonels were given the rank of 1st lieutenants, and lieutenant colonels were honoured with the rank of 2nd lieutenants . From major downwards, they were generally ranked non commissioned officers. However this wasn't always the case, as was the example of both Major Martin Mayuen Dut and Captain John Koang Nyuon who both defected from the Sudanese armed forces and maintained their ranks of Major and Captain respectively. This was different to Anya-nya 11 members who did not hail from any military background or from professional armed forces. But Anya-nya two members who might have obtained military training or knowledge anywhere else in the professional armies, were absorbed or commissioned in different ranks.

If Captain Makol underrated the rank allocated to him by the Movement's leadership because he was previously a major general, then his decision was unbearably wrong. Those who were commissioned with him eventually progressed in the Movement and became top military commanders, during the war of liberation. This included his own stepbrother, Pieng Deng Kuol, who was commissioned as 1st lieutenant at the same time he was commissioned as a captain. He reached the highest military rank during the war of liberation, let alone the positions he held before and after the independence of the south. Makol Deng would have made a magnificent contribution towards the liberation struggle, had he not decided to end his life in such tragic circumstances. As the saying goes, "we cannot cry over the spilt milk" and unfortunately Makol would never return. Even though he left us too soon, he was still remembered as one of the many heroes who had fallen during the war of liberation.

General Pieng Deng Kuol, had a different point of view on why his stepbrother, Captain Michael Makol Deng, had committed suicide. He believed Makol committed suicide because he was picked, detained and taken to Bilpam by security personnel following orders of CDR Kerbino Kuanyin Bol. The reason he was detained, was because Kerbino lost one of his relatives during an Anya-nya 11 battle under the command of Ring Madut. Kerbino saw Makol as a blocking stone on his way to arrest Ring Madut for the death of his brother. Both Makol and Madut were intimate friends during the command of Anya-nya 11 forces. Captain Makol saw weakness in the top leadership of the Movement, questioning why he was taken detained and the fact Commander in Chief, Dr. John Garang de Mabior, didn't come to his defence . Makol saw a bleak future in the Movement since such behaviour could occur in the full knowledge of the chairman and not be condemned. The situation was worsened by the death of Captain Bolbek, making him believe there was no reason for him to stay alive in such a movement. So, the suicidal decision was a combination of his early arrest by Commander Kerbino Kuanyin Bol and the death of his half-brother Captain Bolbek and that the Movement had no certain future.

I mentioned earlier the cramped conditions in the Makuach village. This small village had received an influx of nearly 3000 – 4000 men within three days. As is the nature of any African village, Makuach was not equipped with important facilities such as toilets and bathrooms that could accommodate large numbers of people. The people who came to this village, had to relieve themselves in an open toilet in the nearby forest. Luckily, there was a certain type of vulture, 'the white hooded head' that relied on meat and human waste as a food source. These vultures admirably cleaned up the human waste from thousands of people who had just arrived from Bonga. We valued those vultures and the splendid responsibility they took on, of removing human waste.

The health condition of the forces around Makuach village, would have been drastically different if it wasn't for the white hooded-head vultures. It would have been a disastrous situation for the soldiers living in the camp. Rules of sanitation and hygiene were not strictly observed by the forces. Flies were rampant, tempting to contaminate food and their storage containers. We were saved by the grace of God and therefore, none of us were affected by disease during our days in Makuach. We had to remain at full strength, both physically and mentally, if we were to succeed in the challenges that lay ahead.

We spent around seven days at Makuach, before receiving orders to move to Mangok village. At 5:00am, the Bilpam battalion commander, Major Wilson Kur Chol, instructed his deputy, Major Kuol Manyang Juuk, to immediately order the forces to move across the Baro river onto the Sudanese side. The water level was very low that time of year. Therefore, the troops didn't require canoes or boats. We were able to walk across to the northern side with no issues. After converging on the other side, the marching order was organised in accordance with military formation. Hence, the first COY took the lead followed by the second COY and so on. Battalion headquarters were to be stationed in the middle, with two COYs behind and three in front, including rear and vanguards. By this time, the soldiers had built a lot of strength and were able to walk the five to six hours non-stop. Due to the increased quality of food available, the health condition of the forces improved greatly at Makuach.

This was the first time I had witnessed 1000 men walking in single file. The sight was elegant and impressive, as they moved along the river changing shape along the way. The soldiers kicked up large amounts of dust, like a fast vehicle. However, some members of the battalion, including myself, were facing the difficulty of wearing military boots over a long distance. For the inexperienced, they were heavy and caused damage to our feet. We didn't want to hold up our comrades, so we continued without fuss. We arrived at our destination of Mangok Village together.

My position in the battalion was a logistician, and there weren't many with a similar qualification. Part of my role was to ensure delivery and distribution of food rations such as; grains, rice, maize flour, bulls and different types of ammunitions. I therefore had to track deliveries and make sure I was available to distribute food at any given time. Therefore, my comrades would keep a watchful eye on my whereabouts! If there were delays, I had to keep everyone calm and provide an update.

Food items were already onsite when we arrived at Mangok. I had to distribute these immediately, as we hadn't been fed all day. Military Intelligent (MI) personnel, Mr. Rin Tweny Mabor, was in charge of all the SPLA food and ammos stores. He was a very tall and good-looking man, who could speak only when necessary. When I met him, he was a sergeant and hadn't yet been commissioned into an officer ranking. After a brief introduction, we explained the reason for our visit. He then provided us with food rations that were desperately needed. The COY's representatives and I, had to cross the Baro River back to the battalion's headquarters, where the food rations were distributed. . Once these had been handed out, I saw them off to their respective corners. There were no thatched huts for the troop's accommodation, so they had to stay under the trees.

Two days later, the commander in chief of the SPLA forces came to see how we were faring. Mangok village was the last point to prepare for a military offensive, against the enemy town of Jokou which was nearby. Dr. John's arrival to Mangok, was therefore much appreciated. He came with mounted vehicles for the forces to use at the war front. We did doubt however, whether the relatively small and low vehicles would safely cross to the other side of the Baro River. Hence a few soldiers were ordered to lower the level river banks on both sides, to ensure the Toyota pickup cars could safely cross while mounted with anti-tank artillery guns. Once the river banks were levelled, a driver named Chol Mawut Malual, successfully drove the Toyota pickup across to the other side of the river, much to the jubilation of the camp! We were amazed when Dr. John himself entered the water and attempted a crossing, following the success of the previous driver. Senior officers along with myself, joined the chairman in an attempt to cross together. Whilst in the middle of the river, there were extreme levels of excitement amongst the group that was crossing. This erupted when the chairman shot his pistol into the air, to the rapturous applause of the troops on either side. One captain, Anyuat Achek Pow, who was also elated by the situation, followed suit by shooting his pistol into the air. However, this action caused him to be disciplined. Not everything done by the chairman, is to be imitated by others.

One of the main obstacles troubling the leaders, was how to ferry military equipment across the Baro River. It was a great outcome that the vehicles were able to cross without hindrance, removing a major obstacle. It was in the pipeline that the army garrison town of Jokou would be our next target to attack and capture. Jokou posed a great risk, due to their listening and observation post which could expose our troops at any time. There was no route to get to Central Upper Nile, without passing near Jokou.

Considering the situation, The Movement's leaders decided Jokou must be dealt with to ensure free movement to and from Ethiopia. Movement of troops was constantly being detected by the enemy spies of Jokou. The decision to mount an attack on Jokou was not revealed to us, so we didn't know this would be our next mission.

The SPLM/A had been operating for two years, and had only just acquired military equipment such as personal rifles i.e. AKM rifles, light machine guns, RPG launchers, hand grenades and different types of light artillery mortars. This was in addition to SAM 7 anti- aircraft shoulder carrier. The troops were able to handle this equipment without problem, while crossing the Baro River and others including the White Nile. The SPLA started to expand in terms of military war machinery. Some heavy artillery was obtained, that needed to be mounted on vehicles and this became a test and a task to ensure they were still able to cross the Baro River. There is an English proverb which says, "you never try, you never know", so Dr. John Garang de Mabior wanted to give it a try, and find out whether the vehicles could still cross the Baro river during the current season. It was proved beyond reasonable doubt that the vehicles could easily overcome the obstacle of crossing the Baro River.

After the successful crossing, we received instructions to move to Marial village, which was a two hour walk away. We were given a double load of 240 rounds of ammunitions each, as we were already in the war zone. The three battalions of Lion, Bilpam and Elephant were stationed in different areas. Elephant battalion was to be stationed at Marial, Bilpam at Nyoplew, while Lion was to be based at Nyaang cattle camp which was very close to Jokou town. Marial is in Ethiopian territory, and therefore the Sudanese government forces cannot under any circumstances, attempt to launch an attack. This might have been the reason why the Movement's leaders chose to station their headquarters in Marial.

We arrived at Marial in the morning of February 1, 1985. The following day, three Commanders from Lion, Bilpam and Elephant battalions, Daniel Deng Alony, Wilson Kur Chol and Isaac Gatlok respectively, met to plan their attack and capture of Jokou. After this meeting, the three commanders were instructed to join the chairman and commander in chief of the SPLA, together with his deputy, Kerbino Kuanyin Bol, and Commander Salva Kiir Mayardit, to put the finishing touches on their plan of attack. Military tactics often depend on swift and surprise action. We had no time to waste. Hence it was decided that Jokou town would be attacked and captured on February 4, 1985. In the evening of that same day, Bilpam battalion was ordered to move to the Nyoplew cattle camp, on the northern side of Baro River. This left Lion and Elephant at Marial. We established Nyoplew as our launching base, for the Jokou operation.

On February 3, Bilpam battalion held a general parade where the forces received their last battle instructions for the following day. The soldier's morale was unimaginably high, puzzling those who were experienced with war, especially officers from Jamus and 104/105 battalions who had fought so many battles the year prior. The high morale was not just unique to Bilpam battalion, but also to the members of the other two battalions. Those who had remained at the Bonga Training Centre, were anxious to get to the frontline and participate, after waiting so long to face the enemy. They loved hearing victory news from the field when it was announced over Radio SPLA. Now, all that the second division had been anticipating, was coming to fruition. There was no excuse for the Locust division not to be satisfied, when their objective lay right in front of them.

February 3, 1985 was a day not to be forgotten, in the history of the three battalions. They had been made aware that February 4 was D-Day, so they were preparing for the immanent attack on Jokou and were counting down the minutes. For some of the patriotic comrades, it felt like time was standing still. They wanted the sun to set quickly so they could start moving towards their target. Indeed, it was 12:00am when the forces began to move.

The force was under the overall command of Lt. Colonel Kerbino Kuanyin Bol, Deputy Commander in Chief of the SPLA armed forces and the deputy Chairman of the SPLM. The distance from Nyoplew to Jokou wasn't far. It's never easy moving onto a military target, therefore many precautions had to be observed. There were obstacles on the road to Jokou. Nyaang cattle camp, manned by the local Nuer, was one of them. Our forces used sophisticated military tactics and night cover to evade enemy positions and avoid detection. Still, despite our stealth advance towards the target, the enemy at Nyaang managed to detect our headquarters and exchanged fire before the attacking group could commence. I was unsure why the shooting died down unexpectedly. Due to my position as logistician, I was made to stay behind in the camp and address other important matters such as administration and meal times . It was 4:30am when the attacking forces began their operation, bombarding the town with mortar shells and other artilleries. The enemy reciprocated, by throwing mortar shells where our forces were positioned. This continued for some time while the ground troops or infantry were advancing towards the enemy frontage. When they were a certain distance from the enemy, artillery forces were ordered to stop the shelling and bombardment, giving the infantry a chance to advance . The fighting continued unabatedly for more than four hours. Our forces faced stiff resistance from the entrenched enemy, and they could not penetrate their defensive lines. In the end, our forces had to make a tactical withdrawal and return to their respective bases. The soldiers with light injuries were the first to arrive at the camps. The news in the camp was the bodies of our dead comrades would not be evacuated for burial, due to the intensive enemy fire at the frontage. You can imagine how this made us feel.

I would like to state that our forces were fighting two enemies at the same time. The government troops at Jokou town and local Gajaak Nuer militia men at the rear. Withdrawing troops from the frontage, meant the escape route would be dangerous. The men who had withdrawn, were targeted by the enemy right up to the peripheries of the camp. Wounded heroes who were tracking the same route, were also not spared. All the wounded officers, which included the commander of the Bilpam battalion, line officers and men, were immediately sent back to either Gambella or the Itang Refugee Camp hospital for further medical treatment. Back in the battalion's headquarters, the troops morale, which was sky high the day prior, dropped quite significantly after the first day of operations.

Only two Companies (COYS) from the Bilpam battalion did participate on the first day. The rest were reserved for future operations.

The COY composed of 204 officers, line officers and men. When they returned to base their numbers had dropped, due to either being killed or wounded in action. Those who sustained injuries, were automatically evacuated to the rear base for medical attention. CDR Kerbino Kuanyin came back and managed to maintain the Nyoplew camp when orders from the battalion Commander came differently. Operations on February 5 were to be cancelled, so the forces could rest and prepare for the final assault on Jokou the following day. Indeed, on the 6th a much larger force was arranged and sent with the hope to capture Jokou. This time, extensive fire power was used and wave after wave of manpower for over 10 hours, from 4:30am to 3:00pm. However, no real advance was made on enemy positions. Our forces were again obliged to withdraw and abandon their position, when they were surprised by enemy reinforcements coming from behind. This ended our mission to capture Jokou.

It was a difficult task, not to be underestimated. Their reinforcement was streamlined and they could move faster than our men. Our men on Nasir road to Jokou couldn't be blamed for allowing the enemy to bypass. We were using short range radios for communication which was why the enemy reinforcement could not hit us hard at the war front. While communicating using short range radio, I remembered, CDR Salva Kiir came from Marial with a relatively small force walking quickly towards Jokou town where CDR Kerbino Kuanyin was. This small force managed to confront the enemy reinforcement on the outskirts of Jokou when 2nd Lt Majak da' Agoot da' Atem and many others were injured. In the end, the enemy reinforcement was forced into the town, while SPLA forces retreated to their respective camps very cautiously and not knowing what would happen with the new reinforcement that had entered the town. Will they have the courage to emerge from their defensive position? The following morning came, and the situation remained stable. The enemy remained calmly in their defensive positions inside the town. There is no doubt that Jokou was besieged from all sides. The SPLA ensured no one was allowed to step in or out of the town.

I would like to give a little explanation about the SPLA two-day operation at Jokou town. What led to the failure of the SPLA forces to capture the town? Was there any mismanagement at command level, that led to the failure? How is Jokou situated in terms of approach routes and geographical location?

In any military situation, mistakes are part of the process. Human errors are expected to occur, resulting in victories. In the case of the Jokou operation, yes, some undeniable errors were committed by the operational command leadership. A standard practice in military tactics when preparing to launch an attack, is for the commanders to draw a sand model for each particular target. This sand model must be practiced and studied by the officers and men of the chosen forces, so when operations commence, each will know where the enemy tanks, heavy machine guns, the enemy command post and others are located. It makes sense to deploy your machine guns in accordance with the enemy deployment of their machinery. Before the attack was launched on Jokou, there was no sand model completed. It was mentioned prior that the three commanders of the three battalions, met and discussed the operational plans for Jokou. They also met with Commanders Kerbino Kuanyin Bol and Commander Salva Kiir Mayardit, to discuss information they had acquired from a soldier, Sergeant Garang Gak da' Ayiik, who defected from Jokou a few months prior. He shared his knowledge about the town's military setting, however this must have been changed by the enemy after his defection.

After this collaboration, did they decide on a common position or strategy on how operations would be conducted? No, I very much doubt it. These discussions didn't take place at the battalion level, but I should have been aware of this planning due to my proximity with Commanders

Wilson Kur Chol and Kuol Manyang Juuk in addition to the six COY Commanders. The only plan the commanders of the three battalions were focusing on, was manpower superiority. We had over 3,000 armed men, compared to our enemy with only 500. Therefore, the military tactic was to move forward and manoeuvre best as possible, nothing further. Hence, no clear tactics were applied in the Jokou operation and as a result we failed to capture the town in spite of our superiority in terms of manpower and morale. We could not succeed to break through the well defended enemy lines, no matter how minimal their numbers were. We lost a severe amount of manpower in the two-day operation, which would make us pay dearly in the future.

The Background of Commander Kerbino Kuanyin Bol before joining the SPLM/A Movement

Prior to the formation of the SPLM/A Movement, Kerbino Kuanyin Bol was a major in the Sudanese Armed Forces. He was the Commanding Officer of battalion 105, deployed in Bor, Pibor and Pochalla where his headquarters was located. He arrived in Bor town when his battalion elements went into loggerhead with the Sudanese army's southern command headquarters in Juba, over issues which couldn't be resolved by people outside the military circles.

Some say the forces of battalion 105 were adamantly resisting military transfer orders from the south to the north, alleging they would be disarmed and dismissed from the army if these orders were obeyed. The other part of the story was elements within these forces were criminals accused of having mismanaged military finances in Bor town. Therefore they did not want to comply with transfer arrangements, that could expose them at some point.

If they were not ready to be transferred to the northern part of Sudan because of the reasons provided, how will they be loyal to the system they are serving while at the same time refusing to comply with it's orders? Surely the system was prompted and obliged to take drastic measures against 105 battalions' members', who resisted the transfer orders. This would damage any military system around the world, when a unit resists transfer orders and remains part of that system. It cannot happen in either the civil administration, nor the international. Hence, members of the 105 battalion undoubtedly had no justifiable reason to resist transfer orders. If the latter claim of criminals being accused of mismanaged military finances, was the core reason for their stiff resistance, this also had no standing. Any group or individuals accused of fraud would face prison, after being sentenced in a qualified court of law. Both allegations did not justify the reasons why members of the 105 battalion refused to adhere to their superiors instructions. The following narratives will seek to explain why Major Kerbino and others under his command, did not obey the transfer orders.

The defiance of instructions by battalion 105, was not just a mere rejection but rather a politically motivated move planned by senior South Sudanese officers within the ranks of the Sudanese armed forces. These senior officers hoped to make South Sudan an independent entity on its own merits and rights, like any other sovereign nations in Africa and the world at large. It was just a clandestine movement circulating it's ideas within their own circles. They aimed to launch this plan in the middle of the rainy season, when enemy forces would be reduced by rains, wetness and other obstacles which would be conducive enough to avoid any misfortune to the leaders of this group. Dr. John Garang de Mabior was among many others behind this plan. This group was of the opinion, there was no reason to allow the southern elements to get their own way. Therefore, those forces were to create obstacles to ensure the

105 forces remain in their positions in Bor, Pibor and Pochalla. Those officers would prevent them from leaving the south, but the rainy season was still very far away meaning they would have to wait until D-Day. With the impatience of a person like Major Kerbino Kuanyin Bol, people were getting frustrated when the earmarked month of August for the declaration of the southern independence, was still a few months away. Bor town, together with Pibor and Pochalla, were due to be attacked in March 1983. However local politicians interfered and requested the southern military headquarters in Juba should be given a chance to sort out the matter with their brothers of battalion 105 in Bor town. That chance was awarded, but to no success. When all diplomatic avenues had been exhausted, Dr. John had to appear in Juba with his family aiming to proceed to Bor then onto his home village of Wangkulei. He met Major General Sadeeg el Banna, who permitted him to proceed to Bor when he was 100% certain that Bor would be under military operations within a short period. Another prominent southern politician, Mr. Abel Alier Kuai Kut who was the Vice President of the Republic of the Sudan, was also in Bor town trying to stop the water from Bahr el Jebel which caused floods every year to his home area. Mr. Abel Alier was attempting to stop the stream, when Bor suddenly came under attack from the Sudanese armed forces on the morning of May 16, 1983.

I happened to be in Bor town when I received advice from my relatives, Mr. Kon Paul Nul Bior and Mr. Dau (Jeres) Akoi Jurkuch, to return to my duty station in Juba. I complied with their advice immediately, leaving Bor town for Juba on May 15, 1983. Upon my arrival in Juba, there were military tanks standing on the eastern side of the Juba Bridge, and I got wind of information they were on their way to attack battalion 105 in Bor town. I knew going to Bor would not be a tea party! It meant a lot considering the manner I had left Kerbino and his troops. It required proper support from the government. Indeed, Bor town came under heavy fire the morning of the May 16, 1983, as it was expected. Major Kerbino Kuanyin Bol with his troops put on a brave and tough resistance in the face of the aggressors, resisting their waves one after another until the evening of the first day. Major Kerbino was injured in action and was evacuated in an unknown direction. The fight resumed the following morning, but the government troops still did not succeed in breaking through to the town. However, it was assumed that those in Bor would yield to the pressure of the government's advancing troops when they tactically withdrew out of the town and melted into the communities. Government troops were not aware that the 105 battalion members had evacuated the town, until a good Samaritan tipped them off the evening of the 17th. There was many casualties, including Senior Officer Major Khamis who acted as Deputy Commander of the attacking forces. The injured were evacuated back to Juba on military vehicles. I wasn't aware of any losses to the 105 battalion, though they were apparently minimal, according to information received from those at the battle, among them private Maker Jiol.

§

Did Kerbino Kuanyin Bol and his Commanding Officers, have the Military Knowledge and Capabilities to Lead the Jokou Operation? The answer to this question is yes and no, due to the following reasons.

Commander Bol participated in the first southern struggle from 1955-1972, until he was absorbed into the Sudanese armed forces at the rank of captain. Military service became his duty, until he was promoted to the rank of major. You would assume someone who served in the regular army for eleven years, would be well trained with superior knowledge. I am unable to provide detail on which military courses or training he had completed, to qualify him as a successful officer when he was serving in the Sudanese armed forces. Mangoak, his preferred name in his private life, performed many successful operations against the Anya-nya 11 rebels in the Upper Nile province, which could be added to his military knowledge. The first most significant battle Kerbino commanded, if any, was the battle of Bor against the huge invading Sudanese government army. This occurred before he could defect to the bush and participate in the formation of the SPLA/M in 1983 in Ethiopia. Commander Kerbino above all, led the very successful Buffalo battalion in 1984 attacking and capturing many Sudanese army garrison towns in different parts of the south. He had indeed dispersed a large convoy between Nakdiar and Mohamed Ajak in February 1984, capturing and destroying many enemy tanks and APCs. Finally adding to this experience, he raided Malakal town before he went back to Ethiopia.

His successes that year brought pride back to the people of Southern Sudan, which had been missing for centuries. This was in addition to victories in Deng-jok and Kir in the Akobo area, capturing weapons and enemy soldiers. All these operations were perceived by the top leadership of the Movement to have provided essential military knowledge to Kerbino and that was another possible reason he was chosen to lead the Jokou operation.

Again, on a separate occasion, Commander Kerbino was assigned the role of Deputy Commander in Chief of the SPLA. He was considered by members of the high command, to be the logical person to tackle that duty. Commander Kerbino as a person, was very brave and courageous. All who knew him, would certainly attest to this. Therefore it was a reasonable decision for the leaders of the Movement to offer him command of the Jokou operation.

The explanation given above was tackling the 'yes' part of the answer, confirming why Commander Kerbino was the right person to have shouldered the Jokou assignment. The other side of the answer was 'no'. Let me narrate why others thought he wasn't the right commander to lead the Jokou operation. Firstly, despite his military background in the one of the best rated armies in Africa (possibly the world at large), Kerbino didn't receive training at the leadership level during the years he spent in the Sudanese military service. Therefore, he only possessed a superficial knowledge that would not entirely qualify him to command the huge forces of four battalions. This included Hippopotamus battalion, which joined the operation later on.

Secondly, although Commander Kerbino successfully managed to conduct operations against the Sudanese armed forces in 1984, those operations were meant for recruitment purposes along with guerrilla hit and run tactics aimed at moving targets. The objective of this was a show of strength from the Movement, no matter how strategic and important that town might have been. Hence, his military capacity didn't include operations on stationery targets such as Jokou town, which required entirely different plans and approaches.

Thirdly, Commander Kerbino could sometimes become distressed when unplanned situations arose. His lack of patience and restraint in this regard would affect his military administration. He would not allow himself the appropriate time to obtain accurate information on a subject and work out the best approach. He became overconfident with his large number of troops, and gave no consideration to the enemies' size, strength and weaknesses. His command style was "advance and move on to the target and capture it". How do you move to capture that target? What was required in terms of manpower, equipment and time would not be his utmost priority. His only concern was humiliation, if you are the commander of a force who was unsuccessful in operation.

These examples illustrate both the 'yes' and 'no' reasons, for Commander Kerbino Kuanyin Bol's leadership of the Jokou operation. This operation went for approximately 50 days of continuous assault, two or three times a day. The first two-day assault exhausted much of SPLA forces. Thus, they needed a fresh force to be formed at the Bilpam general headquarters under the command of Captain Chol Deng Alak. They couldn't undertake training at the Bonga Training Centre due to their poor health condition. They were referred to the Itang Refugee Camp for medical treatment during military training at Bonga. That force totalling 1,000 men, was a mighty force that would have added reasonable strength to the men already fighting around town. Their armament came from the wounded casualties of the 2-day Jokou operation. The Jokou situation also didn't spare the female battalion either, who were under the command of Captain Deng Alor Kuol. Their presence in the area, in my opinion, was to boost the morale of the real fighting forces. Especially because they didn't participate in any of the military operations. Commander Kerbino wouldn't risk committing them in Jokou, until the whole operation was over.

To highlight the determination of the SPLM/A when trying to capture the town, they planned a siege from all directions giving little chance of the rescuing forces to penetrate. Remnants of the Jamus battalion who were either illiterate or hadn't attended Cadet College, were stationed in Jerusalem to the northeast of the town near the Ethiopian border. Why the remnants of Jamus battalion? Because the majority were from Cadet College, who were trained and graduated as officers. They were now commanding the current forces operating in Jokou along with other forces all over Southern Sudan. Hippo battalion was based in the northwest of town, while Lion and Bilpam battalions were based to the west of the road into Nasir. This was the route that enemy forces advancing towards Jokou would take. The Elephant and Female battalions were situated to the south at Marial, inside Ethiopia's border which was acting as the headquarters and logistics base for the operation. I must remind you that there are two Jokou towns. Ethiopian Jokou, which falls to the east, and the Sudanese Jokou falling to the west. These are only separated by the Jokou running stream. The presence of the Ethiopian Jokou was unsettling the SPLA forces, as they had to determine whether the Ethiopians were the Movement's friends. If bombardment or shelling was launched on the town from the western side, you may mistakenly hit the Ethiopian Jokou, which the Movement would not dare to entertain. It had become a sanctuary position for the enemy troops, placing their defensive lines close to Ethiopian Jokou. This meant the Movement required superb control over their falling shells, so they didn't accidentally hit one of the Ethiopian targets. Therefore, we took extraordinary care not to harm our friends on the other side of Jokou.

The operations in Jokou continued. The SPLA forces would launch attacks in the morning and raid after a raid at night, which prevented the enemy from having space and time to rest. This continued despite the fact the Movement was paying a hefty price in loss of manpower. To capture a town, we knew the price we had to pay. Blood would be spilled and lives would be lost, however we understood the importance of capturing Jokou. From the enemy's point of view, nothing much had changed since the first reinforcements arrived in town. Demand for more rescuing teams to Jokou, was a priority. According to information received from intercepting radio communications, the enemy was preparing for another reinforcement to be dispatched helping alleviate the situation around the sieged Jokou.

This didn't go down well with us. All we wanted was to capture the town before the enemy rescuing convoy could arrive. And the SPLA command were motivating the forces to cut short the enemy attempts of reinforcing Jokou. As they say, sea-men don't wish the storm to occur while in the sea. The long-awaited enemy rescuing convoy arrived on March 3, 1985, under the command of Colonel Abd el Rohaman Ahmad el Balaa. At 3:00pm their forces commenced operations against Hippo battalion. Commander Kerbino instructed the Lion and Bilpam battalions to rush to the frontage with reinforcements for Hippo battalion, which they did without delay. All the forces converged on the frontage, finding Hippo battalion a bit shaky and overwhelmed by the enemy forces.

In the opinion of military experts, there is nothing that provides a greater relief to a fighting force, than the arrival of reinforcements. This is no matter how small or ill equipped that force may be. The confrontation ended at 6:00pm with the death of the enemy commanding officer, el Balaa. Many of his officers and men also perished. Supplies such as; trucks, heavy and light machine guns, different types of mortar guns with shells, ammo and food items were captured. Only two lorries from that convoy narrowly escaped and entered Jokou town without men except the drivers. Some lucky officers and men from the SPLA, managed to run away with an unaccountable amount of Sudanese money. Some Sudanese soldiers fell captive.

The soldiers coming back to Nyoplew camp travelled till midnight carrying their gear. As mentioned earlier, the brave and courageous Mangoak (Kerbino Kuanyin Bol), could not stay away from the frontage despite his position both in the army and the Movement. He was fighting alongside soldiers, until things subsided. We in the Nyoplew camp where Commander Kerbino stayed, felt nervous until he arrived sometime late in the night and the camp was marred with the slogan of SPLA Ohyee. This had to be loudly echoed by all in the camp with the same SPLA Ohyee running after him. Surely Mangoak and everyone else, were fully intoxicated by the huge triumph and victory of the day if not the year. Those around Jokou, felt like people who had already liberated Southern Sudan. But the mayhem of capturing Jokou was still haunting us in the camp.

Early morning on March 4, Commander Kuanyin returned to the

battlefield to witness what had occurred the day prior. I had to remain at camp, registering the value and importance of items that had been captured with the Movement. One Magerus lorry mounted with 12.7mm heavy machine guns, 120mm mortar and many other items were taken to the rear to be examined for damage. At the battlefield, Commander Kuanyin Bol prayed for the souls of the commander of the government army convoy, Colonel Abd el Rahman Ahmad el Balaa and his men, blaming the repressive regime of Gaffer Mohamed Nimeiry in Khartoum, to be responsible for the current war.

It was a commendable day in the history of the SPLA/M and its radio, when news of this victory was broadcast in the afternoon of March 4, 1985. This victory and other SPLA/M successes brought joy and happiness to the Southern Sudanese masses and the sympathisers, wherever they were. Around Jokou, we celebrated this victory for some time, but also kept in mind the enemy in Khartoum may have heard the calls of their people in Jokou town. This meant more reinforcements, possibly the worst to come, could be expected soon. Days went on and the SPLA forces continued their mounting attacks on Jokou, with the aim to finish and capture it.

One evening, a routine raiding force was ready to advance towards Jokou for the normal night raid. This time, the force started marching into town earlier than usual. Reason being, the raiding force would sometimes miss the target if they deploy their artillery when it's dark. Therefore they wanted to deploy at last light, so they could maintain accuracy of hitting the targets when commencing the raid on the town. This move however, worked against them because they were spotted by enemy guards who had binoculars and were stationed on the trees. They were detected before they could deploy their weapons. They were already inside the enemy artillery range, and started to mercilessly bombard them until they dispersed, running in different directions. It was a marvellous victory from the government forces at Jokou, by preventing the raid. Surely that night, they must have slept comfortably and undisturbed. The SPLA could not organise another raid that night.

There was discontent on our side, because Commander Kerbino was unhappy and forbade all in the camp to rest. We had to correct the error from yesterday and the raid was successfully accomplished the following night. That was one incident I couldn't forget among many others, but I would like to share two more incidents that have stayed in my memory.

Commander Kerbino Kuanyin Bol was a person of unique character. He would admire a person for one reason or another. For instance, he befriended Major Kuol Manyang Juuk who succeeded Major Wilson Kur Chol, in the command of Bilpam battalion when the latter was wounded in day one of the Jokou operation. Major Wilson Kur Chol was evacuated for medical attention after he suffered a chest injury. He admired Major Kuol because he would remain with his forces on the battlefield during the assault. This was uncommon amongst the other battalion's commanders. He would always return to base with his forces at the end of every operation. Mangoak, made these observations within the first two days of the Jokou operation. It was protocol in the forces, for a commander to work with officers within his headquarters comprising of a logistician, the long and short-range radio unit, intelligence officers, and other unassigned or undeployed officers. Commander Kuol would follow this protocol in the days he spent with us. This changed when Kerbino suddenly removed Commander Kuol from our group, stating a brave and courageous man like Kuol must join him at his headquarters.

A new plan for Jokou emerged, which involved a night operation to be led by one of the commanding officers. That operation became a total mess. The commanding officer of the raiding force had to part ways with the main attacking body, and attempts to rescue the situation failed. The short-range radio operator did not cooperate and allow the Commander of the forces and receive instructions from the overall Commander Kerbino Kuanyin. Despite the persuasive language used by the overall commander to rescue the situation, the radio operator did not adhere to him. Everyone at the Nyoplew camp that night, surrounded Kerbino trying to work out the best route of communication for the current situation. These attempts were unfortunately unsuccessful. The radio operator would switch off the radio if he was overwhelmed, to avoid orders and possible communication with him. In the end, Commander Mangoak threw his hands up in frustration after so many attempts, promising the radio operator that he would track him down. Mangoak went to bed then the rest retired to their respective sleeping places. Those operations failed to materialise that night.

Commander Kerbino's headquarters included many respected officers such as, 2nd Lt Johnson Guny Biliu and 2nd Lt. Jumaa Babo Kaka known as Abu Hadeed, to mention a few. The two officers ensured the short range radio operator would learn a lesson for a lifetime. They didn't go to sleep with the others and instead deployed some personnel on the route to Marial, so they could confront him on his return. Exactly at dawn, they caught the radio operator while returning with the force and rushed him to Commander Kerbino's headquarters, across the Baro River. We all woke upon hearing the shouts of Mangoak, who was threatening to shoot him. The shouts continued for some time. It was chaos between the defending and opposing groups.

Those of us who were new to the situation, took his word for it, but those familiar with his behaviour were more relaxed. 2nd Lt. Atem Zachariah Duot, although aware of Kerbino's behaviour, became the victim of the situation when he jumped in front of Kerbino to protect the radio operator. He was slapped in the face by Commander Kerbino, telling him he needed no justification to shoot someone. If Napoleon Bonaparte and Adolf Hitler had free hands to shoot their subjects, as both were commanding national armies of their sovereign states. But Mangoak was a guerrilla fighter unlike the former commanders. Anyway, quick justice was applied, and the radio operator was immediately given 50 lashes, arrested and sent to the Marial base for detention. This event along with many others that passed unnoticed, would have made an impressive film - if only we had the cameras.

In the morning, the force which failed to conduct operations the previous night, was instructed to proceed the following night, but with a change of command. Commander Kuanyin Bol could not find a brave enough alternative to execute this operation, except for Major Kuol Manyang Juuk from the Bilpam battalion. Indeed, commander Kuol succeeded in conducting the operation and the government forces in Jokou were made to pay dearly. That was in accordance with the intercepted radio messages received from our radio operator. When Commander Kuol returned to base the following morning, he was praised by Kerbino for a job well done, and his expectations had been met. I believe Commander Kuol Manyang remained in Kerbino's good books until his death, due to the bravery he displayed. May God the Almighty put his soul in eternal peace.

My assignment in the battalion as a logistician, was to control whatever food and ammunition stores were available. Distribution of ammo would be dealt with separately depending on the battalion's needs and only when operations were conducted. It should be used as a form of replenishment, to those who used their rounds in previous battles. Food items were brought to the battalions from the headquarters at Marial, on a specified distribution day. Ration masters from the COYs would flock to the battalion headquarters, where I was required to distribute rations and in their turn distribute it in accordance to each platoon. This would also occur when bulls arrived for distribution. Initially, each battalion was provided with rifles and their 303 1914 ammunition to exchange for bulls, which went like hot cakes with the local population.

It was an indication that the local Gajaak Nuers, were armed with these types of rifles, unlike the SPLA whose armaments were mainly AKM Kalashnikov rifles. A message would be sent to the leaders of nearby cattle camps on auction day, advising them to bring their bulls in exchange for ammunitions. The exchange would be amicably carried out at our camps, according to the needs and requirements. Once this exchange was completed, the bull's allocation to the COYs would be done in accordance with the COYs seniority. Larger bulls would be taken by the senior COYs and the smaller ones would be allocated to the lowest ranked COY, which was the headquarter of the battalion. The overall commander of the headquarters and the Bilpam battalion, would share the relatively small bull. This was because they were fewer in numbers and lower down in participation levels of the operation. I wasn't sure if my name was in the bad books of those personnel from the two headquarters.

The bulls would sometimes become wild when they were about to be slaughtered, and would occasionally attempt to run away if mishandled by the COYs members. This would leave them with nothing to consume. I raised a complaint with the commander of the battalion, requesting permission to shoot the wild bulls so they didn't escape the slaughtering. Commander Kuol was well aware of the standing camp orders from the overall Commander Kerbino Kuanyin Bol, yet accepted my request. This could have been viewed by others as violating the standing orders, that shooting in and around the camp was completely prohibited.

I had concerns, through personal observations, that Commander Kerbino had a negative attitude towards me. I felt I needed to be extra careful when dealing with people from his headquarters, so no one would report me for bad behaviour. On one occasion, someone reported me to Kerbino in relation to the way I was handling the logistics in the camp. I was ordered to see him immediately. I explained the situation and reassured him of my competency, however I still received a warning to not repeat that behaviour again. This was enough for me to conclude that Kerbino, for reasons known to him, was not entertaining me and I should do my best to win his favour.

Commander Kuanyin Bol would frequently hold parades with members of the Bilpam battalion, whenever he felt like doing so. I would always opt to translate his speech from Arabic into Dinka and vice versa. A Nuer man would translate into Nuer, another local language. After making this extra effort on three occasions, Mangoak started to prefer myself for the job. If I was unavailable for any reason, I was made to complete the job to show I held no grudges and was willing to cooperate. It seemed he started to admire my style of translation without my notice.

§

One day, we had a bull which was very difficult to handle. I ordered an aircraft gunner, Sergeant Garang Akok Adut, to shoot the bull which was tied under Nyoplew's only sausage tree. Sergeant Garang stood next to those who were ready to skin the bull afterwards. He took aim at the bull and successfully fired a bullet into its head, but unexpectantly, the bullet came out the other side and hit and injured a soldier in the arm. The soldier was standing in line with Sergeant Garang Akok Adut. As soon as the incident occurred, a message was sent to Kerbino advising Sargeant Garang Akok had violated his orders and shot a soldier in the arm while shooting a bull. It was early in the morning when the incident occurred, otherwise it could have been a different story had happened later in the day. In no time at all, Sergeant Garang was standing to attention in front of Kerbino. There are standing orders in the camp, that no one is allowed to shoot in that area. Kerbino asked, "I have just heard that you have shot a soldier while shooting a bull?". Sergeant Garang replied, "Yes, it happened comrade!". "Who gave you the order to shoot the bull and where is he?" 1st Lieutenant Jurkuch Barach he answered. I knew I would be called immediately, so I was near the vicinity.

Surely enough someone came to salute me, then told me I was wanted by Commander Kerbino. I came to where he was and found Sergeant Garang standing to attention, and I did the same. Comrade Kerbino said, "Sergeant Garang has shot a soldier just now, and when I asked him who gave him the order to shoot the bull, his answer was you". Without any hesitation, I admitted it was myself who gave him the order. Commander Kerbino asked, "But what about yourself, who gave the order to shoot a bull, that led Sergeant Garang to shoot the soldier?". "From my Commander Kuol Manyang", I answered. Kerbino asked, "And where is Major Kuol? Let him come now." The messenger searched to find him, but had to report he was unable to be found. Sergeant Garang and I remained in attention, meanwhile comrade Mangoak was still sitting in his chair brushing his teeth with locally invented material. Suddenly, comrade Kuol emerged from nowhere finding us still in attention. Major Kuol followed suit. Comrade Kerbino narrated the whole issue to Major Kuol, and Kuol admitted that he was behind the orders because the bulls would run away if mishandled. Commander Kerbino knew Major Kuol was aware of his standing orders, and if he did, this would have been a serious concern. Kerbino favoured the way Major Kuol manages the battalion's affairs. He finally instructed the Chief Intelligent Officer to arrest Sergeant Garang Akok Adut, because he shot the soldier. However they found his action was under instruction from his senior and there was no ill intention, just a mere unfortunate incident that could have been committed by anyone.

Commander Kerbino Kuanyin Bol restrained himself and behaved that way because of the following two reasons. Firstly, he admired the way Major Kuol was managing the battalion as it was mentioned before. Secondly, my relationship with him had improved of late, due to the way

I was managing the logistics in the battalion. I had ensured things were functioning and with no grievances with commanders of the COYs. My role in making the translations, also would have contributed. So, we had a mutual respect for him.

Sergeant Garang Akok Adut was arrested at 7:30am but was released at 8:30am, with only one hour in detention. The reason comrade Kerbino provided his release, was Sergeant Garang Akok was the only successful and well trained person in an anti-aircraft (SAM-7 surface to air missile) shoulder carried launcher. Suppose the government's jet-fighter was to launch a raid on the camp with comrade Garang under detention, who else would take his role in firing at the attacking aircraft? Kerbino understood it would have been negligent if Sergeant Garang was under detention, should an enemy raid occur. The other reason Garang was released, was the injury sustained by the soldier wasn't fatal or life threatening. The soldier only required medical treatment at Marial and returned to camp immediately. What I would like to highlight here, is that it was very difficult to predict Commander Kuanyin Bol, but if he finds a positive trait in a person, it will carry in their favour for some time.

I will now return to the siege of Jokou, and how the enemy would plan to rescue their men. The enemy in Khartoum were very much disturbed by the developments in Jokou. This disturbance was felt at the highest level of government and military. Two reinforcements had already been dispatched to rescue their forces, but to no avail. They had lost the lives of two very dear and important officers including Colonel Abd el Rehman Ahmad el Balaa and others. Before this occurred, the Khartoum government or army general headquarters, wanted to manage the Jokou operation single handed, with no involvement from the southern friendly elements of Anya-nya 11. This time, they were able to prepare a larger convoy under the command of Major General Awad Abasher. The commander of those forces was advised to include some elements from the Anya-nya 11 forces, using an English proverb which says, "Hit the iron with an iron". This force was now amounting around 6,000 men including the Southern Nuer bandits of Anya-nya 11. The forces of Anya-nya 11 had parted political ways with the SPLM/A in 1983 and made them pay an allegiance to the government of Sudan. The support to the government by the forces of Anya-nya 11, would in return be paid back by the government, in terms of armament and other military equipment. This would enable them to fight the SPLM/A on equal footing. The plan of attack was Anya-nya 11 would fight the SPLA/M at the rear, while government forces would face them from the front.

All the enemy forces were to get assembled in Nasir town. After plans were completed, they commenced from Nasir town advancing towards Jokou. The troops were full of confidence, to the extent they were following the main road which previous reinforcing convoys would avoid. Our forces were 3,000 plus, but they were exhausted due to the continuous operations over the last month and a half. Some of the troops were lost in action and many who sustained injuries and were evacuated to medical centres. This resulted in a drop of morale amongst the SPLA troops. But nonetheless, we were prepared to meet the challenge of the two combined enemy forces of Anya-nya 11 and the Sudan regular armed forces. They arrived at our location at 12:00pm on March 18, 1985 when we were already in our defensive lines. As usual, they began with shelling to the Nyoplew camp. We intentionally refused to reciprocate, in order not to expose our defensive position. The ambush site was in a baron valley with no trees or other vegetation that would provide cover for military personnel. We therefore had to remain in the fox holes for three hours before the battle could commence. The enemy applied a single file formation when they arrived at our ambush position.

Our plan was to let the whole enemy force into the ambush site, then the members of Lion battalion - who were at the front - would have to strike first. But the plan was thwarted by our recce elements who had been sent to Marial Forest, northeast of Nyoplew, anticipating the enemy might come from that direction. Those recce elements recognised the enemy had emerged from behind, so they wanted to rush back to defend Nyoplew. Upon sighting them, the enemy stopped, took position and began shelling. That was enough for the main body to begin the fight. It was exactly at 3:00pm when the fire exchange started. It was the first time that myself as logistician, took part in the battle and fired my first bullet from my AKM rifle, since graduating from the Bonga Training Centre two months prior. I had to remove the shame of not having physically participated in the Jokou operation, which I had felt right from the beginning. A depiction of cowardice towards myself, was in the mouth of every soldier in the camp. They did not understand how my role of logistician was relevant in the assignment. So my assignment, to those who hailed from the cattle camps and others, was nothing more than being a coward. The fact the enemy was at my doorstop, was an opportunity to prove to everyone in the camp that my assignment wasn't the illusion they were fixated on. We assaulted the enemy equally with those who fought the enemy in Jokou town so hard, to the extent that I felt like I performed better than those with more experience. The battle continued until 8:00pm, then it temporarily ceased until resuming at dawn on March 19, 1985. It resumed the following morning, but this time the fighting became fierce and a tougher assault and counter assault continued until midday, when our men decided to vacate the area. Of course, the Bilpam battalion Commander Major Kuol Manyang Juuk was injured in the dusk of March 18, 1985 and had been evacuated to the rear base for treatment.

All the SPLA forces after losing their ground, regrouped at Mangok village inside Ethiopia's border. The Chairman of the SPLM and Commander in Chief of the SPLA, Dr. John Garang de Mabior, came to the village of Mangok together with Commander Salva Kiir Mayardit, to address the officers and men of the Movement. They assured the troops it was the battle that we had lost, but not the war at large. This was a morale boosting moment, especially after losing the Jokou operation which would have been a significant achievement, had we succeeded. Our overall Commander Kerbino Kuanyin Bol, also addressed the rally and I was there to translate his speech as usual. Hadeed (Iron) battalion also withdrew from Adura (Thiajak) when they learned of our eviction from Jokou, leaving local Nuer elements to man the area for the day. The entire force was reorganised and ordered to go to Adura (Thiajak) under the command of Lt Colonel Francis Ngor Machec, who had left the area two days prior.

Iron battalion's withdrawal and abandonment of Adura (Thiajak), brought a rift between Commander Kerbino Kuanyin Bol and the Commander of Iron battalion, Francis Ngor Machec. Kerbino believed there was no reason for Iron battalion to vacate the strategic town. Lt Colonel Francis thought differently on the situation. After the SPLA/M forces had been evicted, Anya-nya 11 forces were accompanying the enemy to Jokou, and Lt Colonel Francis was concerned these two forces along with the local Nuer people, would converge and capture the town. This would leave them with significant loses in terms of manpower and equipment. Lt Colonel Francis was attempting to save the lives of his men and the equipment by moving to a relatively safer place, before the convergence of the Anya-nya 11.

Both men were in the Sudan armed forces before they defected to the bush and participated in the formation of the SPLM/A Movement. However, the two men had developed a sour relationship since the Movement's inception in 1983. Lt Colonel Francis Ngor was the most senior among the rest, except for Dr. John Garang de Mabior who became Chairman of the SPLM and Commander in Chief of the SPLA. Lt. Colonel Francis Ngor was sidelined by the group during the formation of the Movement, for reasons unknown to me.

The forces marched the entire night until they arrived on the morning of March 21, 1985. This time I was lucky that Commander Mangoak advised everyone that I was permitted to use the vehicle, for the night journey to Adura (Thiajak). On arrival, we almost clashed with the local Nuer but they rushed out of town before we could take action. Two days following our departure from Mangok village, Commander Kerbino Kuanyin Bol came to Adura (Thiajak) and called for a rally with the forces from Iron, Lion, Bilpam, Elephant and Hippo battalions. A friend of mine advised me to stop translating Commander Kuanyin speeches for the fear that I might end up at his chaotic headquarters. I took this advice on board and did abstain from attending that rally. I was later told that Commander Mangoak was frantically searching for me, but I was nowhere to be found. He then opted to select another officer from Iron battalion to complete the translation.

What is Jokou Town in Terms of Size and the Routes of Approach?

Sudan's Jokou was and still is, a very small town situated on the northern side of the Baro river, at the Sudan/Ethiopian border. There is also an Ethiopian Jokou, that falls to the east of the Sudanese Jokou. A small water tributary named after Jokou runs on the eastern side of the town, which is the waterway that divides them. There is also Nyaang Cattle Camp which falls on the western side of Jokou. Residing here are a few small government institutions including an army unit, police, local administration and local chiefs of the area. It has a small market poorly stocked with local produce and some items normally supplied from Malakal. These are delivered by small boats during the rainy season and by trucks in the dry season. Sometimes domesticated animals (cows, goats and sheep) are sold at this market. Jokou town drew its importance because of the proximity to the Ethiopian border as it was mentioned earlier in this book. Jokou town was found to be reporting to the Khartoum Government all activities made by the Movement. This would prompt the leadership to decide whether to proceed.

Jokou town is located on a plain in a swampy area, which gets flooded in the rainy season and dries up during the dry season. It does not have the capability to grow trees to form a bush or forest, so it remains very open to the eye. This means an approaching person or animal can be detected from three to five kilometres away. This factor wasn't thoroughly considered by the commanders who manned the Jokou operation. In an exposed town like Jokou, it's always difficult to approach or withdraw during the light of day. This is the reason the SPLA forces didn't succeed. Instead, we lost significant manpower from those killed or wounded in action and failed in our prime objective to capture the town.

I must reiterate that the Movement's leadership have given Jokou town a weight it didn't deserve. In my opinion, more than 5,000 men who were assigned to capture Jokou could have been given different tasks. For instance, if that force was tasked to prevent movements of the enemy in between the towns applying guerrilla tactical warfare, that alone should have been able to paralyse or hamper the enemy's transportation system. This should have occurred not only in the Upper Nile region, but also in the other regions of the southern parts of the country, by decentralizing the force into COYs instead of battalions. At that time, a COY consisted of a formidable force of 204 able officers, non-commissioned officers and men. It was a formidable force and capable enough to operate alone and be victorious against the enemy forces if permitted.

I am aware of some difficulties this plan could have encountered if we were to apply that tactic. The problem could have been centred in the communication system, given that each battalion was assigned with either one Racal or TRC 340 long range communication radio, plus an unspecified number of short-range radios. Surely if this was taken as a policy by the leadership of The Movement, they could have acquired reasonable numbers of both long-range and short-range radios to the levels of COYs of the five battalions. Surely, the Movement's presence would have been felt all over the south in the second year of operation, instead of hearing it around Jokou or in most cases around the Upper Nile region. This does not negate or deny missions of Buffalo battalion who were sent to Aweil to destroy Lol Bridge in 1984 and Zendia battalion's mission to eastern Equatoria for mobilization and recruitment of new manpower in 1985.

Concentration of operations in one region had a negative effect on the Movement at the later stages, because the majority of the SPLA forces at that time originated from tribes of Upper Nile and Bahr el Gazal. Most of the officers hailed from the two regions mentioned, depending on the time they joined the Movement. This gave seniority to the officers from the two regions, which was seen by members of the other tribes, especially from Equatoria, that the Movement only belonged to the Upper Nile and Bahr el Gazal regions. But this was not the case. In a military system or hierarchy, promotions are granted to members according to their seniority at the time of their arrival to the Movement's headquarters. This is along with what military training has been completed in the Movement's training centres. This issue could have been avoided completely if a decentralisation policy was adopted and implemented during the initial stages. Recruitment could have been conducted in every corner of the south simultaneously, leaving no chance for future complaints from aggrieved comrades. Some officers from the area of Equatoria raised complaints to the leadership of the Movement, requesting promotions to senior positions in order to be equal with their comrades from the Upper Nile and Bahr El Gazal regions.

Life in Adura (Thiajak)

After two months of operation in Jokou, the life of the forces in Adura (Thiajak) became remarkably difficult as living conditions were not conducive. Food sources dried up as supplies from the Itang Refugee Camp became unreachable and therefore the limited stocks were exhausted by the thousands of troops living in the area. In the first week of April 1985, Commander Kerbino instructed Lt Colonel Francis Ngor from Iron battalion, to organise a force ready to attack a small government army garrison town of Malual Gahuth which was along the Baro river, not far from Adura (Thiajak). Orders of Mangoak were to be implemented immediately. Battalions of Iron, Lion, Elephant and Hippo were selected for the mission under the overall command of Lt Colonel Francis Ngor Machec. These four battalions started to move at dusk that same day. Four Jeeps mounted with anti-tank launchers were prepared to escort the forces. They departed and deployed near the target. At dawn the following day, they commenced proceedings around town, but the whole operation turned out to be disastrous. Local Nuer militia attacked our men from the rear while we were facing the enemy in front. We lost the Commander of the forces, L.t Colonel Francis Ngor Machec, along with 103 officers and men. It was the first time in SPLM/A history, to lose such a huge number in a single battle including the commander of the forces. Even Jokou, which was known as a graveyard to the SPLA forces, didn't result in as many casualties in a single day. Life at the camp was gloomy, due to the loss of our dear comrades and particularly the loss of Lt Colonel Francis Ngor Machec. I fall short in providing proper emphasis or a description about the personality of Lt Colonel Francis Ngor Machec, as I didn't know much about him at that stage. According to information I have gathered, he was such a gentleman in every aspect of life, it is beyond description.

I will reiterate, why was such a huge force not able to cohesively fight and defend itself? After nearly two months of deadly Jokou operations, the morale of the forces dropped to its lowest level. The forces were not ready or willing to fight further battles, at that point in time. Loss of morale in the army is a major setback. Those forces were not even ready to hear a bullet, let alone fight in a battle. The military psychologists would agree, our army at that stage was not ready for military operations. What they required was rest and time away from the area, in order to recoup and regain confidence. Unfortunately, this was not in consideration from our leaders. They still believed they had a force to reckon with, which was why they sent troops to conduct an operation which turned out to be a disastrous result.

After returning from the Malual Gahuth failed mission, the situation in the camp remained unchanged. The entire force spent a difficult three days without food to eat. Soldiers were shooting randomly in every direction, in an attempt to fish with bullets in a small running tributary near the village. Disorder reigned in the camp for those few days. Rifles were being sent to nearby cattle camps, to be exchanged for bulls. The inhabitants of the area had a guilty conscious for their act against the Movement, and they had to distance themselves from Thiajak (Adura). It therefore took messengers some time to complete the mission. Assorted food items were airlifted from Itang to the camp, in addition to the bulls. That was a huge relief to us all. Life had to return to normalcy, before things got out of hand. There was no control over the army who were shooting in every direction, prompting senior officers to take cover or hide in order not to be mistakenly hurt.

After the food situation at Thiajak (Adura) had slightly improved, we received some uplifting news. Boma town had fallen into the hands of our gallant forces from Scorpion battalion, under the Command of Major Nyachigak Ngachilok, in the morning of April 1, 1985. This was announced from the mouth of our own overall Commander Kerbino Kuanyin Bol, who was so keen to share the news he didn't want to wait for the usual announcement to come from radio SPLA. He came out from his compound shouting the slogan of SPLA hoyee! He congratulated every person who passed by. I think he purposely performed this to boost the morale of the troops, which was very low due to the reasons explained above. The entire camp was amazed to hear this marvellous and exciting news! After the Jokou operation failed, we never thought an SPLA force operating elsewhere would inflict and score a major victory against the enemy force, by capturing a garrison town such as Boma. Thankfully our morale was on the rise again. Congratulatory messages for the triumph in Boma, were exchanged amongst the forces at Thiajak (Adura) and from other units in different parts of Southern Sudan. Everyone waited to hear the official news from radio SPLA at 3:00pm, to confirm what had already been heard.

Boma is a strategic town situated near the eastern border of Ethiopia. It connects Pibor and Pochalla, with eastern Equatoria through Kapoeta. Losing Boma meant a great deal to the regime in Khartoum. On the other hand, gaining Boma meant a strong foot hold for the SPLM/A, enabling them to launch future military operations to the south of the country, to the north and to the interior of southern Sudan. It was the first town to officially fall to the SPLA/M since the inception of the Movement two years prior. Indeed, it was a springboard for the SPLA/M operations to Kapoeta in eastern Equatoria to the South, and Pibor and Akobo to the northwest of the Upper Nile Region. Meanwhile Bor was left shivering, waiting for its own turn to come in the near future.

Equally, another motivating piece of news had emerged this time from Khartoum (the heart of the Sudan), that General Jaffer Mohamed Nimeiri's government had fallen on April 6, 1985. Also that General Abd el Rahaman Mohamed el Hassan Siwar el Dhab, had ceased power in the country. Demonstrations and public unrests reigned for weeks in Khartoum and other cities of the Sudan, calling for the President to abdicate or step down. President Nimeiri had travelled to the United States of America for medical treatment, allowing the Sudanese masses to demonstrate as they wish. The developments occurring on home soil, left President Nemeiri wanting a hasty return from the USA. The coup was announced while he was traveling on a flight bound for Egypt. He was bestowed with a presidential welcoming by his counterpart, Hussini Mubarak of Egypt, at Cairo International Airport. Completely unaware of the rapid political escalation of affairs back home, President Nimeiri wanted to fly to Khartoum when the hard facts of political change in his country were revealed. He was adamant he must go back to Khartoum, but President Mubarak firmly prevailed and made him accept the matter, as difficult as it was.

President Jaffer Nimeiri came to power via a military coup on May 25, 1969 by overthrowing the democratically elected government of Ismael el Azhari and his Prime Minister, Mohamed Ahmad Mahjoub. He ruled the country with an iron fist resisting any coup attempts against him. The first incident Nimeiri's government encountered, was the Ansar problem at Gezera Island Aba in 1970. He defeated the Ansar and eliminated their leader, el Hadi el Mahdi, when he was about to escape to Ethiopia. Many coup d'états were mounted against him from Hashim el Ata in July 1971, Hassan Hussein in 1975 and the Libyan invasion in 1976, just to mention a few.

President Nimeiri himself aggrieved the southern people mostly because of his unpredictable and contradictory behaviours. He attacked Bor town in May 1983 for a simple administrative reason that could have been addressed without bloodshed. Again, he divided the southern region for no other reason than applying the divide and concur policy, plus carried out many other offences against southern people. We had meticulously understood the oppressor's policies against the south, and that was why we undoubtedly supported the liberation of southern people from the oppressing elites in Khartoum. Learning the news that President Nimeiri had been overthrown, we were excited to the point we forgot our own difficulties and challenges being faced on the ground.

The intention of the coup leaders in Khartoum, was to address what northern people called southern issues, but we in the SPLM/A termed it a problem of the Sudan. In fact, there were two administrations in the country. There were military junta, or supreme council, led by General Siwar el Dahb and the council of ministers, run by civilians and led by El Gezouly Defa'alla. The latter was to deal with civil parts of the administration, meanwhile the former took the name of the supreme council. The military junta's role was to tackle the national affairs on behalf of the civil administration. From their first inception, the military wing commenced work dispatching envoys or emissaries to Addis Ababa to meet the SPLM/A leadership. Their aim was to seek ways on how they could address the southern problem, however this was where they missed the point. Dr. John Garang de Mabior and the leadership of The Movement, called it a problem of the Sudan. All attempts made during that time were unsuccessful. Instead Dr. John considered them a group of military junta that hijacked people's power and therefore, there was no point attempting peace talks. He instead considered and called it 'May Two'. The two administrations were assigned to conduct free and fair elections, at the end of the first year. They were trying to convince the Movement to join them in the democratization process taking place in the country, but this fell on deaf ears, as the Movement leaders wanted the solution to the real root course of the problems in Sudan. These problems were marginalisation, Islamicisation, Arabization and other concerns around elites and how they applied their managerial way of ruling, which would not permit those descending from the south, east and western parts of the country to rule. Sudan must be ruled on a new basis of equality in terms of religion and ethnicity, each according to his or her capabilities. In the Islamic world, an infidel (non-believer) cannot rule Muslims under any condition. They must instead be subject to Islamic rulers. The clique rulers of the Sudan, mainly from the far north and central, believed in their Arabic origin, when they were in fact being considered by those Arabs, to be of African origin.

I will quote here an article from an Egyptian lecturer's teaching at the University of Khartoum, from the late 1960's. The author is Mohamed El Nuwayhi from the book of Dr. Mansur Khalid, titled "The Paradox of Two Sudan's". He preached, "Northern Sudanese writers and poets attach greater value to the Arabic literature to the complete expulsion of their African heritage and environment." He went on to argue, "the Sudanese having been defeated and humiliated by the Anglo-Egyptian forces, needed psychological reassurance which they could neither find in their African past or the realities of contemporary Africa. Instead of empowering them to regain self-confidence, Africa would have accentuated their feeling of inferiority to the British and Egyptians".

Mudathir Abdel-Rahim, an eminent Sudanese political historian, corroborated that judgment by saying that in the eyes of that generation of northern Sudanese, "Their non-Islamic present, like their pre-Islamic past, was for them, the Jahilliya (the age of ignorance), and they could not, therefore, identify themselves with either. That the northern elites identify themselves fully to the Arab and Islamic world ignoring their African origin, was the reason why southern people, who had been Christians, picked up arms on two occasions to fight against the unjust system in Khartoum. This was to correct it or fight, to separate themselves and have their own country". The quotation is from the book of Dr. Mansur Khalid, "the Paradox of the two Sudan's"

Indeed, the Junta and civil administration conducted elections exactly after a year as promised, when they toppled General Nimeiri's government on April 6, 1985. El UMA Party of Sadig El Mahdi won the election and formed a coalition government with the Democratic Unionist Party (DUP) of Molana Mohamed Othman el Margani, ending the doubt and speculation that the junta would not relinquish power as claimed. Sadig's government aimed to work towards realizing peace, and they put every effort behind achieving this goal. Instead of this, the administration escalated the war culminating in committing unprecedented atrocities like the el Dhaeen massacre in which hundreds of Dinka women and children were killed or injured, and the war in the south intensified. Children in the areas of the south adjacent to the north were moved on and sold for slavery in the northern markets. Northern militia men were rampantly roaming and raiding villages in northern Bahr el Gazal and northern Upper Nile. The Prime Minister el Sadig Sadeeg Abd el Rahaman Mohamad Ahmad nicknamed as el Mahdi, met with the SPLM/A Leader Dr. John Garang de Mabior in Addis Ababa to discuss how peace can be achieved in their war-torn country. This meeting went for nine hours, but to no avail. We were very much pleased to hear the news of the regime changes in Khartoum and that General Nimeiri, who ruled the country for 16 years, was finally unseated.

At Thiajak (Adura), food supplies were not as plentiful as they had been in Jokou. There were shortage of grains and only a few bulls for the forces to live on. CDR William Nyuon Bany Machar took over from CDR Kerbino Kuanyin Bol, who became sick at a certain point and was referred to the rear for treatment. This change in command didn't unfortunately improve the food supply situation. Although CDR William was a Nuer by tribe, the army did not consider him worthy to contribute a bull for the army to feed on. Though in comparison, CDR William's presence was more highly regarded than CDR Kerbino. This may have been because of the linguistical factor.

While in Thiajak (Adura), two more incidents occurred in the month of April in addition to the capture of Boma and fall of the Nimeiri government. One of those events was the capture of alleged coup plotters, who were arrested and sent to Bilpam for detention. Those alleged coup plotters were all officers from Bor Dinka. What's important to mention in this matter, are the deaths of two members, 2nd Lts. Ateny Mayen Deng and Majok Chol Nai. They were part of this group, but died before they could reach Bilpam. They were subjected to severe torturing by a group of military intelligent (MI) personnel at Mangok. This was the way they would cruelly treat those accused of subversive activities in the Movement. It was exactly the same way Dr. Juach Kerjok and Engineer Manyang Diu were eliminated at the Bonga Training Centre, some months prior. The security personnel didn't have experience on how to deal with the accused comrades. It's accepted worldwide that you are innocent until proved guilty in a competent court of law. The SPLA/M security personnel were still unexperienced in following correct security procedures that would have saved the innocent lives of the suspects. There were a total of 25 people accused. Twenty of them perished and became martyrs on the war front, fighting against the enemy and putting doubt on whether they were fairly suspected as coup plotters or enemy informers. To them, the accusation had no tangible substance and you could still observe a terrible bitterness in the tone of the survivors, despite a long period of time elapsing.

The second incident to mention, was regarding a Dinka man who was assimilated into the Nuer community some years prior. This man recognized a soldier who descended from his original home area of Dhongjol Dinka section. He coaxed him into accepting a visit to his house outside Adura village. The soldier and the members of the family exchanged visits on several occasions. One fateful day, two sons of the Dinka man visited the soldier in the military camp at Adura (Thiajak) and asked him to come home with them. As they were walking, the older son speared the soldier in his stomach, inflicting serious wounds. The two sons ran away after the incident, and the soldier had to struggle back to Adura village. He explained what had happened to members of his battalion, when they wanted to obtain the truth. The soldier was attended to by nurses who had insufficient medical supplies, and due to this, they unfortunately could not save his life. CDR William Nyuon Bany ordered the local chiefs to surrender the members of the accused family immediately. He was outrageously stunned by the boy's behaviour. The father and son who speared the soldier were immediately sentenced to death by a special military court, and were executed on the spot. CDR William Nyuon Bany held a rally with the local population demanding and threatening that such an act, under any circumstance, should not be repeated.

What prompted the young man to perform such a senseless act against a person thought to be their relative? Those who knew the young man, claimed he committed this crime because he wanted the rifle of the soldier. All his peers in his community had firearms, except himself. He was so desperate to acquire a gun, he was prepared to do anything, including killing a soldier who was a relative. Initiation in some of the Nilotic tribal customs would occur when a boy is heading towards manhood. This is acknowledged with six marks to the forehead, showing that when a young boy reaches a certain age (generally around 15 years), he must shift socially from a boy to a man.

With this considered, the youth of the area were coming in possession of firearms illegally. It became a habit and culture in the eastern Nuer community that young men must be armed with firearms. However, this young man did not anticipate he was playing a dangerous game, which would result in him losing his life, along with his fathers. My thoughts were, the judgment was too harsh for the family, especially the father. I didn't agree that he should receive the death penalty, considering the son was found to be responsible. The life of the old man should have been spared, but this was not the case. The wrath of CDR William Nyuon was beyond control, because he felt the father would bring a bad omen to the life of William Nyuon himself and his forces, should he be left alive and free.

Life at Bukteng

The whole month of April had passed. As colourful as it was at Thiajak (Adura), we were then instructed to move to Bukteng village inside South Sudan, in May 1985. My role as logistician of the battalion, ceased around this time and I had to assume the role of a second COY Commander. We commenced our journey to Bukteng in the evening and we passed through the village of a prominent chief by the name of Kunthuol Kuach, just before sunset. We were to rest at Bar-alual for the night. At dawn the following day, our journey continued passing through Lak-nhom and Kuanylou villages, until we arrived at Bukteng at 4:00 pm. It was now the beginning of the rainy season and the inhabitants of the area were busy clearing the farms around their homes. The soldiers had no accommodation, and therefore had to share residential tukuls with the owners. This created an unimaginably peaceful and friendly atmosphere, making the Bukteng village appear like a military defensive locality. Foxholes and communication trenches could be found on the perimeter. The reason was that Anya-nya 11, who were allies to the government of Sudan (GOS), were in close proximity and could launch an attack at any given moment.

Upon arrival, we were shown the defensive area earmarked for Bilpam battalion. Other battalions occupied their positions. Again, food supply was limited which made conditions tough. The scarce supplies weren't enough to satisfy the demands of the army, which is a common issue during a guerrilla struggle. It was not only the food that was lacking, but many other essential items such as clothing, boots, sleeping materials and mosquito nets. This was of particular concern as the rainy season was about to commence, and the mosquitos would become rampant.

Desertion Phenomena

An incident occurred one day when group of soldiers, suspected to be members of either Hippo or Lion battalions, secretly slaughtered cows from a nearby cattle camp. It was owned by local people, and the cows were grazing in the vicinity. They were lucky not to be detected at the time of the incident. The owners discovered that some animals were missing, when the herd returned to the cattle camp. They reported the missing cows to CDR William Nyuon the following day. Detective personnel were quickly dispatched to inspect the camp, but could not find any tangible traces. A few members from the battalions mentioned above, were arrested on suspicion of stealing and killing the cows. The accused came from one ethnic group, Bor Dinka, which prompted Commander William Nyuon to take immediate action and dispatch members of those three battalions (Lion, Elephant and Hippo) to their respective native areas, bringing an end to that chapter. However, no legitimate resolution was found.

Another incident took place when a group of soldiers from one ethnic group, Ngok Dinka of Padaang including Pan Arou, thought of leaving camp and returning to their home areas. They deserted one night, watched by all in the camp including CDR William Nyuon Bany himself. This desertion phenomena, was taking place in every battalion trying to undermine the Movement's objectives and achievements. The deserters were leaving their battalions due to the poor quality of life, and possibly also due to home sickness. They wanted to return to their relatives, friends, and the community at large to demonstrate what skills they had acquired and how strong they had become. This behaviour was both disappointing and embarrassing to the SPLM/SPLA Movement's leadership due to the following reasons;

1. The battalions became weak and vulnerable in their defensive localities, especially in the areas where Anya-nya 11 bandits were rampant.
2. The deserters themselves became more vulnerable and exposed to the danger of Anya-nya 11 bandits, as many lost their lives in transit at the hands of those forces.
3. The deserters themselves were the source of armament to the bandits of Anya-nya 11.
4. They were exposing their relatives in their hometowns to the enemies of the Movement (Sudan Government and Anya-nya 11 Bandits).

CDR William Nyuon and the commanders of the battalions were extremely disappointed and tried to arrest those officers who were from the same areas of the deserters, accusing them of instigation. Captain Lam Cholkeny and 1st Lt John Mayar Mayiik plus others, were the first accused. They were later sent to the headquarters in Bilpam for detention.

The last group of deserters were from the Nuer of Ayod and Pangak. CDR William Nyuon Bany Machar and Major John Koang Nyuon, hailed from the same area. Major John Koang tried his best to prevail over the deserters and ensure they did not proceed with their plan, but this was to no success. The desertion phenomena became short lived, as many deserters later returned to Bilpam (the SPLM/A headquarters) in less than a year. They were seeking ammunitions and other important materials, which they were unable to obtain on their own. As they say, if you never try – you'll never know, and they believed it would be easy to remain quietly at home. On the contrary, they faced real challenges on the ground that caused them to think otherwise. It was more preferable to be deployed by the headquarters, than opting to deploy oneself. Conditions were issued from the general headquarters, which were returned and accepted by the deserters, and they continued to move in the Movement's choice of deployment.

Peace with Anya-nya 11

We stayed at Bukteng for two months, managing with the difficult conditions. Commander William Nyuon was in constant peace talks with the Anya-nya 11 command at Nyandieng. On one occasion, a group under the command of Gordon Kong Chol, sent a delegation to Bukteng to negotiate peace with the SPLA/M. General Bol Kong was among the Anya-nya 11 delegation. When considering the differences between the SPLM/A and Anya-nya 11 forces, it was determined there was no justified reason to fight one another, since we were not enemies to ourselves. Previous differences were in relation to leadership aspiration, which we now considered not fundamental enough to culminate in blood shed between the parties. Instead, we agreed to unite our ranks to face our common enemy, which were the oppressors in Khartoum. We all rebelled against the type of rule we had been subjected to by the northerners, since Sudan received its independence on January 1, 1956. After three days of intense deliberation, the delegation returned with a message of peace to the command of Anya-nya 11. This command at Nyandieng, reciprocated by inviting the SPLA/M, under the command of CDR William Nyuon Bany, to visit the area. The SPLA delegation dispatched to Nyandieng village, the headquarters of Commander Gordon Kong Chol. The two groups performed the same way they did in Bukteng. They determined and outlined how peace should be achieved between Anya-nya 11 and the SPLM/A. I personally was not part of the delegation that travelled to Nyandieng, but the information received from those present was convincing enough that peace was around the corner. We indeed ceased hostilities between the two parties, which had been occurring for quite some time.

Release of War Prisoners

One day whilst in Bukteng, the Chairman of The Movement and Commander-in-Chief of the SPLA, Dr. John Garang, considered releasing the Sudanese Government's war prisoners as a gesture of good will. This action from the side of the Movement, was none other than a pure political tactic and manoeuvre. The prisoners in question, were to be released through Bukteng under the Command of CDR William Nyuon. The deal was to be implemented from Bukteng to Nasir town under the control of the Sudanese government forces. Commander William himself was the one to execute the mission. It was only a one day walk to Nasir from Bukteng. A reasonable force plus three mounted jeeps, were arranged to escort Commander William and the prisoners to Nasir town. This occurred without any hindrance, and a very cordial ceremony was held by Commander William Nyuon and the commander of the Sudanese armed forces, in Nasir town. The atmosphere between the SPLA and the Sudanese armed forces was peaceful to the extent that some members of the SPLA were able to cross the Sobat River to Nasir town. As the saying goes, sailors don't wish storms to occur while in the sea, and unfortunately the peace enjoyed for two days around Nasir town didn't last. Members of Anya-nya 11, who we had just promised a peace deal with some days prior, mounted an unprovoked and unexpected attack on our forces. Commander William Nyuon narrowly escaped unhurt, by the Anya-nya 11 endeavour. The battle lasted a whole day. It's a known fact, when southerners clash amongst themselves, it takes a long time before they can separate. I lost one of my strong light machine gunners, Mr. Deng Chol, plus many others. Second Lieutenant David Manyok de Barach da' Atem who fought bravely, was among the injured officers from that battle.

We were in shock and couldn't work out what had prompted the Anya-nya 11 Commander Gordon Kong Chol and his group, to make the fatal decision to attack the SPLA/M. We were amidst a peaceful settlement to the long-standing differences between the two southern groups, so it did not make sense. All in Bukteng were astonished and infuriated by the unexpected act by Anya-nya 11 when a peace deal seemed so close. No doubt, it was an act of war, so we dug more trenches anticipating they would follow us in the next few days to our defensive positions. They wrongly thought they had been victorious in the Nasir battle. We received instructions to prepare for the worst.

When analysing the reason for the Anya-nya 11 surprise attack, it was concluded that the Anya-nya 11 command thought the SPLA/SPLM was attempting to forge a peaceful settlement with their allies, the Khartoum Government. The Sudanese armed forces were the only source of military supplies to the Anya-nya 11 movement, which enabled them to fight the SPLA on their behalf. The process of handing over the Sudanese government's war prisoners in Nasir, was wrongly conceived by Anya-nya 11 as an undermining move. The Khartoum government could stop provision of military support to Anya-nya 11, in accordance with their narrow-minded thinking. Therefore, the SPLA forces that came to Nasir must be fought, so this process ends before they sign a peace agreement with the Sudanese government.

In contrast, Dr. John Garang de Mabior did not intend to make peace with the Khartoum government by releasing the war prisoners at Nasir. His intention was to embarrass the Khartoum government, who were not preserving the lives of SPLA war prisoners who had been captured on different war fronts. The SPLM/SPLA (who were a guerrilla movement), were considered by international observers to be fighting for a just course while preserving the lives of their enemy captives. The act of returning war prisoners was a source of disappointment to the established Khartoum government, because they believed executing the opponent's war captives is against the international laws and regulations. War prisoners are meant to be protected by their captors, no matter how grieved the situation might be. With the scenario of events stated above, the returning of war prisoners in Nasir was not done with the intention to make peace with Khartoum. However, this was misinterpreted by Anya-nya 11, and they cancelled their relationship with their allies. The real intention was to belittle the Khartoum government internationally, but not to undermine Anya-nya 11's good relationship with their military allies, the Khartoum Government.

The SPLM/A had not considered Anya-nya 11 as real enemies, worth throwing their full weight on to fight. They were just considered southern Sudanese whose grudges in fighting the Movement were based on the Movement's leadership. They prepared different leaders for the Southern struggle, compared to those leading the Movement at the present time. The SPLM/A considered them brothers, to share one road towards the liberation of southern people. It wasn't long after this, that peace between the SPLM/A and Anya-nya 11 was achieved in 1988. Their leaders were fully absorbed into the ranks and files of the SPLM/A. Their top commander, Gordon Kong Chol, became the Alternate Member of Politico-Military High Command.

Whilst preparing my defensive sector, I was confronted by an officer, 2nd Lietenant Lul Chol, regarding a foxhole dug a few days prior. His challenge was in full disregard of military norms and procedures and occurred in such a belittling and humiliating manner, that I was extremely offended and felt I must defend myself. I retreated to a strategic position which enabled me to closely monitor his movements. In a short period of time, he started walking towards the battalion headquarters, which was 600m – 700m away from my defensive position. Upon seeing him move in that direction, I immediately slipped away unnoticed by my bodyguards. I caught up with him approximately 400m away from his destination. I immediately asked him to stop and put down his AKM rifle, so that we could battle it out by hands, a traditional way Bor Dinka people wrestle. The officer, 2nd Lt Lul Choll, was baffled by the way I was confronting him. There was no third person around to intervene or separate us. "Just show me your strength", I told him. As I was also ready to show mine. In no time at all, I wrestled him to the ground at a communal farm with a dura plantation, which had grown so high you were unable to see anything on either side. To his good luck, and my misfortune, my right shoulder became dislocated as we fell to the ground. Instead of teaching him a valuable life lesson he would never forget, I instead took a defensive position as he tried to struggle back to his feet. Over my dead body - I promised to myself – as I tried my best with only one arm, to hold him on the ground. The whole affair turned out to be a nightmare, disastrous on my side. We fought for around 20 minutes, after which two soldiers thankfully emerged from nowhere to rescue the worsening situation. The conflict was put to an end and we were separated. I breathed a huge sigh of relief, since the battle was turning in his favour.

After the show down with the 2nd Lt Lul Chol, my next challenge was how to return my dislocated shoulder to its correct position. The ill-trained military nurses, who were also poorly equipped, tried their level best but to no avail. A good Samaritan who was a friend and colleague of mine, 1st Lieutenant Malony Akou Nai, successfully fixed my shoulder, to my great relief. The dislocation caused intense pain which I had to bear for the days following, because there was no pain relief available. By then, I had only myself to blame for the show down. That notorious officer and

I were immediately placed under arrest until the case could be settled in the special military court, which would be established by the battalion Commander Major Isaac Gatluk. We spent a total of three weeks in detention, until our case was finally settled by the military court. We were sentenced to extra work duties for a month and received a serious warning never to repeat such an act again. Whilst under detention, rumours of Anya-nya 11's eminent attack on Bukteng village were circulating daily. The residents of Bukteng were confident that Anya-nya 11 forces would not dare attack the SPLA position. If they were foolish enough to attack, they would pay the consequences very dearly, because the SPLA were far superior in terms of equipment and manpower. These predictions were correct, and Anya-nya 11 did not attempt to attack Bukteng that year. However, there were a few slight skirmishes that occurred around the base when missions were dispatched outside the Bukteng defensive area.

A Brief Stay at the Itang Refugee Camp

After dealing with the harsh conditions at Bukteng, Locust division members who were eligible for attending shield three were notified through their commanding officers. They were released and moved to Bilpam headquarters, then onto the Bonga Training Centre for officers training. It was a rare opportunity to get a quick release from Bukteng's hell. I lodged a request with my commander to be released for the upcoming training. My direct commander, Captain Paulino Deng Ajuong, didn't hesitate to approve with immediate effect, pending final approval from the overall Commander William Nyuon Bany Machar. He accepted and I was able to leave for the Itang Refugee Camp. I was fortunate to have an Ethiopian chopper arrive at Bukteng at 8:00am, to transport me to my destination. Some heads of units would deny their eligible officers this rare opportunity. My Commander General William Nyuon Bany was no exception. He later prevented his officers for attending the training, thankfully after I had already left. Real guerrilla life was experienced at Bukteng, for those living in the area.

The helicopter landed at the Itang Refugee Camp, following a half hour flight from Bukteng. The SPLA security personnel quickly escorted me out of the air strip, because I was dressed in full SPLA military uniform which was prohibited at the refugee centre. It could be wrongly misconceived by others that the camp was for the SPLA military organisation, and not for legitimate refugees. The wife of 2nd Lt Bior (Asoud) da' Ajang Duot, Madame Ayen Kon Deng Malual, whom we knew very well, did not recognize me when I greeted her, telling me I wasn't the same man she knew. This was simply due to my emaciated health. I was shown my relative's place of residence, inhabited by 1st Lt Kuoreng Akoi Yaak, 2nd Lt Isaac Marol Mangok and 2nd Lt Chol Alaak Ajak plus, three sisters from the female battalion namely, Achol Dau Ngiwei, Amira Achol Bul Malith and Anei Garang Deng Ngor. The sisters had immediately noticed my lean body weight, and quickly rushed to prepare some food, which I devoured. Coming from Bukteng to Itang refugee camp, I felt I had moved from the hell where everything was missing, to heaven where so many things were at reach and on demand.

I acclimatized to a new life at the Itang Refugee Camp. Itang's administrators tolerated me, as I was a stranger to them. I lacked everything required for both modern and guerrilla life. The time of miracles and good luck, when you can make something out of nothing, had elapsed long ago. I therefore had to endear myself to the Itang administration group, to satisfy my many personal needs. The hot cakes from the Gambella market was the edible oil, but to find it was like climbing to the peak of the tallest mountain. I had to rely on them to provide all my requirements. On top of this, I had lost my bag containing all my different clothes when we were evicted by the enemy in Jokou, four months prior. Uncle Kuoreng Akoi and I were thankfully honoured by the Itang administrators with some cartons of oil, which were a rare commodity, along with bags of maize. This was a motivating factor for both of us to rehabilitate. In order for us both to rehabilitate, Uncle Kuoreng was a wounded hero who required special care from a kind-hearted humanitarian. For myself, I had to recover from a walking skeleton returning from the war front.

To transport the essentials obtained to Gambella, we had to search for a vehicle. It took us a whole day to locate means of transport to Gambella town. Our health situation had improved rapidly when we received some Ethiopian Birr in exchange for items sent to the market. We acquired some new clothes and extra food supplies, which improved our health within days. The days in Gambella were carefree and exuberant, having the opportunity to spend time with friends. We had to return to Itang after a few days in Gambella, as our pockets were duly and clearly exhausted. The opportunities to return to market were rare, and big personalities were required to find highly valued and marketable items.

Shield Three Cadet Training at Bonga

I came to Itang with a clear purpose to accomplish. This was none other than joining the SPLA Officers Military College. The Chairman of the SPLM and Commander-in-Chief of the SPLA, Dr. John Garang de Mabior, had instructed the Commander of Officers from the Military College, Capt. Chol Deng Alak, to open the college for shield three cadet training. The eligible group to attend shield three, were those of Locust division. Uncle Kuoreng, Captain Philip Chol Biowei, myself and many others were transported to the Bonga Training Centre via a Toyota pickup vehicle. We spent two to three hours in Gambella looking for necessary items to use at Bonga. We departed for our final destination (the Bonga

Training Centre) at 8:00 pm. As is the nature of military training centres, we were subjected to a rough reception from the camp administration, then shown to our rooms. To give you an indication of what these rooms were like, they should not be misconceived as standard or modern rooms. They were long and built with temporal structures. The roofs and walls were thatched with grass, aimed at accommodating around twenty cadets in one building. They were roughly and hastily constructed by the cadets themselves. There hadn't been proper consideration given to the size and number of cadets it would be able to accommodate when constructed. At dawn the following day, a whistle was blown to wake up cadets for morning drills. Military drills were conducted before we could break for breakfast. We first attended the general parade and were organised into COYs, platoons and squads. I became part of the third COY, third platoon and third squad. Cadets' administration was set up following under officer, COY's, commanders, platoon's commanders and squad's commanders were selected. Minor duties, such as constructing personal beds, was to be done at a specified time. After finalising the cadet's college administrative formalities, the real military training commenced.

Instructors converged on the morning of October 15, 1985, ready to begin their duties according to the work timetable. The day commenced with drills at 4:00am and at 6:00am cadets would break for breakfast. Following this, cadets would converge again and move in a military march towards the lecture hall at 7:00am. The lectures hall was a guerrilla one, meant for training bush cadets. It was a high structure also with a thatched grass roof, but with no walls to prevent blowing wind or rain. There were also no chairs for the cadets to sit on. The cadets would look for a space and a relatively smooth stone to use as chairs. Lectures continued until noon, when the cadets broke for lunch. They resumed at 1:00pm until the next break at 5:00pm. The cadets then had free time until 7:00pm, when the final parade was conducted before retiring for the night. This daily training routine would systematically continue, but differed when cadets attended demonstrations. On these occasions, we would attend a short briefing in the lecture hall, then move to the field for demonstrations until our lunch break at noon. These were the proceedings followed for the first month.

One day, a situation occurred when a fellow cadet, Professor Bari Wanji, lost some American Dollars (USD) in his room. He innocently made the mistake of reporting this to the college administration. This incident made the cadets pay dearly as we were forced to face disciplinary measures. After the official daily routine ended, the cadets were paraded at 7:00pm. This continued until 1:00am, when all the cadets shouted until the Ethiopian college instructors came to the cadet's rescue, advising the South Sudanese instructors to let the cadets rest before the next day's preparations. The cadets had to wake at the usual time of 4:00am, even without considering last night's punishment. Those who felt they may be offered a reprieve, fell short in understanding the expectations of military training. Training in a military college is as rough as can be, to build resilience and prepare the cadets for real military life conditions.

After the hectic day which followed the money stealing incident, we continued with business as usual. One morning, the head of the college administration, Capt. Chol Deng Alak, appeared at the front of the parade with two pistols hanging from his waist (as he always prefers to appear), and holding two documents in his hands. He began calling out cadet names, of which my name was amongst those called out. We were paraded separately from other cadets, and informed we had been promoted to the rank of captain. As you can imagine, the group was elated to have succeeded in progressing their military career, hoping to make a difference in the near future. Captain Chol Deng congratulated the group on their new rank. While we were still standing, he started calling out names from another list. My name was called out for the second time, so I had to comply. This group was ordered to stand in a different line and was a mixture of different ranks, including captains, 1st Lieutenants, 2nd Lieutenants, none commissioned officers and cadets. Captain Chol Deng didn't reveal why this second group was called out, but only signalled for us to return to our positions in the general parade, according to our position in the COY.

The Trip to Cuba

On the 15th of November 1985, members of the second group called out were instructed to pack their belongings and move to the headquarters across the Bonga tributary stream, to receive their final instructions. On the journey way to headquarter, I was conversing with two brothers, 2nd Lt Akur Garang Akuein and 2nd Lt Dut Achuek Lual, when they disclosed that we were heading to Cuba for further military training. It came as a complete surprise and was amazing news. Unlike Akur and Dut, I hadn't considered why we were singled out from the rest of the cadets, nor the purpose. I thought it would have been a regular posting to the field for another military operation, which I now felt comfortable with. On arrival at the headquarters, our numbers increased as we awaited for transport to Zinc, the Ethiopian's military base adjacent to Gambella town. The transport to Zinc arrived at 8:00pm, and we met with the colleagues also earmarked for the same training. The hosting personnel quickly took us to our respective rooms for the night. Zinc was also hosting some of the heavyweights from the Movement's leadership, Dr. John Garang and Salva Kiir. The reason for their presence was to see us off at the Abobo air strip the following morning. We converged at the air strip on the morning of November 16, at 8:00am. We waited for the plane to land whilst the chairman briefed us on the mission we were to implement in Cuba. Among us was Yusif Kowa Maki, the SPLM representative to Socialist Republic of Cuba, Ambassador Gabriel

Acuoth Deng Acuoth, Captain Bior (Asoud) Ajang Duot and Captain Biar Atem Ajang along with many others. After the short briefing by the chairman, a huge military airplane landed. The two commanders had to farewell our group, composed of 100 officers, non-commissioned officers (NCOs) and men (mainly from the VIP protection unit), as we marched to board the plane.

It was a short one hour journey from the Abobo air strip to Addis Ababa. As we landed at Bole International Airport, the SPLM/A representative Captain Deng Alor Kuol, was at our reception. We were taken to a special bay where all necessary arrangements were processed and completed. After completion, we boarded an Ethiopian airline heading to Angola and the Luanda International Airport, which took four hours. We were following the plan precisely, from the briefing by Chairman Dr. John Garang at the Abobo air strip. We noticed the difference in time zones, as it was 4:00pm according to East African timing, but 2:00pm Angolan time when the plane touched down in Luanda. The plane was directed to a special corner for us to disembark. The Cuban friends who were present in Angola were at our reception. They generously served the group with tea, coffee and cigarettes. These were things some of us (especially those descending from the Bonga Training Centre) had long forgotten. Two to three hours quickly passed at Lawanda International Airport. We were then signalled to board another plane for the remainder of the journey. It was at 6:00pm when the six hour journey to Cape Vert Islands commenced. This time it was a Russian airliner who transported us to Cuba. On board of the airplane, many strange irregularities were occurring. It was a diverse group of people from different social backgrounds. Some were from the countryside and some from urban centres, but there were not many who could understand the services aboard an airline. When food was served, it was a real challenge for some of our comrades to feed alone. These people had to seek support from those with knowledge and experience, on how to feed. The moist hand towels provided were misused. To eat with knives and forks was a challenge to those who had only ever used their hands and fingers to feed. Cuban friends distributed cigarettes to the smokers who lit their cigarettes and filled the plane with thick smoke. This was very intense, so the crew had to signal the smokers onboard to stop smoking. The plane landed and we spent one hour at the Cape-Vert Islands refuelling for the final leg part of the journey to Havana, Cuba. It was midnight when the eight hour journey commenced. All on board retired to sleep in their seats, when by chance I spotted a gentleman, who I assumed to be an aircraft technician, passing by. He was carrying a wooden hammer and heading towards the tail of the aircraft. It was an alarming situation that caused fear among those who witnessed it. The gentleman started hitting something at the tail of the aircraft, which caused great concern. Has this caused serious damage to the plane? Will we be able to complete the journey to Havana? How far away is the destination? These queries and speculations began to circulate in the minds of those who were awake. The gentleman with the hammer then returned to his normal position. Thankfully there were no strange movements made by the plane, and things remained stable despite what had occurred. Confidence was fully restored and our journey continued. We arrived at San Hose Martin's International Airport at dawn on November 17, 1985, to our great relief.

It was still dark as we disembarked the plane. We collected our luggage from the arrival hall, then met our Cuban comrades who came to receive us. We were composed of different groups coming to specialise in various fields. The infantry was the first and the largest group, and this was the group I was a member of. The second, were the VIP protection personnel (security guards) and the third was the political squad who were joining the political school along the SPLM Cuban ambassador. Each group was received by its own host, and we immediately left the airport to our respective destinations. Our group was taken to the Havana Hospital for a medical check-up. It is worth mentioning, that Cuba is a malaria free country, therefore any African person visiting must be quarantined or subjected to a thorough medical examination. This is a requisite, no matter what your political or social status. All necessary hospital requirements and medical check-ups were implemented. Whilst waiting for our results, we were provided with malaria tablets to swallow. I avoided these tablets because I was 100% certain I did not have malaria, which was confirmed when my test results came through a few days later. We spent three days in hospital, when those without malaria were discharged leaving their positive comrades behind. Those with malaria who remained in hospital, had to wait 5 days and return a negative result, until they could join us for training. We were transported to the training school via bus, on November 20. The school was very isolated and situated in the Pinar de Rio region. On the journey, we explored the area which was sparse apart from the sugar cane plantations. Cuba as a nation that depends on sugar and livestock as their only source of national income.

Life and Training in Pinar de Rio - Cuba

Captain Biar Atem Ajang, who was the head of the group and the most senior, along with Capt. Ayuen Alier Jongroor, arranged the sleeping order of the group. We were housed in one big building, that could accommodate more than 100 people. Opposite this, was another long building composed of two classrooms and a dining hall. Water tanks that supplied water to the school, were located near the dining hall. Adjacent to these two buildings, were the bathrooms which were well facilitated with wide washing basins and many water taps. The ground was paved and levelled with mixed aggregates and asphalt, which made it firm and strong. The compound was fully surrounded by tropical forests, and a manmade freshwater lake stocked with cultured fish. To the northwest of the compound, was a tall mountain range of up to 1000 metres above sea level. At the foot of the mountain, you could practice military training drills, to consolidate what had been learnt in the classroom. In the far distance was an area designated for shooting practice. Considering we were new to the area, the guiding personnel showed us the surrounding areas of the compound. We faced difficulty in communicating with the Cuban representatives, as no translator had been assigned. The Cuban comrades who accompanied us had to return leaving nothing for us to do. Leisure equipment was limited with no books, footballs, basket balls, tennis racquets and above all no grounds to play any of these outdoor activities. The only way to entertain ourselves, was to build chess pieces out of mud and play with those, until proper pieces were later provided by the school administration. Many chess players were among the group, myself included. This was to pass the time, as those interested in chess were playing while the others would spectate.

It was 1:00pm when a food provider assigned to our group arrived with food already cooked in large white containers. It was off loaded then immediately taken to the dining hall, where the group on duty welcomed everyone. The food was exceptionally delicious, with pork and other components provided. It was appreciated by the whole group, especially those who descended from cadet's college where the food had been extremely poor. After quickly devouring our first lunch at the compound, it was a self-service affair, whereby everyone was expected to wash their dish and return it to the correct position. The duty group was required to clean the dining hall. We all returned to our areas of business, and wished that 8:00pm would come soon, and we could queue up again for dinner. Following this, the group could retire to bed at their discretion. Our Cuban friends continued to feed us for one and half months, until they officially declared training opened on January 2, 1986. The one and a half months spent without official duty, was a probationary period aimed at strengthening our emaciated health. The Cubans knew our mission was not a picnic, but important business that required strong and well-nourished candidates, unlike the training conditions provided in Bonga. Indeed, the condition of our health had improved immensely

For security reasons, our hosts provided us with different names that would match the Cuban naming. I was given the name of Agua, which means water in Spanish. Also, when training was due to commence, we were supplied with military equipment, a khaki uniform, boots, knapsacks and hammocks for training purposes. Field materials were provided, as we began to visit the field and practice what had been learnt in the classroom. One morning, the Cuban trainers arrived early and called us to organise ourselves into two groups of 25, which was later increased to 26 when two female colleagues arrived, Ajieth (Siayama) Chol Atem and Aluel Gabriel Ayiei de Chath. The classes were marked as class A and class B. Each class would practise drills and train separately from the other class. We began the daily activities by climbing to the top of the nearby mountain mentioned above, that reached nearly 1000m above sea level. On the first day, the two classes climbed to the top of the mountain together, with the Cuban trainers showing us the best route up and down. On top of the mountain, we delightedly converged and began to sing SPLA/M revolution and morale songs with high and loud voices. It was like we had been victorious against the enemy on the war front. After those praises were sung, we started our descent back to the school compound a little tired, to some extent.

Those who originated from flatter areas (myself included), found it extremely difficult to climb the mountain. I would feel like retiring after 600m, when I witnessed the young strong comrades walking down swiftly after reaching the top. The fastest people from class A were Gabriel Jok Riak Makol and Yen Makuach (Magirgir). The fastest from class B were Kathekiah Ruei Pout and Deng Atem Aper. We would pass them around the 600m mark, when we were ascending, and they were descending after already reaching the summit. This indicates how the age factor affects the fitness levels between those in their mid-thirties (such as myself), and the majority who were in their early 20's. We completed this training every second day, over a three month period. On the final day, the Cuban trainer instructed both classes to climb the mountain three times, to farewell the mountain and this exhausting task.

Below I will outline the class structures, explaining how they were conducted, when they would commence and when they would end.

Classes would commence at exactly 8:00am, after breakfast which ran from 6:30-7:30am. Lectures were delivered in Spanish, but translated into English by translators. The translators were also able to assist us by translating any queries from our side into Spanish.

The subjects covered provided a typical military education;
1. Tactics and its sub subjects
2. Topography
3. Weaponry
4. Shooting
5. Mapping

Lectures commenced at 8:00am and I vividly remember an occasion when a lecturer posed the question 'What was the meaning of shooting?' It was correctly answered by a student, and the teacher commended them with the phrase "Cinco Ponto", which means five points. It was the first time for all of us in the class to learn those two Spanish words. Lectures would continue until 1:00pm, according to the timetable. We then broke for lunch and had the wonderful opportunity to decide what each would like to accomplish, until classes resumed the following day.

We took part in intensive learning sessions for the first two weeks, before we received instructions to prepare for a three day mission into uninhabited areas. Our mission was to journey through thick forest to reach the top of the mountain ranges, then descend on the other side into the valley. We took three days' worth of food rations, including dried and canned food. This was a heavy load to carry in addition to other items. None of us knew where we were heading, which direction to take, or what distance we were required to travel. All we had established was the time length of three days, according to food rations received. As mentioned, we left from the school compound at 9:00am walking through thick forest while ascending a much higher mountain than the one adjacent, which we had previously climbed every two days. As the group ascended, we aimed to take only two or three rest breaks, but this would increase if there was an unforeseen event, such as sickness or an injury. Upon reaching the summit, the group would assemble and begin to move in single file until we came to a point of departure where we could descend down into the valley. In the valley, we would meet at a designated camp site at an agreed time of day. Succinctly, we would tie hammocks on four trees to use as beds since it was prohibited to sleep on the ground. We were allowed to rest and feed briefly before heading to the demonstrations, which was the main purpose of our mission. The instructor and translator then lead the group to the demonstration site for practice. Regarding the camping situation, there was no system agreed on whether the camp would be required for one night or more. So it was unknown when we set up, how many nights we would be staying for. It would all depend on the progress of what we had come to implement.

This was a unique mission, the first one conducted in the area. It was considered unique, because we would walk aimlessly from morning to evening then camp for the night, resuming the next day for another aimless walk. This continued for three days until we returned to the school compound. The purpose of this mission was to acquaint ourselves with the terrain and geography of the area. This was never revealed to us, possibly due to communication issues and no translator being assigned. One of the challenges, was racing to an area assuming it was the targeted place to rest, all to no avail. However, we stuck to the mission because we had come to Cuba to complete our duties and training, no more.

Cuba was a safe-haven for mosquitos, despite the fact African visitors and others coming from tropical areas were coerced into thorough medical examinations or quarantine to ensure they were malaria free. Immediately on arrival, our Cuban friends distributed mosquito nets to shield off the mosquitos that were rampantly roaming. These mosquitos however, were malaria free, and that was the very reason why those coming from tropical areas had to be isolated. Cubans were more welcoming of an AIDS positive person arriving without much concern, than admitting a malaria positive traveller. They had a strong perception on the damage malaria causes to those communities living in a malaria contaminated area or zone. At every point during our trek through the valley, we ensured mosquito nets were erected to shield off mosquitos. This occurred not only in the forest, but also in the school compound.

We continued with our normal school duties, attending lectures as scheduled for three months. One day we were surprised when the Chairman of the SPLM and Commander in Chief of the SPLA Dr. John Garang de Mabior, Commander Arok Thon Arok Member of Politico Military High Command and Captain James Hoth Mai accompanied by a senior member of the Cuban Government, paid a visit to school in February of 1986. We paraded outside the classrooms where they greeted us and we responded by chanting a highly charged series of revolutionary and morale songs. Deng Atem Aper along with myself, were the initiators of the songs. We were asked to continue with our normal business but would meet the chairman in the meeting hall, later in the day. Our dignitaries left, and we returned to the classroom to resume our lecture. At 2:00pm, a bus arrived to transport us to the meeting hall in the nearby compound, where we met the delegation and family of Dr. John. Again, SPLA revolutionary and morale songs flared up from the two persons mentioned earlier. We were asked to be quiet, to provide Dr. John and his delegation an opportunity to address us and announce any relevant updates over the last 4-5 months. Commander Arok Thon spoke first. In his statement, he encouraged us to fulfil the mission to the letter and with spirit, as it would benefit the entire movement in the future. It was not common for a guerrilla movement to send troops for training abroad. Considering the Movement was blessed with such a chance, we must utilize it for the benefit of our marginalized and oppressed people. Commander Arok Thon, also proclaimed we will be true cadres of the Movement in terms of military knowledge acquired when we graduate from the friendly country of Cuba. Interruptions were flaring as he spoke. Next Dr. John was provided the opportunity to address us. He confirmed what his colleague Arok had stated, that the expectation and success of the Movement and southern Sudanese people was lying in our hands. He encouraged the trainees to study hard and apply the knowledge obtained on the war front, on return to South Sudan. He was grateful to the president and people of Cuba for the valuable opportunity to train cadres of his movement. While he assured us of military stability and the progress of operations back home, the crowd erupted with more SPLA revolutionary and morale songs. Three hours passed without notice when he concluded his speech.

Dr. John and Arok Thon Arok, although well acquainted with the happenings of war, intentionally refrained to reveal the death of their colleague Major Nyachigak Ngachilok, who was Commander of the Scorpion Battalion plus a member of Politico- Military High Command, who perished on the war front around Kapoeta town. Maybe this was because they didn't want to disappoint or embarrass the group, if setbacks were revealed. We farewelled Dr. John and the accompanying delegation, then returned to the school compound to continue with business as usual.

I must confirm that our group was in total isolation in Cuba. As previously explained, we were in the region of Pinar de Rio and we were not allowed contact with the SPLM/A Movement in particular. There were no newspapers available to acquaint ourselves with world events that had been occurring. Also, there were no telephones or means to communicate with our relatives back home, to obtain any grievances they may had. Due to this lack of communication, we did not receive the news on the death of Commander Nyachigak Ngacilok. We truly were in the middle of nowhere, even the local inhabitants were hard to sight. What I am still unsure of, is whether the isolation of the group was intentional or not.

The Role of Cuba in International World Politics

It was not the SPLM/A alone who were lucky to win the support of Cuba and their socialist administration, but all struggling socialist movements were also receiving support from Cuba. Being a small, poor nation naturally endowed with nothing except agriculture and livestock. However, it has contributed immense support to many wars of liberation, of which the SPLM/A was a beneficiary. It's no secret that the Union of Soviet Socialist Republic (USSR) was behind the strength of Cuba. Every need in which the Cuban administration was falling short to achieve, was hence being provided by the USSR. Examples of this include energy, gas and fuel supplies, food supplies (e.g. wheat, rice, cooking oil) and means of transport (sea, land and air), were sufficiently supplied by the Soviet Union, in addition to military support in the form of armaments and ammunitions. This therefore enabled the Socialist Republic of Cuba, to support oppressed people in different corners of the globe. Cuba, in addition to our delegation, hosted 600 South Sudanese youth and school children. These school children studied and specialised in different fields of interest including inter alia, medicine, veterinary, pharmacy, agriculture and different military specialisations. In brief, Cuba and the Soviet Union did not fall short of their physical and moral obligations to effectively enhance support to the oppressed and struggling people of the third world.

Back in the school compound, Captain Biar Atem Ajang had no real difficulty in managing the group. All knew why they were in Cuba and therefore no grudges were mentioned. One day, a comrade accused another of abusing a member of Politico-Military High Command. The scenario occurred when Cuban comrades provided us with two to three bottles of red wine, to commemorate one of their national days which was celebrated across the nation. Six of us sat together and enjoyed drinking the bottles of red wine. We were conversing in Dinka and discussing issues of concern. A non-Dinka man who was sitting near us and didn't fully understand the Dinka language reported to the senior person among the group, Captain Biar Atem Ajang, that one of us had abused and insulted a Politico-Military High Command member. It was seen as disrespectful for a junior officer to behave in such a manner to his senior. A board to tackle the issue, was quickly established. The group of six was summoned and the accuser was called to deliver his accusation. The committee determined there was no tangible evidence since the accuser was not well versed in the Dinka language. The accuser belonged to the same tribe as the Member of Politico-Military High Command, who he thought was insulted by a junior officer who hailed from the Dinka tribe. The whole issue should have been put aside, but since ethnicity was a sensitive topic, it had to be addressed in that specific way to avoid any political favouritism or crossing of tribal lines. Both parties received stern warnings never to repeat such an unnecessary disagreement, otherwise deportation could ensue to the guilty party.

Training continued as normal, with all performing their required tasks. The dry season passed with no unusual incidences among the group members. We would attend lectures, then practice what was learnt over the next two to three days in the valley. Journeying to the field for drills and practice sessions, was much easier during the dry season. Seasonal changes would present some difficulties. When required to walk through the rain, the load we were carrying became much heavier than usual. Or if it rained during the night, it would disrupt our sleep. All in all, the rainy season was repugnant to us, due to the disturbances experienced in the bush.

Our Cuban comrades were doing their best to keep us happy so we didn't feel the isolation the group was being subjected to. One morning, a bus arrived to take us to a beach between Havana and Pinar de Rio, where we were staying. It was a very colourful site to watch the families, friends, young girls and boys and young adults socialising and swimming in the ocean. People were playing a range of different games and enjoying themselves in whatever manner they felt like. We were no exception, swimming and joining in the games when given the opportunity. Some even enjoyed a few alcoholic drinks, until evening came and the buses took us back to the school compound. I have very fond and vivid memories of this day, which made some lasting changes amongst our group. Such outings were indeed a rare occurrence during our time in Cuba.

Another day of R&R worth mentioning, was when we visited the capital, Havana City. We were facilitated to visit all corners of Havana, which included historical sites in the old and new city, including the old port. We passed through a tunnel which had been dug under the sea to the old port. We were able to marvel at the many different types of ships, both big and small. Old canon guns along the port were exhibited to us. We were also lucky to be shown around the new Havana City. This was another fond and memorable occasion during my time in Cuba. We were then taken back to the San Hose Martin International Airport and the Tropical Hospital where we had been quarantined the first time we landed in Cuba.

The most appealing thing about Cuba, are the Cuban people. In Cuba, you are free to interact with anyone you are interested in conversing with. If there is a challenge, it is most likely due to the language barrier as most Cubans speak Spanish, unless you are lucky to find someone you can interact with in English. Cuba, along with Brazil, are the only two nations where this is possible, in my opinion. It does not matter if you are black or white, there is very little discrimination experienced amongst the citizens. This is rare in today's world and it does even occur in one of the largest known democracies in the world, The United States of America. I could cite many obnoxious examples of the USA relating to discrimination. Many of these are often disguised or hidden to a certain degree.

Back in school, different military sciences were being taught. More importantly, guerrilla warfare tactics that suited bush life were discussed. A guerrilla men can disguise themselves by smearing with mud or any other related material that would enable them not to be noticed by the enemy. Following the lesson, we were asked to demonstrate what had been learnt in the field. One comrade and I were selected to be smeared with mud to test out the tactic. Our bodies were smeared with mud and we then laid down and hid in a well-known area. The rest of the comrades were ordered to find us. Although they knew roughly where we were located, their search was in vain and they failed to find us. All were astonished when we were asked to reveal our hiding spot. Many useful guerrilla tactics, on how to evade the enemy, were taught. We learned further valuable tactics in regards to day/night attacks, raids, reconnaissance missions, patrols, ambushes, advance to contact, battalion attack and moving into hostile areas These were all fully explained and illustrated. We were shown how to make home-made bombs, composed of TNT and other devices made from local materials. Invented means of delaying the enemy were also taught, for example fishing hooks and others in addition to planting land mines and booby traps. Some other important standard subjects such as topography, weaponry and shooting were pursued and taught to the group. The months continued with theories learnt in the classroom then practiced in the field. To my best knowledge, all students mastered shooting and were at the level where they could shoot moving targets. I remember at this point, I was even capable of shooting tiny targets such as birds while flying, using different types of short and long-range weapons. We received comprehensive training on how to use all types of weapons and would be kept up to date with any new types entering the market.

Weapons or firearms are divided into light and heavy categories. The light ones, are either urban or battlefield weapons. Short and light guns are used in the urban operations, while long and light personal guns are applied on the battlefield. These can also be used in urban operations, depending on the operative situation. In a necessary military operation, every available weapon is logically available for use. I won't detail all what was learnt in the classroom, but just enlighten you with some relevant details.

One day our school had an unannounced visit from the SPLM/A Movement's ambassador or representative to the Socialist Republic of Cuba, Comrade Gabriel Achuoth Deng Achuoth with his family and the family of the Movement's chairman Dr. John Garang de Mabior. Visitors to our school compound, provided great motivation to every person in the group. The reason being, we were in complete isolation in the region of Pinar de Rio and many were homesick. We quickly gathered in a classroom and were anticipating any significant news from home. No doubt, our visitors had many items to discuss. We never knew what to expect, as news could either be sweet or sour. The SPLM/A representative Comrade Gabriel Achuothdit and Madame Rebecca Nyandeeng de

Mabior revealed some good news from back home, from both a personal and political perspective. Some upsetting news was shared regarding the shocking death of one of the Movement's Alternate Member of Political Military High Command, Major Nyachigak Ngachilok who's demise occurred on a battle field around Kapoeta on December 6, 1985. Our heads were all bowed as a sign of disappointment and respect, as we learned of his death. The death of General Nyachigak occurred in December 1985, just a month after we left South Sudan. As mentioned earlier, it was not revealed to us by the Chairman Dr. John Garang and his delegation when they met with us previously. They wanted to wait until our return to Sudan, before revealing the news. It was a logical plan because it would have been utterly disappointing to discover the news on our return. The following days were marred with gloom so clearly seen on the faces of everyone in the compound. We mourned the death of Nyachigak Ngachilok for three consecutive days.

After receiving the sad news of Major Nyachigak's death, we resumed our classes until the end of August when exams were held, marking the end of our training period. The results were announced during a parade with our Cuban trainers. Our friends held a ceremony marking the end of the training course.

After the official closing, Our Cuban friends provided us with some casual clothes along with an additional two sets of our military uniform. In the middle of September 1986, the first group were preparing to journey back to Africa. Members of that group were beating drums with joy and happiness, and were excited to reunite with their families, relatives and friends after almost a year. These feelings of elation were in direct contrast to those remaining in Pinar de Rio. The remaining group were disappointed, because it meant they had to remain anytime between 14 to 30 days. The reason it was difficult to secure flights, was because the USA had imposed flight restrictions on Cuba due to the socialist system of governance it had adopted.

The only flights that would risk coming to Cuba, were the USSR's airline and her allies which flew in once a month. The departing group were collected by bus and transported to San Hose Martin's International Airport, leaving the second group (including myself) miserable in the school compound. There was nothing official to do, except playing chess, cards or reading books which we rarely had time to do. Life in the compound continued as normal, but dreams about home were hoovering in the mind of every individual. Although every need was made available to us, nonetheless, the days were slow and rotation seemed stagnant. At times, we were mindful of the real situation back home including the living conditions and every aspect of life.

Two weeks had passed by very slowly, until we received instructions from our Cuban friends that we would be transported to the airport the following morning. It was a huge relief. Indeed, a bus arrived to transport us to Havana city's San Hose Martin's International Airport, as promised. We promptly boarded the bus, as luggage had been packed immediately after receiving our departure information. It was an hour long journey from the school compound to San Hose Martin's International Airport. On arrival, we were directed to a special bay at the airport where details of our departure were to be arranged. We immediately noticed dogs who were controlled by security personnel checking and inspecting the luggage. This was strange to those who hadn't experienced this before. An announcement was made, calling passengers to board the plane immediately. Our plane took off and the eight hour journey to the Cape Verde Islands commenced. The second journey to Africa was different from the first, which was marred with many irregularities. Lessons were learned by members of our group, and they better understood the etiquette expected during flights. The plane landed safely in Cape Verde Islands to refuel and our journey resumed. It would be six more hours until we landed at Luanda International Airport, the following morning. The Angolan comrades took us to a place out of Luanda city to wait until evening, when we were transported back to the airport to board an Ethiopian Airline to Addis Ababa Bole International Airport. All check out processes from the airport were completed.

After departing the airport, we found the SPLM/A representative to Ethiopia, Mr. Deng Aloor Kuol who had seen us off on the journey to Cuba. He was the one who received us again on arrival in Addis Ababa. Paradoxically, symptoms of the guerrilla system started to emerge upon our arrival from Bole International Airport. The representative had arranged a long trailer truck to transport us to Tata Military Training Centre outside Addis Ababa city, where we spent the night. Tata village was a military training centre where Ethiopia's fresh recruits would be duly trained when the need arose. When we arrived at the training facility, there were no recruits currently undergoing training, which meant there were no administrative members to direct us to where to sleep.

Luckily the guards could show us the rooms and we were asked to choose our own beds. The rooms were dusty and dirty, and sleeping beds were mounted in three levels. The sleeping materials, especially the blankets, were so dirty we couldn't imagine sleeping with them. The weather in Addis Ababa at that time of the year was freezing and there was nothing to feed on, during the coldest parts of the night. When there is no solution, you must find a suitable one yourself. We managed to sleep despite the unsettling situation. When we woke the following morning, there was no free tea available like there had been in Cuba. Tea was available, but only on a commercial account. Some comrades among the group who originally emanated from the Itang Refugee Camp, luckily possessed some Ethiopian local currency and managed to rescue the situation. They were able to buy tea for those who did not possess local currency, not on a commercial basis but on brotherhood account. We had been advised by comrade Deng Alor, that we would be collected early the following morning. Although it arrived late, a bus was sent to Tata

Military Training Centre to transport us to meet with the Movement's representative, comrade Deng Alor Kuol. We then had to work out how best to transport the group to Western Ethiopia (Gambella district), our final destination. We alighted at a hotel where we enjoyed our first meal since we landed in Bole International Airport the day prior. I failed to locate that hotel when I returned to Addis Ababa three years later. After the meal, money for transport and a feeding allowance (TFA) were given to each of us. We bid farewell to each other with the Addis Ababa group and then continued our journey to Western Ethiopia as planned. It was a two-day journey to Gambella, and we arrived at approximately 4:00pm.

In Gambella, Commander William Nyuon Bany Machar who was currently in town welcomed the group back home. He assured us he was pleased, we were among our colleagues and our services were greatly missed by the Movement, relatives and friends. He quickly arranged transport for us, to return to the Itang refugee centre to reunite with families and friends whom we'd been missing for almost a year. My case was exceptional, as the absenteeism was about three years since I departed my family in September 1983. Our members couldn't wait to reunite with their loved ones. Mama Yaak (Madame Racial Achol Juach Diing), relatives and friends were at my reception in a compound that consisted of many families, each in their own Tukul according to the arrangement.

I must mention, that transporting the group via a trailer lorry upon arrival in Addis Ababa was an indication that things were still not easy for the SPLM/A Movement, even at the Addis Ababa level. This observation was made by some of us while on the trailer truck. It was a meaningful reminder to the group that nothing much had changed and spending a year abroad for training didn't bring changes at the level of the SPLM/A. We were still a guerrilla movement that was immensely lacking everything even at the Addis Ababa level. Some of us thought otherwise, having been transported by bus after landing, but just for that moment.

Cuba, although considered a third world country, is far more advanced compared to many independent African countries. There's no doubt, it would be considered a first world country in the eyes of a guerrilla movement like the SPLM/A. Guerrilla life is not pretty, so a trailer truck could transport us like a bus or any other means of transport to where we were aiming to reach.

The Movement's leadership permitted us to stay in Itang with our families for at least a month, until the last group arrived at the end of October. Following this, we received instructions to report to Bilpam general headquarters where we would meet Dr. John Garang to receive our final orders of deployment. A military Ural truck was sent to transport us to Bilpam. The vehicle had to stop on the right-hand (northern) side of the Baro River opposite Bilpam southward. Crossing the river at the beginning of the dry season was not posing any obstacles. Therefore, we waded across to the left hand (southern side) of the river and eventually walked to Bilpam in less than one hour.

Major Chagai da' Atem de Biar, Commander of the area welcomed us and directed us to our accommodation huts. Commander Chagai had ensured the area was at an acceptable standard and all administrative duties had been actioned. There was an officer's dining hall, where meals were served and the residential quarter. After four days, Dr. John landed via helicopter. It was evening when he arrived, so there weren't any immediate tasks to be done. The expectation was that we would be interviewed the following morning, which would surely result in deployment after a full year of training and being out of the field. Indeed, things emerged as expected. The chairman interviewed us one by one, until all comrades had been spoken to. His trip to Bilpam, was a dual mission. His other intention was to interview political cadres who had just graduated from the political school at Zinc, led by Colonel Makuei Deng Majuch and Lt. Colonel Aru Man Chot on the military side, and Justice Bullen

Panchol Awal Alier and Michael Makuei Lueth Makuei on the civilian side, just to mention a few.

The following day, we were instructed to supervise the cadet's examinations for comrades hoping to attend shield four (4) then mark the exams to the satisfaction of the Chairman. After accomplishing all the required assignments, Dr. John instructed those who were being deployed out of Bilpam to travel with him to Itang. It was dark when we came to the Baro River for crossing. A Ural truck earmarked for the transportation to Itang, was waiting for the Chairman and the group on the other side of the river. All except Dr. John crossed to where the vehicle was waiting. A canoe was provided to ferry Dr. John across. As the saying goes, there is nothing beautiful about guerrilla life. Nearly 30 of us packed into the Ural vehicle and we finally arrived in Itang at midnight. The following morning, we converged at the gathering point then another vehicle arrived to transport us to the Bonga Training Centre. We rested for a while in Gambella then proceeded to Bonga, our final destination. The process that occurred at Bilpam was also to be carried out at Bonga. Candidates interested in joining the college, had to pass an exam before they could attend shield four. University graduates were excluded or exempted from sitting the examinations. Instead, they were granted direct entry into cadet's college. The candidates were able to sit exams in the morning, which meant marking was completed and results were announced on the same day. The successful candidates were able to join the college immediately. We had assumed the process would take a long time, but it could be done in one day due to the many officers available for marking. The Chairman was relaxed and happy. He knew he had qualified manpower who could accomplish a large job in a short amount of time. Most of those who completed the marking were already deployed to the headquarters of the Chairman of the SPLM and Commander in Chief of the SPLA. Our mission in Bonga was brief, as the screening of candidates for shield four was successfully accomplished.

In the afternoon, as part of screening process, the Chairman ordered the head of his bodyguards, Commander Captain Bior (Asoud) da'Ajang Duot, to prepare for a meeting in the hall as soon as possible. Captain Bior instructed the guards to quickly move to the hall. The group that had recently come from Cuba and had already been assigned to the Chairman's headquarter, were not part of the Chairman's body guards. Nonetheless, Captain Ayuen Alier instructed us to join the guards at the meeting hall fully armed with our AKM rifles, like the bodyguards. This was strongly objected to by Bior Asoud. Dr. John followed immediately and found a group of cadets whom he wanted to interview sitting impatiently waiting for him. He commenced the interview with strange questions, difficult to understand. This was not because the questions were difficult in meaning, but because of their application. Dr. John Garang knew what he was aspiring for, but we were no doubt falling short of understanding their exact meaning and application in the cadet college. We stayed with him until the evening when he finalised the interview.

After some months, we got a slight inclination of Dr. John's intention. He was interviewing two groups at the same time. The first group was potentially joining the political school in Addis Ababa (Yakatit). The Movement's ideology then was a socialist system of governance and therefore the Movement was to do something synonymous to that. Candidates or able personnel within the Movement were to be sent to Cuba, Addis Ababa or Zinc to attend political training in their respective political schools. Dr. John was duty bound to interview them regarding anything related to political work in the army. The Movement's leadership for the first time in its history, decided to have political cadres sent to the Addis Ababa Political School for training. That was why it was difficult to perceive why Dr. John was interviewing those cadets at the initial stage.

The other group being interviewed were earmarked for a special mission in central Equatoria (in South Sudan). Questions were asked on whether each of those cadets knew how to swim or not! These questions along with others, were difficult to ascertain in our minds. To question a cadet who's applying for military college about anything geared towards aquatic matters was puzzling. We understood later that the second group were meant for a special mission aimed at executing a big military target, which was the destruction of the Juba Bridge, to destabilize transport in and around Juba town including the river. Indeed, both groups departed for their different missions. Political cadres went to the Addis Ababa Political School for the two-year training course, whilst those assigned to destroy the Juba Bridge went to Equatoria (Juba City particularly) but failed to succeed in accomplishing their targeted mission.

The Fall of Pibor Town into the Hands of the SPLM/A 6/3/1987

The Chairman Dr. John Garang was a determined and motivated person who would be busy even late into the night. One of his plans among many others, was to attack and capture the Sudanese army garrison town of Pibor. After a few days in Bonga, the Chairman instructed his headquarters to move to Pinyudo. It was in the afternoon of December 15, 1986 when our convoy was due to leave for Pinyudo. Captain Ayuen Alier, Captain Samuel Ater Dak Kwong and myself (also a Captain), were allocated one Ural lorry for transport during this mission. The seating arrangements on the truck were allocated due to seniority. I took a back seat and gave my seniority seat to Captain Samuel Ater Dak due to his age. He was to share the front seat with the most senior Captain Ayuen Alier. We spent the night at Pinyudo and then proceeded the following day to the Gilo river crossing point, which was already established as a military base. The road to the crossing at that point in time, was under construction on the left-hand side along Gilo River to the crossing point. The road to Pochalla was under construction since there was no road connecting Ethiopia with Sudan in that region. Dr. John himself was the one in charge of directing the road construction team to Pochalla town. It was not an easy mission. The road passed through a densely thick forest that hadn't been penetrated by humans previously, although it is an Anyuak land.

The mission of opening the road across that area was successfully accomplished by Dr. John Garang. He had a map which was enabling him direct contact with the Ethiopian engineers in charge of the road construction. The movement of people and equipment to Pochalla and thereafter to the interior of South Sudan, became a much more simple task as one could travel from Gambella to Pochalla in one day. Previously, it would take two to three days by foot from Pinyudo to Pochalla. The decision by Dr. John to construct a road from Ethiopia to South Sudan through an area that had never been surveyed, was like hitting two birds with one stone. Once the mission was successfully accomplished, it was a great achievement in itself and facilitated the SPLA/M movements to and from Ethiopia. Not only was the road an important civil development, but to Dr. John it meant an easy way to reach the war front with its requirements - manpower and war materials - in the shortest time possible.

When we came to Pochalla in December 1986, the road construction engineers were already clearing the road linking Pochalla with Pibor with their equipment. Things became easier from Pochalla to the interior of the southern part of the country, as roads already existed, they just occasionally needed to be graded or trees removed that were in the way. Roads had not been repaired or graded since war broke out in the south, four years prior.

A surprise visit was paid while we were in Pochalla, by three newly appointed alternate members of Politico-Military High Command namely, Dr. Lam Akol Ajawin, James Wani Igga and Yusuf Kowa Maki. I didn't know the purpose of their visit, but assumed it was an exploratory mission to acquaint themselves with the route they would soon take with their forces in about two months. Commander Yusuf Kowa remained behind at Pochalla, but the other two returned to Ethiopia immediately. As of now, our mission with the Alternate Member of Politico-Military High Command, Commander Yusuf Kowa Maki, was to supervise the road construction protection unit under the command of 2nd Lt Chol Chiman Garang. In the first two days, we would join the road construction team from morning to evening. The protection unit would be left to sleep on the side with motor graders, then come back to Pochalla to spend the night. Due to distance, we could not find an alternative except to camp with the team and resume early the next day. At the junction of Pibor Pochalla Boma road, we branched off to Boma road which took 14 days of continuous work. Dr. John would make frequent visits in order to keep supervision.

After the road grading to Boma was completed, we turned back to Pochalla where Dr. John had arranged a huge rally attended by Anyuak's King Agada Cham and all the chiefs in the area. A large local dance was held in the morning by the Anyuak youths and members of other tribes who happened to be in Pochalla town i.e. Dinka Bor and Murle (mainly from the SPLA Soldiers). The objective of this was merely as motivation, as plans for the Pibor operation were underway. Dr. John was dancing with every group that opted to dance that day. Anyuak's young female dancers would shy away from dancing with the Chairman Dr. Garang, but the girls would be forced back to continue dancing with him, providing a very eloquent and interesting site to watch. I came across and encouraged Dr. John to perform better, so he could attract the girls. But he had just told Captain Bior Asoud that "those young girls have utterly rejected to dance with me, but it is simply because of my position as the

Chairman of the Movement, that is the only leverage that is forcing them accept to dance with me". It was an entertaining and enjoyable day, with jokes told and Anyuak's young girls dancing with the very jolly Dr. John.

Preparations to move on to Pibor were in progress. Forces from the Joseph Akuon battalion which mainly composed of Anyuak sons, were reorganised into new forms. Captain Bior Asoud received instructions to replenish the newly reorganised Joseph Akuon battalion, with whatever was missing in terms of armament, uniforms, boots and etc. Captain Bior went ahead with preparations to implement the plan, by distributing uniforms to members of that and other battalions. Providing uniforms to the soldiers of the Joseph Akuon battalion was not appreciated by the Chairman. Dr. John, who was obsessed with desertion menace as most of the members from this battalion were deserters from different battalions. They didn't seem to be ready to serve on different war fronts, other than their own home area of Pochalla. His plan was to pull them away from Pochalla to a location nearer to the target, where provision of military equipment can be distributed as peacefully as possible. With this in mind, Dr. John disagreed with the actions of Capt. Bior Asoud, of handing out the uniforms. To the relief of everyone, Akuon battalion did not intend to desert their battalion and return to their respective home areas. It would have been a serious setback to the Movement if the Akuon battalion, who they were hoping would capture Pibor town, together with otherswere to desert.

Transport arrived to transfer the forces to the Okello military base. Myself and other members of the forces, while on the way to Okello military camp, hunted many wild animals such as the white-eared cob. The Chairman would later on take these animals back to the recruits undergoing military training in Bonga, to feed on. Dr. John returned to Okello after a short visit to the Bonga Training Centre. He called the officers to his headquarters for a briefing. After a short briefing, I was then assigned to command a reliable commando task force composed of experienced officers, non-commissioned officers and men. In the evening, I received instructions that myself along with the whole force, would leave Okello for Kong-Kong the following morning, to establish it as a base. The forces and I departed as instructed the following day for Kong-Kong. It was 32kms away, which took us six to seven hours on foot. Commander of Joseph Akuon's task force and myself had to perform a quick tactical deployment of the forces to secure the area. We realised the area we had come to, were unfriendly towards the Movement's members. Therefore we had to ensure the security of the area was tight, since Pibor town was just 15kms away from Kong-Kong.

The Murle tribe's men had long ago established militia armed groups friendly to the government of Sudan but opposed to the SPLM/A. The SPLA/M fortunately already had presence around Pibor town. There was a strong contingent of the SPLA/M under the command of the son of the area, Captain Kennedy Gayin, who had been manning the area for over a year. Their command headquarters were in Panahoth, just five to six kilometres from town. The presence of that force, settled the security situation in the Murle area. Murle militia men who were commanded by Murle paramount Chief Ismail Konyi, were forced to retire into Pibor together with the forces defending the enemy. The SPLA/M forces could shell the town at any point, leaving the town dwellers with no real commitment to the enemy to desert it for good. Many members of those militia men joined the SPLA/M. Our arrival at Kong-Kong was a strong addition to our fighting force compared to our presence at Panahoth. This eventually sent continuous waves of alarm to the government and militia forces in Pibor town.

As soon as the two task forces controlled the area, a radio for communication was erected to communicate to the Chairman's headquarters, and other important units. It was a surprise to see the Chairman had dropped in just hours after our arrival at Kong-Kong. His quick surfacing to the area, indicated his serious commitment to the state of affairs. Sending forces ahead of time to Kong-Kong signalled his pending visit, and he arrived in a timely manner even though the area hadn't yet been fully secured. It was a sign of Dr John's dedication, bravery and full commitment to the course he was leading.

One of the challenges faced by the forces at Kong-Kong, was a shortage of drinking water. It was an important issue that needed to be raised with Dr. John, plus a remedy had to be found. Ethiopian friends provided a water tanker, in addition to the road construction team's equipment. The Ethiopian team constructing the road were thankfully permitted to return to Ethiopia and left the machines to the South Sudanese teams. This meant they could continue the road grading from Okello to Kong-Kong and from there to Pibor afterwards. Standing orders were laid for the water tank driver to supply drinking water to the forces from Oboth River twice a day. The water tank's driver, Private Majur Akok Adut, a brother to 2nd Lieutenant Garang Akok Adut (mentioned earlier as a Sergeant), performed his job as required. Internally, we made the rule that no one was allowed to use the water for bathing, it was only to be used for drinking or cooking.

While Dr. John was busy preparing for the Pibor offence, we were stunned by news of an enemy reinforcement convoy entering into Pibor town. Thorough checks were carried out in Panahoth and Kong-Kong, following the news. We became vigilant, unsure of what action the enemy may take in Pibor town. Will they dare to attack Panahoth or Kong-Kong, or both at the same time? Will they offload supplies and quietly slip out of town and return to Malakal, where they came from? Panahoth was only six kilometres from Pibor, which was a disturbing factor to the town's inhabitants. They did not want the rescuing convoy to return, without addressing the challenge of Panahoth.

So, on February 23, 1987 at 10:00am, the enemy launched a mortar shell attack on Panahoth, the SPLA defensive position. We heard the sound of bombardment at Kong-Kong. Upon hearing this, our overall Commander Captain Ayuen Alier Jongroor relayed this information to the Chairman's headquarters, updating them on the latest developments. My reaction to the new situation at Panahoth was to instantly send reinforcements to that end. However, Captain Ayuen thought otherwise, and wouldn't dispatch reinforcements until given the approval by Dr. John Garang. We received instructions to move to Panahoth, three hours after the fighting commenced. Myself and the commando task force, were assigned to the rescuing mission. The distance from Kong-Kong to Panahoth was an exhausting three-hour walk. This was too long of a delay, to rescue anything at Panahoth. Military actions such as this, are quick to execute. We found the enemy had already dislodged our forces from their defensive position and had returned to Pibor with the only Zu 23 anti-aircraft heavy machine gun, which our force at Panahoth had in their possession. We had to track back to the base at Kong-Kong before dawn. In our minds, was the threat they could attack our position at Kong-Kong the following day as their morale was skyrocketing, due to their victory at Panahoth.

Dr. John understood the situation, so he dropped in with task force one from Zalzal (Earthquake) division, under the command of Capt. Malony Akou Nai, and jeeps mounted with anti-tank launchers. This was an encouraging step, since we had been dispossessed of our only heavy machine-gun at Panahoth a few days prior. Attempts to restore military balance were mounted. A force under the command of 1st Lt Deng Adeerdit da'Adhor, was sent to Panahoth to regain control. A recce team commanded by 2nd Lt Makuach Diing Arok was dispatched to Pibor to assess the situation around the town. That reconnaissance force was unfortunately detected by the enemy in town and they began to bombard them with mortar shells. Serious wounds were inflicted on the commander of the recce force and many others. The force had to withdraw back to the base at Kong-Kong and then 2nd Lt Makuach and the injured soldiers were quickly rushed to the rear for medical treatment. We were disturbed by the recent development of affairs, but the enemy in Pibor town was infuriated by the SPLA/M encroachment. Task force one, commanded by Capt. Malony Akou Nai, was instructed to join 1st Lt. Deng Adeerdit da' Adhor at Panahoth, then begin launching attacks on the town. I was ordered to move to a different area called Manyirany to the north of Pibor, with my forces which composed of 400 men. We were required to establish a defensive base. My force would be moving under the fire cover of 1st Lt Deng Leek (Majook) Deng Malual who was ordered to attack the town from the east, as I would be advancing to Manyirany. We took our position at Manyirany early in the morning of February 26, 1987. Upon our arrival at Manyirany, all forces were instructed to dig fox holes as a precaution due to our proximity to the enemy position in town. The troops were busy digging fox holes and pounding grains for food.

There was huge relief at Manyirany, as the forces were able to find enough water for drinking as well as bathing. Also, we acquired plenty of grains from the local stores when the owners weren't present. Instantly, the cows and goats in the vicinity began to penetrate our defensive lines in search of water and became easy foray for the forces. The entire force, as mentioned earlier, did not bath for a good number of days at Kong-Kong. The food supplies had been tight, as soldiers had only been rationed one cup of grains every two days. Both grains and meat became available in abundance, to the extent all soldiers were now feasting.

As forces were busy with their own activities, the enemy launched a surprise attack at 3:00pm with mortar shells falling heavily on our defensive positions. We assumed it was an attack mounted by the enemy from

Pibor, attempting to send us away from Manyirany. Our men were ready to confront the enemy from any direction. I immediately sent two COYs to flank the enemy from different sides and our frontage remained firm. We managed to dislodge them in a short amount of time. The third COY under the command of 1st Lt Lual Malong, was to take the left hand side flank across the river while 1st Lt Kiir Dau took the right hand side. The enemy quickly rushed back to town as they felt threatened by our forces.

Our only short-range radio 77 operator, private Jok Anyeth Jok was overwhelmed by fear and ran away to Kong-Kong. This left us with nothing to use for communication to report the situation to Kong-Kong, Panahoth and other SPLA stations. We therefore had to report to Kong-Kong headquarters via a handwritten letter, carried by two messengers. The report stated the enemy came from Pibor town and attacked our position at Manyirany this afternoon. We are in full control of our defensive position. We lost one soldier in action with three wounded. None of the wounded are in serious condition. We also communicated that we were short of ammunitions and requested reinforcements to be dispatched asap, as we are not certain what the enemy will do tomorrow. The messengers had to leave Manyirany for Kong-Kong at 5:00pm. The distance to Kong-Kong was approximately 15kms. The message arrived at 3:00am the following morning, with the recipients fearing the worst. False information that we were dislodged from our defensive position had been reported, with our whereabouts unknown. This shock was short lived, as the messengers arrived and provided the correct update on the Manyirany military situation. Upon hearing the news, Captain Ayuen Alier with a sigh of relief, organised a force to start moving to Manyirany on a mounted jeep to rescue us. Captain Ayuen ordered the whole force to evacuate Kong-Kong for Manyirany, instead of rescuing us.

The following morning, we heard the abnormal sound of machines moving from the direction of Pibor. They resembled the sound we experienced the day before when our position was attacked. Surely, it's the enemy tanks from yesterday's clash? We quickly took our positions ready for the challenge. We were quickly rescued by the SPLA force at Panahoth, as they launched a mortar attack on the town. The enemy advancing towards our position started to retreat as the town came under heavy bombardment from the SPLA forces. We remained attentive in our positions waiting for the enemy, which was not forth coming. We weren't aware the attackers had already retreated to defend Pibor from the SPLA attackers. From our defensive position, we didn't realise they had withdrawn back to town. We had cause for sudden alarm, coming from the opposite direction. This development was from our own forces advancing from Kong-Kong. A mounted jeep arrived with ammunitions and soldiers, which was a huge relief to those in the camp. The jeep was followed immediately by all the forces that remained in Kong-Kong. The enemy in town was in two minds. If they attempt to attack Panahoth from the south, the SPLA at Manyirany could come from behind and attack the town. The opposite applied for Panahoth. If they attacked Manyirany to the north, Panahoth would deal with them from behind as had happened that morning when they attempted to attack Manyirany for the second time.

The government army in Pibor were in total confusion, not understanding which operative was the best action to take. Those who brought supplies to Pibor and managed to capture Panahoth had seized an anti-aircraft heavy machine gun (Zu 23). They did not know whether to leave the town for Waat, then head to Malakal with their loot? If they left, what will mitigate the situation in town when the SPLA forces are approaching? If they stay in the town with the defending force, the SPLA will surely attack and capture it. The enemy force that came to Pibor, decided to leave town for Malakal on the morning of February 28, 1987, pulling along the Zu 23 they had captured at Panahoth. This was instead of leaving it behind, to be used to defend the town from the immanent SPLA attack. They were anxious to take the recently captured Zu 23 to Malakal and exhibit it as a point of pride to Malakal's town inhabitants. This would demonstrate the Sudanese army was courageous enough to inflict a heavy defeat to their enemy, the SPLA forces. The whole affair however was propaganda against the SPLA/M Movement. The Sudanese government would historically belittle the SPLA, as an ill-equipped movement using out of date weapons that didn't match their war machinery. But to find war machines such as the Zu 23 in possession of the SPLA/M, was in fact sending shocking waves to the army and the towns inhabitants about the real level of armament possessed by the Movement. If anything, it indicated they hadn't quite anticipated the Movement's strength.

As the convoy left Pibor for Waat, I was instructed by my operational overall Commander, Colonel Agasio Akol Tong, to move in a parallel line with the enemy forces coming from Pibor towards Waat town. We did as we were instructed. We followed them up to the point of no return to Pibor town, after which we had to return to base. On the return journey, we encountered a local Murle man identified by those at Panahoth to be an anti SPLA/M, rearing his herds very close to town. We told him enough was enough, and not to stay near Pibor town at this juncture. We took him along with his cattle, to our base.

Captain Malony Akou Nai with his task force 1, was already at the base sitting with Dr. John Garang de Mabior when we came in. A sand model in preparation for the Pibor operation was already conducted, according to the battalion members who had remained at the base. It was immanent the fate of Pibor had already been determined. Captain Malony was to kick start the operation with his Zalzal's task force 1. Captain Malony would use night cover on his route to attack the town. They launched the attack at dawn of March 1, 1987, capturing the front of the enemy lines but were forced to withdraw by 9:00am. My role was to cover Captain Malony's forces from the rear. When we arrived at the base from the covering mission, I found Captain Malony reporting the situation to Commander in Chief Dr. John Garang. The next attack to Pibor was assigned to the commando task force, under my personal command. Again, we would move towards the town at night. We failed to mount an attack the following day due to technical reasons, but we successfully managed an attack on February 3, and the remaining forces caught up with us in town.

The town was divided in two. The enemy forces were in their fox holes to the southwest of the town, and we were directly opposite. Both sides began shelling each other. As all forces were in town, Dr. John took the role of chief cook. He was directing the cooks to quickly do their job, so food and water could be rushed to the soldiers on the front line. Night time halted the battle, until February 5, when another tougher confrontation resumed. This continued until 8:00pm when a flare light was fired into the sky by the enemy. It came as no surprise, this was a sign of the enemy withdrawing from town, indicating the fall of Pibor into the hands of the gallant SPLA forces. The event could not be celebrated until the following morning, when we moved into town to take firm control. Commanders of task forces; Captain Malony Akou Nai, Captain Kenedy Gayin, Captain Maciek Akuochpiir from task force three, Captain Bior Asoud of the Chairman's headquarter, Captain Ayuen Alier, Captain Gilo Agada Cham, Captain Peter Pitia, myself plus operational staff, moved into the town at 4:30am. This was followed by operational overall commander Colonel Agasio Akol Tong at 7:30am. When the Chairman of the SPLM and Commander in Chief of the SPLA Dr. John Garang de Mabior arrived, he was congratulating officers, NCOs and men who exerted a magnificent effort capturing the town. He was hugging every officer and soldier he came across. The whole affair was celebrated by people breaking into dance and members of every community danced according to their own style. Every success must be marked with joy and happiness. Therefore Pibor town was marred with shouting, shots being fired into the air, the singing of revolutionary songs and war cries of the SPLA hoyee by the SPLA fighters.

The different cultures and nationalities could easily be observed in Pibor when the men who captured the town were busy collecting the booties. One could identify a Murle and an Anyuak man from a Dinka, a Shiluk, a Nuer and others by their behaviours when collecting the booties. The Murle and Anyuaks were occupied with a collection of different types of firearms and ammunitions. Culturally, their means of defence centred on firearms and therefore prepared to search for ammunitions. This would be beneficial to them by either using it in self-defence (in the case of aggression by a neighbouring community), or using it for the purpose of wealth collection from nearby tribes (cattle raiding and child abduction), or otherwise used in hunting for food. Ammunitions could be sold or exchanged for cattle, goats and sheep or it could be used for acquiring valuable materials, such as clothes and food.

Unlike other nationalities, Nuer, Dinka, Equatorians and Cholo (Shiluk) focused their interests on food collection and other important materials such as clothes, beds, mattresses, shoes and mosquito nets. This made the former group vulnerable in terms of food supplies, because they ignored their main sources of living. In the near future, the group collecting ammunitions started to beg the other group for food supplies.

Following the capture of Pibor town, Dr. John Garang left for Ethiopia for reasons only known to him (possibly to secure additional military support). We were disciplined to the extent that a person need not enquire of the Chairman's whereabouts, asking where he is going and when he will return. It was enough to farewell and welcome him on return, without asking any questions. This was due to security reasons.

Dr. John returned to Pibor within two days with another task force under the command of Major Geu Erjok (athorkuei) Deng. The new task force was stationed at Pibor's old air strip 7kms west of Pibor town, awaiting orders for their next deployment. The commanders of the task forces were all asked to attend an important meeting with the Chairman Dr. John Garang, at Lokurnyang across Pibor River. The meeting explained the new deployment of forces that would match the defence of newly captured town. My task force was ordered to Likuanglei, which was 32kms north of Pibor. Task force one under command of 1st Lt Malong Chol, was deployed to Gumuruk, while Captain Kenedy Gayin, Captain Ayuen Alier and Captain Malony Akou Nai were to remain in Pibor. The task forces instructed to deploy outside Pibor town, were scheduled to depart the following morning. Two gentlemen, namely Mr. William Kon Bior Duot and Dr. Richard K. Mulla arrived in Pibor with the Chairman Dr. John Garang. Their mission in Pibor was to enlighten the Murle community about the Movement's objectives in their cattle camps. William Kon was assigned to me, meanwhile Dr. Richard K. Mulla was to go with Malong Chol to Gumuruk and be escorted to the cattle camps by the son of the area, 1st Lt Clement Nyilma Katinya. It was currently the dry season when the population move their herds to different places in search of greener pastures and water. The two gentlemen were expected to move to those faraway areas where they could meet with the population and educate them about The Movement's policies and objectives. It was not an easy endeavour, as they had to move on foot in search of the scattered population across different locations. Dr. John left Pibor for Ethiopia, after handing out the new instructions for deployment.

News of Pibor falling into SPLA/M hands, caught the attention of the international media. On BBC radio the 'Focus on Africa' programme interviewed an SPLM/A representative in Addis Ababa. They confirmed Dr. John was the commander in charge of the operation that captured

Pibor town. That statement was a slip of tongue from the SPLM/A representative, Commander Martin Manyiel Ayuel. Those in Pibor upon hearing the interview, concluded that something unpleasant would surely occur to the residents of Pibor tomorrow. The reason they felt this way, was because of Dr. John's presence in town. The enemy (Khartoum Government), wanted to eliminate Dr. John Garang to weaken the SPLM/A. Hence, confirming his presence in Pibor town was reason enough for the enemy to launch an air attack hoping to hit their target. This caused the residents to be on edge, expecting an air attack at any given moment.

That evening, we packed all our belongings ready to depart at dawn the following day. My forces were overwhelmed by the booties they had captured in Pibor. Heavy loads of food and rounds of ammunitions were not easy to transport along the 32km journey.

The Establishment of Likuanglei Military Base

Our journey commenced early in the morning. I was faced with hesitation and resistance from those carrying the heavy loads. It was a tough challenge convincing them to walk out of town. My job was made easier, when expectantly two jet fighter planes started bombing the town with the then prohibited napalm bombs. They could burst into fire once they touched the ground, leaving those who had been dragging their feet to move faster than ever before in fear of their lives. They managed to catch up with us on the way as intensive bombardment continued for quite some time.

Mr. William Kon Bior who had been assigned to us, was walking by my side. He had come from London and was not yet trained, so I doubted his ability to cope with the walking. Unlike those who had completed an intensive training regime . To the surprise of everyone including myself, the man was up to the challenge and was faster and stronger than some of his ccnx counterparts. He had been trained in how to handle an AKM rifle which was issued the day prior. Due to the heavy load our men were carrying, we decided to rest at a water point and prepare some food. The task force vanguards of Joseph Akuon had managed to encounter a local Murle man rearing goats with an AKM rifle. It was not an ordinary sight to see an untrained and a non-SPLA member carrying that type of AKM rifle. He was immediately seized and brought to the headquarters for questioning. Following this, he was handed over to the Boma task force whose members all hailed from the area, for better communication and custody.

We moved along the Pibor River and camped close to the final destination of Likuanglei. We arrived at Likuanglei and deployed our forces according to the sectors. When we departed Pibor, the road construction team also departed, leaving the road grading to be completed by Likuanglei village. There were no inhabitants of the village that we could find and communicate with. We had to ensure every soldier dug a foxhole, because we were unsure whether there were enemies lurking in the surrounding population. Also, we could not easily anticipate which direction that had been taken by those government forces who were , defeated in Pibor a few days ago. By then, our forces had encountered one of the local enemy collaborators who wrongly thought those who had just arrived in Likuanglei village, were government forces. He approached the SPLA soldiers with a wide smile, thinking they were the friends he had departed with. He was lured in by the SPLA soldiers but was deeply shocked when he realised they were not the true friends he was looking for. He was sent back to his community in the nearby village and advised not to collaborate with enemy forces again.

The government forces together with Murle militia men under the command of the paramount Chief Ismail Konyi, preferred to go to Akobo for reasons best known to them. It could have been because Akobo was relatively nearer to Pibor, than to Bor. Also the community they would be travelling through was friendly towards them, compared to the hostile and unfriendly Bor Dinka community. The third and main reason of not traveling to Bor, was the lack of water sources along the way, which they would have to track by foot. Meanwhile the route to Akobo was naturally endowed with the Pibor River. Therefore, they had to follow the route to Likuanglei, and we eventually arrived after them. We could have caught up with them , had we not been delayed with the celebrations for the fall of Pibor. Though we could not find many people at Likuanglei, but we were visited by the parents of the late Nyacigak Ngacilok the Alternate Member of Politico-Military High Command. They were paying their allegiance and support to the SPLA, in which their son was killed in action around Kapoeta two years prior. We were grateful and appreciative for their visit, assuring them their son did not die in vain.

After firmly securing Likuanglei, we instructed the forces to build residential hut and shelters, since we were planning to reside for a while. The forces were confronted with the challenge of scorpions during the construction process, although it did not hamper their mission. That time of year, is the scorpion breeding season. It's still a vivid in my memory that every person in Likuanglei base was either stung once, twice, or even three times by the scorpions including the current President of the Republic of South Sudan, his Excellency General Salva Kiir Mayardit. General Salva Kiir dropped into the Likuanglei military base on his way to reinforce his colleague General Arok Thon Arok around Akobo town. The enemy intended to reinforce the garrison town of Akobo, while the SPLA were trying to prevent this from happening. When General Salva came to Likuanglei, he was aware of the scorpion issue and wanted to evade being stung at all costs. But sailors don't wish storms in the sea to occur. After finishing his duties, Commander Salva wanted to exit his well secured tent, so he irradiated at his sleepers to make sure there were no scorpions around before he could step on them. . As soon as he stepped on, he was unfortunately stung right away. He immediately shouted loudly at his guards declaring that he had been stung. Then, the giggling bodyguards came rushing to his call. You could tell they were thinking to themselves that if all in the camp were stung by the scorpions, why not you either? There was nothing that could be done since it was too late. Commander Salva had to endure the intense pain of the scorpion's poison for the rest of the night and into the following day. News about the scorpion was broken to us the next day, when we visited him for morning salutation. The scorpions at Likuanglei village were rampant and could be found or seen in every corner of the camp. I was once stung when a scorpion crept into my clothing while I was relaxing in the evening. It stung me at the waist, making my night very uncomfortable, and I was still in pain until the following afternoon.

Likuanglei became an important stopover point for forces advancing towards Akobo then heading to the Northern Upper Nile. Task forces of Lazim, Khor Flus battalion and other forces passed through Likuanglei on their way to Nanam stream. The Joseph Akuon task force, which was part of my forces at Likuanglei, also joined them at Nanam. The focus was to deny access to the enemy trying to reinforce their isolated and besieged forces in Akobo town. Our forces were deceived and wrongly fed with misleading information that the government had organised a huge force to retake the recently liberated town of Pibor. The SPLA leadership upon learning the news, decided to keep those forces around Nanam to stop the advancing enemy forces from recapturing Pibor. It was a military war and tactics aimed at dividing the SPLA attention, instead of concentrating on Akobo Waat road. The commander of those forces, CDR Lam Akol Ajawin, was the last to join them at Nanam. Dr. Lam spent a miserable night with us at Likuanglei, but proceeded to Nanam the following day. The night was miserable to Dr. Lam because we had no food available to feed him the meal he deserved.

Lies usually don't live long, and it became clearer to the forces at Nanam that the enemy forces at Waat were directed to reinforce Akobo, rather than recapturing Pibor. Commanders Salva Kiir and Lam Akol with the forces starteding to move to Akobo town, when the revelation confirmed the only enemy objective to implement was to reinforce Akobo town. They then had to race against the clock, as the enemy forces were already on the move from Malakal to Waat and from there to Akobo. The area the enemy could not detour on the road to Akobo, was the Kaibui Bridge. Therefore, the SPLA forces built-up their position at the bridge, in their attempts to prevent the enemy from entering town. Efforts were futile, as the enemy broke through the SPLA defensive lines and went to Akobo and then back to Malakal.

To understand why the enemy penetrated the SPLA lines despite the large presence of their forces, was due to many factors;

1. Lack of war experience as our forces had just returned from the Bonga training centre.
2. Lack of equipment capable of destroying the enemy's war machinery e.g. tanks and artillery.
3. The enemies capability of destroying our equipment from a distance, due to the level of training which could not be matched by our own forces.
4. Enemy superiority in terms of mobility and military war machines.
5. SPLA forces were distracted by desertion, wanting to exercise operations in their home areas and therefore deserting the battlefield.

After the operations around Akobo town concluded, the top three commanding officers, CDRs Salva Kiir, Arok Thon Arok and Dr. Lam Akol had to leave for their respective assignments. CDR Arok Thon had to remain at his headquarters around Akobo, meanwhile CDR Salva Kiir returned to Likuanglei then to Pibor and afterwards proceeded to Boma. Dr. Lam Akol became Sector Commander, and upon his appointment was required to lead troops for a long walk to the Northern Upper Nile where he was expected to establish his command headquarters. I would like to reiterate that the Movement's leadership had appointed five commanders to the newly created position of Alternate Members of Politico-Military High Command. This was less than the position of permanent members of Politico-Military High Command. Those newly appointed Members were as follow:

1. Lt. Colonel Dr. Riek Machar Teny
2. Major Dr. Lam Akol Ajawin
3. Major James Wani Igga
4. Major Yusif Kowa Maki and
5. Lt Colonel Daniel Awet Akot

This was in addition to Major John Kulang Puot and Major Nyacigak Ngacilok who had already been appointed to the same position of Alternate Members of Politico-Military High Command in 1985.

Back in Likuanglei base, the forces had constructed grass thatched shelters. To enable the force to be self-sufficient, we were provided with motor-graders to clear trees and a tractor to cultivate the graded land. About ten areas were cleared of trees and cultivated with maize and sorghum. This left us with high expectations of a good harvesting season. But unfortunately, a drought unexpectedly occurred and destroyed the crops and hopes of a good harvesting season were dashed.

Life at the Likuanglei camp was tough. There were no food supplies and the population had left with their cattle looking for greener pastures and water. Even if they remained in the area, they would not willingly attempt to collect food rations for the soldiers, as they were unfriendly towards the Movement. The Murle mind-set under the leadership of their paramount Chief Ismail Konyi, was geared towards our enemy in Khartoum. Hence, unit officers and men were at my throat, due to the lack of food supplies. I don't think there is a commander on earth who could successfully manage a guerrilla force, if they are unable to feed them. Therefore, the months of April, May and June of 1987 were terribly demanding especially when the local population returned with the animals to their residential settlements. Soldiers would sneak out of camp and try to befriend members of the community to at least provide them with something to consume. It would be a different story altogether if they failed to find anything to feed on.

I would like to explain an issue I once encountered at the camp. It was dividing the camp between native soldiers and those from other areas. Red army soldiers (a nickname given to the child soldiers) managed to kill a bull owned by the father of the late Commander Nyachigak Ngacilok. They took the meat they planned to carry, leaving the rest of the meat in the bush. As mentioned, the sons of the area who were already members of the Movement, saw this as an act to devastate the wealth of the Murle community. They demonstrated their discontent in a manner that almost lead to the division amongst ourselves. I tried my best to diffuse the situation and compensated the lost bull by giving a cow to the family of the late Ngachigak. That was one challenge among many others that I need not mention here in the book. That incident occurred before things could turn good for all the forces in and around Pibor. The friends of the Movement (Ethiopia's Government) transported food supplies by air to Pibor town. The food items supplied were enough to cover us for the rainy season from July to December. The outposts of Likuanglei and Gumuruk, would dispatch teams to Pibor on the day of distribution to bring food rations to the two respective areas. These would include; rice, maize, beans, lentils, salt and edible oil plus some non-food items.

It is a known fact that the Murle community have limited interest in farming. They are a cattle owning society. Therefore, they befriended all the soldiers at the camp. On the day of food distribution, you would witness masses of women flocking to Likuanglei camp to obtain food stuffs from their friends. We also had acquired a few bulls, which were an important source of meat for our men. The soldiers would move into the community looking for their friends to provide them with some rare food commodities to change up their diet. The community we thought were enemies against the Movement became peaceful and friendly to the SPLA forces to an extent of metaphorical depiction. They drained basic rounds of ammunitions from SPLA soldiers to the extent that if we were to confront any military challenge, it would have been a disaster.

Through our relationship with the community, we were able to recover abducted children from the neighbouring communities and reunite them with their families. Child abduction and cattle raiding are habitual norms of this community, and as a result they inflict terror among neighbouring communities. Sons of the area who happened to be members of the SPLA, did their best in persuading the Murle community to leave in peace, with the SPLA soldiers. Captain Kennedy Gayin Ngare, 1st Lt Marshall Stephen Baabanen, 1st Lt Kitchener Mothan, 1st Lt Clement Ketinya, 1st Lt Jashua Konyi Ereer and 1st Lt Alan Kuju among many others played an instrumental role in calming the Murle youths from infringing into the Movement's affairs. The youths were advised not to lynch an SPLA soldier with the intention of robing his rifle. From our side, we cautioned our soldiers to be vigilant and always walk in groups when entering the community, to avoid being targets of the Murle youths.

All Community Chiefs of Likuanglei, approached me and I had a close relationship with them all. The best chief among them, was Chief Loki Mano. Also, Ayicho Lual, Nganthow Kabula, Kerewa, Barchuch, Guryay and many others gave us their un-wavering support. Despite strict precautions and outstanding orders for our men to follow, we still encountered unimaginable disasters. On one occasion, three soldiers were ambushed and killed by members of the Murle Youths who took their AKM rifles just two kilometres from the camp. This occurred when Murle communities and their youths, returned to their settlements after visiting different grazing areas during the dry season.

The second incident occurred when a soldier permitted to go home, left Likuanglei for Pibor after assuring us it was safe for him to do so. This soldier did not reach his intended destination of Pibor. We enquired with his friends to find his whereabouts but did not yield tangible results. A few days later, a youth from that location came to our camp wearing the late soldier's military cap. He was arrested and investigated in relation to the cap, but with the relaxed attitude of the guards, he escaped and was never held accountable. This incident took us by surprise, because it occurred at the time when the Murle community were peaceful and friendly towards the SPLA soldiers. Local dances were being held at Likuanglei. Local women and children could interact with the soldiers as they wish.

The third incident occurred to an officer who hailed from the Murle community. 1st Lt Alan Kuju committed and dedicated his life to serving the Movement on all fronts. He was against the rampant ownership of firearms by local youths, and felt it was dangerous to the authorities in the area. Alan decided to move out of the camp to search for firearms in the communities. This was a mistake committed by Alan because he made the decision alone without consulting with the administration of Pibor and Likuangle. The youths became furious and outraged and decided to eliminate him for that reason. We were utterly shocked upon learning of Alan's sudden demise at the hands of his own relatives. The SPLA will have to react in retribution of his soul.

The fourth incident took place when a young Murle man, who was a light machine gunner, was assassinated while hunting. The accompanying colleagues came back with the fateful news of his death. He was known as a strong man who exerted a remarkable effort during the capturing of Pibor town some months earlier.

We Those in Likuangle camp, wrote to the overall commander of the SPLA in Pibor, Captain Ayuen Alier, requesting ammunitions and authority to launch a revenge attack against the community who assassinated Alan Kuju. We began preparations to visit those who murdered Alan. When the day came, forces under the Command of 1st Lt Marshall Stephen started moving to check where Chief Ayicho Lual's men were located. The confrontation was light. Youths of that community had run away with the animals leaving no real fighters to face, if at all. Murle tactics are always hide, hit and run away after causing heavy damage to the opponents. A Murle man can hide himself in a very clear and open area, but it would be hard to locate him. Our men had to return to the base with only one comrade lost in action. It was already dry season when the communities leave their homes for areas in search of green pastures and water. With the absence of the youth, our men became in full command of the area. It became a daily routine, to send people in the early hours of the morning to shield off Murle youths from the vulnerable places. That policy bore fruits and we didn't lose any of our soldiers during the whole dry season of 1988.

The killing of Alan Kuju and others, as mentioned earlier, signalled a sign of unrest and rebellion in the whole Murle area. My wife, Achol Juach Diing, who had joined me at Likuanglei four months prior, had to be escorted on foot to Pibor. From there she would be transported to the Itang Refugee Camp in Ethiopia. The Movement's leadership took the death of Alan Kuju as a serious challenge to its authority. A force was prepared from the rear under the command of Captain William Deng Garang Bany, to be sent to north of Pibor (Likuanglei county) to counteract Chief Ayicho's challenge. The operation was delayed due to the upcoming rainy season, when the population would have returned to their settlements. Since the defeat and eviction of government forces from Pibor a year ago, Paramount Chief Ismail Konyi who was also a Murle militia commander, had been away from the area. This is why peace throughout the area had prevailed. As the community was about to return to their settlements, rumours of Chief Ismail coming back to Murleland were speculated.

In May 1988, Captain Deng Garang arrived at Likuanglei with his forces. Commander Salva Kiir Mayardit was named as Commander in Charge of those expected operations. The Pibor area was falling under his command axis. South Sudan was divided into five axis points, among the five permanent members of Politico-Military High Command; Dr. John Garang de Mabior, Deputy Commander in Chief of the SPLA Lt. Colonel Kerbino Kuanyin Bol, Lt. Colonel William Nyuon Bany, Major Salva Kiir Mayardit and Major Arok Thon Arok. Therefore, Commander Salva would follow Deng Garang as an overall commander of the operation. Before he could come to Likuanglei, there was an enemy convoy code named as 'deterrent' moving from Malakal, coming towards either Waat, Bor or Pibor. We were uncertain of its target, so needed to remain vigilant to ensure the enemy did not surprise Pibor town or Likuanglei village, my current headquarters. Equally those SPLA Forces around Bor town were not spared either. One evening, we received the news that the wondering enemy between Waat, Bor and Pibor had emerged at Akuai-deng village very close to the SPLA headquarters at Baidit, 16 miles from Bor. We in Pibor and Likuanglei breathed a deep sigh of relief, confirming the proverb which states, God changes events to the better. To the better here, means the betterment of the forces in Pibor and Likuanglei, but not the entire SPLA forces. This is because it was going to be disastrous to our headquarters in Baidit, where everything was stored. Nonetheless, those at Baidit laboured all night, removing important items and leaving behind the non-essentials.

After the emergence of the deterring enemy convoy in the Bor area, Commander Salva Kiir prepared to leave Pibor for Likuanglei with the aim of seeking revenge against the murderers of 1st Lt Alan Kuju, five months earlier. He joined Captain William Deng Garang Bany and myself at Likuanglei. Commander Salva spent two days in the area before instructing Captain William Deng to commence operations in the north of Likuanglei. The SPLA force was to clash with the rebel force of Chief Ayichu Lual the following morning. There were casualties from the battle, that were immediately evacuated to Likuanglei and were transported to Pibor then Ethiopia for further medical treatment. The wounded comrades from that battle were lucky to be given first aid treatment by Dr. Dau Aleer Abit in Pibor. They were immediately given first aid, before being evacuated to Gambella for further treatment. Meanwhile, Commander Salva opted to continue the operations against the outlaws in that territory. It was no surprise, Chief Ayichu went into hiding never to be seen or heard of. In pursuance of the rebels, Commander Salva went up to the Nanam area and turned southwards to Nanam Mountain, which was a known hideout for the rebels. After three weeks of an unfruitful search for Chief Ayichu Lual, Commander Salva surfaced at Gumuruk military base on the way to Bor, and west of Pibor. He finally went back to Pibor town after a month of searching for chief Ayichu Lual and his men. Commander Salva ordered the base commanders to Pibor for a meeting, to present their grievances and challenges. I immediately left Likuanglei for Pibor with my escort. News of former Paramount Chief Ismail Konyi returning to Pibor was discussed at the meeting, in relation to the security situation. After the meeting, I requested permission from Area Commander Captain Ayuen Alier to travel to Itang to see my newly born son. With his permission granted, I accompanied General Salva on his return journey to Gambella the following day. We flew by military helicopter to Gambella and proceeded to the Zinc military base, where we met Dr. John Garang de Mabior. He called me into his office, enquiring about the general situation in Pibor. After this was discussed, he caught up with Commander Salva Kiir Mayardit for the remainder of the day. We could then finally depart for Itang, our last destination.

When the unrest started to surmount in Pibor, the local population was receiving news about the outlaw Paramount Chief Ismail Konyi returning. Indeed, his presence in the area unleashed many disturbances. Some of his followers did not leave with him, when he left with defeated Sudanese armed forces in Pibor on March 5, 1987. Instead, they melted into the Murle community making what we termed as 'sleeping cells'. These cells started to cause havoc and insecurity, targeting SPLA supporters among the communities. This happened in the case of Mr. Boyoy Gola, who's house was raided and cattle stolen during the night. He was killed during a fight when he sought assistance from the SPLA forces. On some occasions, the cells would attack SPLA soldiers when vulnerable, e.g. travelling from a location to another, when they were hunting, fetching fire wood or gathering construction materials. The SPLA administration in Pibor made many attempts to reconcile with Chief Ismail Konyi following his return, all to no avail. He left the SPLA frustrated and with no other option apart from military confrontation. This would be implemented during the upcoming dry season of 1989 when Commander of the Sector (Axis), Salva Kiir Mayardit unexpectedly surprised the chief at Nanam Valley, distributing the Sudanese government's newly supplied arms and ammunitions to his militia men. He narrowly escaped death with his forces abandoning those supplies to be captured by the SPLA forces. The traitor, Paramount Chief Ismail Konyi, was given a real hot pursue by the SPLA with the hope to capture him but to no avail. He tactfully applied guerrilla warfare by using the community as his shield. The whole rainy season passed, dodging the SPLA forces. However, his days of staying in Pibor were numbered, because the SPLA had managed to bring in many forces under overall command of William Nyuon Bany Machar and the direct command of Commander Anthony Bol Madut. Chief Ismail resisted the dry season offensive of 1990, until he escaped to Juba at the beginning of the rainy season in May that same year. Following are some important factors that allowed him to evade the SPLA forces;

1. Terrain - there is a thick forest along the Pibor River that allowed Chief Ismail to manoeuvre the SPLA movements without being detected.
2. His knowledge of the area, enabled him to dodge any attempts to capture him.
3. His ability to hide among the Murle Community members.
4. Vastness of the area - this could allow him stay in areas far away from the reach of the SPLA forces.
5. The community was too secretive to release any information about the Chief.

That was not only for Chief Konyi alone, but for any criminal who committed crimes in the Murle area. Emphatically, a Murle man is ready to lose his dear life instead of releasing a secret he knows about a fellow Murle person. The news of Chief Ismail disturbing the area were relayed to me while I was attending the Addis Ababa political school, as he arrived after I had left my base at Likuanglei.

Three Months at the Itang Refugee Camp

Life at the Itang Refugee Camp was a known routine. Food rations were as usual being distributed twice a month. Everyone receives even rations, however sometimes you can receive more rations if you know someone from the refugee's administration. I enjoyed a bit of a luck due to my friendship with the Camp Manager Samuel Ater Dak, who was head of the administration's committee. Camp Manager Ater, thankfully honoured me with one hundred Ethiopian Birr to help support my family. I was very grateful to Ater because the amount of money he offered me, was not easy money back then. I was granted permission to visit Itang for a few days only, but this was extended beyond a specified time, because the only way the SPLM/A could transport me back to Pibor, was via air. Heavy rainfall had caused floods within the camp.

During the two months spent at Itang, I had to manage my own affairs since there was no official duty assigned to me. Commander Salva Kiir, whom I had been in contact with, had nominated me to attend political training in Addis Ababa, which was due to commence in about one month. As he was going back to his operational sector (Axis), I was to accompany him to Pibor to collect my personal belongings. We travelled via helicopter to Pibor from Gambella. On arrival, Pibor was looking like an island submerged under water with only a small portion of the air strip still dry. We landed safely and Commander Salva and members of his headquarters disembarked from the chopper. After we bid them farewell, I received my luggage from my bodyguards and was advised not to take any guards with me. The chopper then departed for the return journey to Gambella, Ethiopia. Joining me on the chopper, was First Lt Clement Katinya Nyalma and his wife Yayi Nyibuyi. He was also nominated to attend the same training programme. The helicopter landed briefly at the Pinyudo Refugee Camp, and Clement alighted with his family and proceeded to Gambella. I returned to Itang to prepare for attending the Addis Ababa political school, in around one month. Other nominees were 1st Lt Michael Manyuon Anyang from Kuanylou, 1st Clement Katinya Nyalma and myself from the area liberated in Pibor mentioned earlier. There were many nominees from other SPLA held areas to attend the same training at Yakatit Political School. Three of us who were from Itang, approached the chairman of the refugee's camp, Mr. Samuel Ater Dak, to facilitate us on our journey to Addis Ababa, which he did without hesitation.

Journey to Addis Ababa from the Itang Refugee Camp

The man in charge of the SPLA's affairs in Gambella, 1st Lt Arop Monyaak Monytoach, invited us to spend a night at his duty station. The following morning, we left for Addis Ababa. It was a two day journey via public transport to our destination. On arrival, we were taken to a nearby hotel where we stayed for few days before being relocated to the nearby town of Debriziet. Life at Debriziet was relatively affordable for the SPLM coordination office, compared to the hotel in Addis Ababa. We were just a small guerrilla movement with no resources to maintain its cadres in the Addis Ababa city hotels. The Movement employed some local cooks to serve their members who visited Addis Ababa for official missions, residing in a rented house. We thought we would commence our schooling on arrival to Addis Ababa, but this was not the case. We had to wait over a month, before we could officially commence. We were briefed by the Chairman of the Movement Dr. John Garang, also present in Addis Ababa and the Movement's representative in Ethiopia, Mr. Deng Alor Kuol. They outlined their expectations on how we should interact with our colleagues, as representatives of the Movement. Discipline and respect were required from every group member, which were basic norms in the school. We were also expected to exert a solid effort in acquiring the knowledge required to run the Movement's affairs in the future, which was highly sorted afterward. Dr. John Garang provided a short briefing, before we were transported to school at 4:00pm. We had to wait a little while at the gate before being permitted entry, possibly due to some administrative tasks that still needed to be completed.

Once we had arrived, the accommodation was sorted by the school management. A few important items were shown to us. It was time for dinner, so we were led into the dining hall. Symbolically, the school was being run by highly qualified cadres from the Soviet Union and some other socialist countries, plus Ethiopian nationals led by Mr. Molugeta as the head of school. The students were all Ethiopian political cadres. Some of our South Sudanese colleagues had already joined the school three years ago. They showed us every corner of the school important to acquaint ourselves with. Members of the group were to attend two different courses. I was among the group attending the one year course, while others were to undertake a two year course namely, Akol Khor Kuch and Bol Malou Gai. We had to spend a week in the school compound, before being allowed to enter the classrooms.

The day always began with early morning drills, followed by a shower, then the dining hall for breakfast. Following this, our lectures commenced in the classroom. We had a break at midday for lunch, then after one hour our lectures resumed. They concluded at 4:00pm, depending on the daily schedule, then we had the opportunity for evening activities (e.g. sports), then dinner afterwards. The feeding at school was excellent and exceptionally colourful, but there were some foods we could skip. Ethiopians could eat raw meat, which didn't match our feeding cultures. Of course, the style and ways of feeding of the citizens in every nation depends very much on their cultures. Some inquisitive people among us, tried to eat raw meat but could not persuade others to do it the Ethiopian way.

After every weekend, we would be entertained by Ethiopia's national social dancing teams in the school dancing hall. They would present a dances from each of Ethiopian nationality, that is part of the Ethiopian nation. It was an event we enjoyed every weekend. A probationary period allowing us to leave the school compound without permission, was introduced. Normally, you would not be allowed under any circumstances to exit the school gate. This was prohibited for newcomers to the school. This condition was relaxed after one month of attendance. Once we had completed that specified time period, we gained our freedom to come and go with the rest of our colleagues.

We were then granted permission to visit relatives and friends around Addis Ababa over the weekends. Socialising with Mr. Chol Chiman Garang, was a particular source of enjoyment. His presence in Addis was infrequent, as the SPLA members were usually deployed to the war front and were not in cities like Addis Ababa. But once in Addis, Chol would make it a condition that I join him at the end of every week that he was in the town.

The main challenge encountered by the students at the Yakatit political school was mainly related to finances. This was a usual problem faced by students, not only in Yakatit but by all students in the third world. It is a necessity for those who live in towns to have liquidity or a source of income in any sense, but that was a nightmare for guerrilla members like us to obtain. We were very much grateful to the school administration for providingthough little, - some bursaries for soap and other necessities each month.

Lectures in the classrooms were well delivered by the school's lecturers. South Sudanese students were in all three classes. There were first and second year students, plus those completing the one year training course, depending on their nomination. I was among those attending the one year course, as mentioned earlier. It was a real challenge for a guerrilla person like me, to suddenly attend regular classes. I was coming from Likuanglei where it was very hard to find a piece of paper, let alone a book! Our knowledge before joining the Movement had evaporated and was replaced with a military vocabulary with which we addressed operations at the war front. The knowledge one has, should be replenished through the reading of different books. Lessons taught in Yakatit were of socialist philosophy and ideology background, which I had never heard of before joining the Movement, given that Sudan was a capitalist system of government. Therefore Yakatit studies were faced with a little bit of difficulty, at least for myself. We had no option other than exerting our best efforts, to cope with Ethiopian colleagues in the class. We all spent long amounts of time in the library to study socialist ideological books and to solve given assignments. Not all the subjects taught at Yakatit were a real challenge, but I had difficulty in coping with dialectical materialism and other ideological related subjects. Some colleagues among us performed excellently in the first and final examinations.

Football and chess were some of my personal favourite games. Captains Majok Mach Aluong, Kuol Deng (Aboat) Kuol plus myself were among the class football team representatives and we were also among the overall school football team. We were awarded with models when the Yakatit political school played and won against the Addis Ababa University. The same thing occurred to Samuel Bullen Alier in the local chess competition, when he won and was awarded a medal.

Nine months of continuous training at Yakatit passed quickly. We were fully occupied with our studies, but in addition to this we were able to enjoy our weekends out of the school compound. Time was spent with our South Sudanese friends who would visit us from the various refugee centres of Itang, Pinyudo, Assossa and Dima. Sometime even those coming directly from the war front, as mentioned earlier. The end of nine months was marked by a tougher final examination, in order to graduate from the Yakatit political school. We were subjected to a very strange system of examinations, not experienced before in Sudan or Egypt when I completed my first degree in commerce. Students had to choose the correct answers from a list of similar answers, for each question asked by the examiners. This system does not offer a chance for a student to manoeuvre around the question. A student's answers are limited and controlled by suggested answers set by the teacher (lecturer). In the Sudan or Egypt, a student is asked about a question, and they are required to answer in the form of an essay explaining what they know about the subject. It's generally a lengthy answer, which was very contradictory to how we were tested at the Yakatit political school.

Again, another odd system at the Yakatit political school was the way they set student's passing marks. Passing marks are set in a way that depends on class performance in the subject in question. For instance, if most of the students in a particular class scored marks up to 90%, the ones that have scored 89% downwards would be considered to have failed the exams and awarded with mark C or D. The student in this case has not actually failed, but they are given lower marks which can affect those students in their final score. In other systems of education, a student is considered to have failed the examinations if they only get a lower mark than 50 or less. This is in the case of Sudan and Egypt.

After the examinations, we graduated in a colourful and respectable ceremony attended by Ethiopia's high-level dignitaries, the highest being the President of the Socialist Republic of Ethiopia, Comrade Mengistu Hailemariam. We were very pleased the objective was achieved, and we would be back to South Sudan in a few days. We were invited for lunch to the house of our Chairman Dr. John Garang de Mabior, marking the event of our graduation. In his speech, he congratulated us all for successfully completing the training at Yakatit. He then started talking to us about the responsibilities and challenges awaiting, as the Movement's political cadres. Following this, we were briefed on the Movement's achievements on the war front.

1989 was the year the SPLA scored tremendous and unprecedented victories, lifting it to a high level of recognition, not only within Africa but also the world at large. The SPLA forces started to sweep enemy forces at Kiyalla, Isoke and Ikotos east of Torit during the rainy season of 1988, exposing Torit town to an unimaginable vulnerability. Torit was the next foray to be consummated by the strong SPLA forces in March 1989. It was followed by Katiri, Talanga, Pajwok, Magwei and Nimule town at the border with Uganda. That was in eastern Equatoria. Then the SPLA ignored Juba and the small towns around it, immediately moving to Bor town in the Upper Nile Region. In fact, Bor is the hometown of the Chairman of the SPLM and Commander in Chief of the SPLA Dr. John Garang de Mabior. Bor was nothing but a besieged town, from all directions. Commander Kuol Manyang Juuk who also hailed from this area, was the one in charge of the forces in Jonglei and around Bor town. Dr. John joined Commander Kuol in their desire to seize the town. There was no euphemism used by the two commanders in the capture of Bor town, but instead they confidently informed Khartoum that it was just a matter of days until the gallant forces of the SPLA would capture Bor. Indeed, Bor was attacked and fell into the hands of the SPLA forces on April 29, 1989. The Commander of the enemy forces unfortunately failed to survive the SPLA attack on that day. News of the fall of Bor was received by southern people with excitement and jubilation. It was a town which had triggered the revolution of the long aggrieved southern people. The last town to fall into the SPLA hands during that successful year of victories, was Waat town which happened in early June that same year. There was no real confrontation that occurred between the SPLA and government forces during the fall of Waat. Formerly, there were some skirmishes outside the town initiated by the enemy with the hope of deterring the SPLA forces around it. When they realised their troops were attempting to block unstoppable forces, they unilaterally decided to withdraw from the town without resistance or conflict. With the fall of Waat town, the SPLA had managed to clear all enemy forces from the eastern side of the River Nile from Nimule to canal mouth in the Upper Nile Region, where the enemy forces could make a break. At the end of this eventful briefing at Dr. John Garang's house, we were grateful to hear the news then returned to our residence at the school compound.

Our mission in Addis Ababa was complete, and we then prepared to return to Bonga to await our next deployment. We received instructions from our representatives, that the following morning we will be transported by bus to Bonga. Pocket money for food and accommodation was provided. It was a two day journey via bus to Bonga from Addis. As soon as we arrived at the Bonga Training Centre, we were warmly welcomed by Majak Da' Agoot Da' Atem, Commander of the Bonga Training Centre. The administration allocated our accommodation in the grass thatched houses, despite the large numbers. Military rank and hierarchy were considered when making such decisions. Rank of Captain was the most senior among the group, which included myself. The second group to follow was the 1st and 2nd Lieutenants. Finally, we had one un-commissioned officer, Timothy Tot Chol, among us who was treated differently from the rest of the group, due to his position. That to him was clear discrimination which he jokingly revealed to me afterwards once he was commissioned as a Captain attached to shield five, when he was taken for political training in Addis Ababa.

One of the challenges the Addis Ababa group encountered at Bonga which I must mention, was the food situation. However, this was not considered by others as an important point of criticism. There was a clear difference between the feeding at the Addis Ababa political school and the Bonga Training Centre. Addis Ababa was fully managed by the government of sovereign nations with different and colourful types of food supplies. Meanwhile Bonga was provided by a guerrilla movement, that didn't have an independent budget of its own but instead depended completely on the support of donors.

We were provided with a well-balanced diet in Addis Ababa, containing a mixture of flavoursome high protein food and carbohydrates. While the diet at Bonga was very poor, which composed mainly of carbohydrates and only two meals per day. The sudden change of diet from a delicious to poor one, had resulted in stomach pains and was causing heart burn to myself and others among the group. The mounting daily heart burn, created general weakness to the point that we required medical attention. Some were admitted to hospital and others were ordered by administration to return to the Itang or Pinyudo Refugee Centres, for a change of diet. People would skip meals for the whole day, but would be obliged to eat the following day, because no one would dare to lose his dear and precious life through hunger strike.

We had hoped Dr. John would appear soon to assign us to new positions, but this wasn't the case. As time went on in Bonga, the thinning out process was implemented. All those from Yakatit in Addis Ababa, nominated by their mother units, were requested to report back to where they came from. I was among the few who remained at Bonga with Commander Majak Da' Agoot (the Commander of the Bonga Training Centre, but not as his official military rank in the SPLA). He, in fact, wanted me to assist him in the managing of the Bonga administration, by assigning me in charge of some units across the Bonga tributary stream. There were four battalions undergoing military training on the eastern side of that tributary in addition to cadet's college. Meanwhile four others were on the western side, where the headquarter was ere located.

There were no significant concerns with my management, except for a few isolated issues relating to officers returning from the war front, awaiting their next deployment. Those officers would sometimes infringe with rules and regulations laid down by the central administration and that led to me being rebuked by Commander Majak da' Agoot. Commander Majak would dispatch to my headquarter on the eastern side, with some newcomers hoping to join the SPLA military training college (shield seven). Among those I received, were comrades Dr. Riek Gai Kok, Luka Biong Deng Kuol (who later acquired a doctorate certificate), Martin Kenyi, Akur Aruai Mabior plus many others. They were to wait for shield seven cadet college which was due to be opened in a few days. Indeed, the college opened and those comrades mentioned eventually joined the college and graduated as officers in 1990. They later served the SPLA in different capacities on the war front.

Differences Between the Host Community (Anyuaks) and the Sudanese, in September 1989

There was a major event which occurred between the South Sudanese refugees and the host community of Anyuak, that I would like to shed some light on. The incident which nearly soured the cohesive relationship between the host country (Ethiopia) and the South Sudanese refugee community, represented politically by the SPLM. It sporadically erupted at the Itang Refugee Centre in September 1989 and was quickly replicated at the Pinyudo Refugee Camp in a matter of hours. It was a devastating event because many lives were lost between two brotherly communities. The leader of the SPLM/A, Dr. John Garang, did not hesitate to allocate strong administrative measures to the refugee administrations in both camps, attempting to curve the mayhem. Two military committees were formed, to temporarily reside over both camps. Alternate Commander Oyay Deng Ajak, was assigned to Itang meanwhile Alternate Commander Gier Chuong Aluong was in charge of Pinyudo. All SPLA officers and men at the two refugee camps, no matter how senior they were, were rounded up and sent to the Bonga Training Centre immediately. This meant, the two areas were placed under emergency laws. Soldiers required to implement this policy were transported from nearby bases of Bilpam and Mangok.

Those forces were instructed by their direct commanders to beat and arrest anyone found roaming in the camp after 6:00pm, be that person a woman, a child, or an adult, a soldier or civilian, officially assigned or loiterer. They went as far as persecuting those they thought to have committed crimes in front of the refugee community. In those days they reigned with an iron fist, which made the Anyuak community believe the SPLA was innocent from the crimes and atrocities committed by the inhabitants of the two camps. There was no verification legally conducted, to prove the SPLA innocent of the crime committed against members of the Ethiopian community. The behaviour of those soldiers, I thought, had restrained the Ethiopian government into thinking there was no ill intention from the SPLA soldiers. Thankfully that situation was quickly brought under control by the two commanders, instead of escalating, and it could have been the SPLM/A who would had paid the heavy price if it was mishandled. The Itang administration was dissolved immediately, and Samuel Ater Dak Kwong was briefly arrested and taken to Bonga. He was later released and taken to the Bonga Cadet College of shield seven for officers training, from where he was confirmed as a captain. Alternate Commander Taban Deng Gai became the head of Itang refugee's administration, instead of Ater Dak. Alternate Commander Pieng Deng Kuol at Pinyudo maintained his position for a while but was relieved shortly afterwards.

The officers evicted from Itang and Pinyudo under marshal law, were brought to the Bonga Training Centre, to wait for new deployment. Many people among them were senior officers. Their presence at Bonga had almost brought disorder, because some of them seemed to be undermining Commander Majak's administrative authority. Commander Majak would always seek advice from his seniors on what to do when a situation arises. The case in question was between the Bonga Training Centre's Commander Majak and Alternate Commander Daniel Deng Ajuong. The latter at a certain stage, did not abide by the norms and guidelines of the camp but Commander Majak could not take the appropriate measures against him due to his position of seniority. Those senior officers were quickly deployed out of Bonga and Commander Majak assumed and restored the full powers invested in him, prior to the senior officers' arrival. It is worth mentioning that Alternate Commander Deng Ajuong was demoted to the rank of Captain and sent to Northern Upper Nile under the command of Commander Martin Manyiel Ayuel.

The refugee camps were a fall back position to all SPLA fighters. Their families and relatives were the camp's inhabitants. A person would go to the war front, to execute his national duty. His assignment in the war front would take an unspecified time, but they would one day get a chance to visit their families y in one of the refugee centres. That permitted person, may intend not to return to his duty at war front for unknown reasons, but instead would seek job opportunities to work at the refugee centre. Some were permitted by their commanders for medical reasons, and they must not have had a desire to return to the war front. These types of people with no official duty, accumulated in the refugee centres over the years. They formed a formidable force capable of creating unnecessary rifts against the host community, pretending to be protecting refugee's violated rights. I am sure there may have been a misunderstanding between the host community (the government of Ethiopia) on one side and the refugee community on the other, over petty issues that triggered the September mayhem which took the dear lives from friends and brothers.

When the South Sudanese came to Ethiopia in 1983, they were warmly welcomed by both the government and the host community (Anyuaks). This could have made the South Sudanese feel like they were equal to the national citizens of Ethiopia in their own country. When the national police personnel would carry out their bound duty in bilateral areas, a refugee would object, claiming their rights have been infringed or interfered with. These objections accumulated and the refugees were accused of disrespecting the national authority. This is another potential cause on the assault of Itang's local administration on that fateful day. I have no concrete evidence on who commenced the fight, but I was told from reliable sources that it was a mere overreaction on the side of the refugees. There appeared to be a long-standing grudge to be settled by the refugees, against the host community. If there were existing differences between the host community and the South Sudanese refugees, there should have been a different forum to be addressed by the leaders of the two communities, instead of the hasty and cruel action that was taken.

The behaviours of the South Sudanese in Ethiopia (both refugees and SPLA members), resembled behaviours of those who had never left their home country. What does it mean if an SPLA officer could travel in Ethiopia from point A to point B, fully armed with his rifle on the watch of security personnel, who would not dare to disarm him? It means that SPLA members were enjoying the rights they did not deserve in a foreign country. This behaviour was occurring in every corner of Ethiopia where SPLA members were present, including Addis Ababa where the seat of government was. On one occasion, a bodyguard of the Chairman Dr. John Garang de Mabior made an unforgiving blunder by firing his pistol at another fellow South Sudanese, while his boss was meeting with Ethiopia's Head of State, Comrade President Colonel Mangistu Hailemariam. I am reiterating this point to validate that South Sudanese were not indeed behaving like foreigners in Ethiopia, but just behaving like nationals of that country. This confirmed what President Mangistu had said in Itang in 1984, when he addressed South Sudanese refugees. He said, "You are welcomed in Ethiopia your second country", and he continued by saying that, "If there is nothing to eat, we shall share half of a bread with you, South Sudanese". We took that as genuine sincerity. Let me assure you, if we were to achieve our independence while staying in Ethiopia, believe me, we wouldn't have known the real bitterness of the liberation struggle. We recognised this after we were chased away from Ethiopia in 1991 and came to Kenya, where we encountered the true meaning of a refugee life in a country of refuge. Thank God the almighty, for showing us that fact. We were warmly received in Kenya at the political level, but not at the lower levels of administration. Kenyans educated us about the real meaning of a refugee. I will dwell more on this topic when we discuss refugee life in Kenya.

While busy completing my assignment across the Bonga stream, I was asked to report to Commander Majak da' Agoot's headquarter as soon as possible, with my personal belongings. I had to respond immediately to the call. Commander Majak said when I stood before him, "You will be accompanying the Chairman of the Movement to any where he needs to travel to, so be ready". I saluted him and sat down. In the guerrilla army, you must not make many inquiries. So, I failed to ask him where we will be heading to? When will the journey start? How many people will be accompanying him? What will be my role in the journey? Moving out of Bonga alone was a pleasing step, but I was not sure whether I will be coming back to Bonga. I didn't stay long, before we were commanded by the head of bodyguards to start the journey.

The convoy was heading towards Gambella town. There was no reason for speculation about where we will be heading to since we were already on the move. We arrived at Gambella, but instead of proceeding with the journey to the western side of the Baro River, we changed the course of direction to the south. The sun set before we could reach Abobo town. We were certain we were heading to the Pinyudo Refugee Camp or we would pass by it if we were to go ahead. Our convoy ended up at

Pinyudo where we were received by the chairman of the refugee community, Mr. Pieng Deng Kuol. We were directed to our accommodation for the night. Chairman Pieng was instructed by Dr. John to call a rally the following morning, hence it was announced over the loud speaker that everyone must attend. . Indeed, everything went as planned and a big rally was held in the morning. I will not mention anything about the rally rather than understanding the concerns with the meeting of the area administration, intellectuals and school teachers.

Some elders spoke about the challenges facing them in the camp and their ideas on how to tackle them. The chairman Dr. John Garang spoke next, and he began by praising the Pinyudo administration wishing them every success in leading the camp. In the end, he mentioned the chairman of the refugee camp Mr. Pieng Deng Kuol would be removed and be replaced by Mr. Jurkuch Barach Jurkuch. He is also a son of the area, like Pieng, and he wished him all the best in implementing the administration of the camp. After meeting with elders, Dr. John instructed us to depart for the Pinyudo military training centre, which was 5km south of the Pinyudo Refugee Camp. The reason being, that it was further away from the eyes of UNHCR administrators. This provided an opportunity for the chairman to implement and exercise his authority in a free atmosphere. Dr. John was a busy man, more so than his other colleagues.

Dry season was approaching, when the enemy normally intensify their operations across the different war fronts. I was summoned by Dr. John and advised that my new assignment at the Pinyudo Refugee Camp, was to run its administration. As a soldier, I was standing to attention. I listened to his instructions, saluted him, then left the room without saying a word. Dr. John was terribly disappointed by my behaviour and ordered me to come back. When I returned, he asked "I told you to be the head of Pinyudo's administration, you kept quiet and went out without saying a word, why did you do so?" My answer to him was simple, that I thought he was giving me military instructions and that orders were not negotiable. He explained, they are orders yes, but you still get a say over the issue, either you reject, or you accept. Dr. John continued, "To run a refugee centre is not like managing a battalion. You will manage a mixture of civilians and soldiers, mixed with foreigners from the UNHCR. It is not a cohesive group like soldiers. I thought you would say yes or no". Upon hearing this, I was compelled to talk and assure him I was in full agreement with his decision. I went as far as telling him that we wish him all the best for the operations on the war front. Dr. John had been preparing to launch a major offensive against the enemy garrison towns in Western Equatoria. He knew what he was doing, but asked for my opinion. Otherwise, he had given me many military assignments over time, without actually knowing my thoughts. It did make me wonder, what was different about this occasion that made him to seek my personal opinion? After we finished, Dr. John ordered his head quarter's personnel to pack and he returned to Gambella.

Alternate Commander Pieng Deng Kuol (the current Chairman of Pinyudo) along with myself, were left at the training centre when Dr. John Garang and his headquarters departed. The host, Commander Pieng, tried to source bicycles for the two of us to ride to Pinyudo. It was difficult for me to ride a bicycle after such a long time. It was late in the night when we arrived at Pinyudo. Due to the newly imposed curfew, this was a prohibited time when nobody was expected to be moving around. Pieng was very conscious about what would happen to me if I fell too far behind. He explained the potential danger if I fell into the hands of those manning the curfew and urged me to ride closer to him. We arrived at the Pinyudo guest house, where I was accommodated. Food was promptly served and Alternate Commander Pieng left for his house.

At the Pinyudo training centre, I met up with some of my class mates and colleagues from the Movement. Amongst them were 2nd Lt Panchol

Jongkuch Kur, William Bior Bullen Alier along with many others. They congratulated me on my new position, of Chairman of the Pinyudo refugee administration. They confessed, since they were my colleagues, there was nothing they would offer as a congratulatory gift for my new position. However, they confided in me that there was a person who won their trust, and said "take this man, Machar Madut Machar, he is a gift we can provide you as a brother". Indeed, Machar Madut that night brought my luggage to where I was staying. It did not take me long to realise that Machar Madut was the right man to do business with. He was very honest and respectful, very diligent, and hard working on top of everything. Machar Madut could get something out of nothing. Thank almighty God for creating such a person, who could not easily be cajoled into pseudo businesses.

In those days, Pieng and I were keeping extremely busy in preparing the take-over and hand-over processes, which were due to be implemented shortly. Alternate Commander Pieng had no time to waste in Pinyudo. He was to be sent to the war front on his new assignment, under the command of Alternate Commander Chagai da' Atem de Biar whose assignment in Bilpam had also come to an end. From an administrative perspective, there was nothing to hand over since the stores were under full control of the UNHCR. Commander Pieng advised that the most instrumental person 1st Lt Elijah Alier Ayom Anyang, was to remain in his position as part of the new administration, since he was well acquainted with everything in the camp. I had no objection to his recommendation, so long as it was for the benefit and welfare of the entire camp.

It is worth mentioning that the Pinyudo refugee camp was a base for the "unaccompanied-minors", who we paid extra-care to. They were later renamed as "lost boys" when they were transferred to the Kakuma refugee camp, in northern Kenya in 1992. One morning, a rally was called by Pieng to declare to the Red Army, a local name for unaccompanied-minors and the general public, to announce the new administrative changes. It was a new visible handing over in front of everyone. Mr. Pieng violated the arrangement's order, by refusing to talk first. He made me present my speech before him, which was unlawful and not logical. The usual procedure, is the former shows up first and then the latter will close the occasion. If I was stubborn and disagreed with Pieng's order of speech, things would have played out differently. But I knew this was the last official act of Mr. Pieng, in front of the Pinyudo public. Patience sometimes serves, I ignored it completely and that was the end of the whole story.

After the official handing over ceremony, I departed for the office to commence my duties. There were many visitors who were lined up with a long list of requirements. Some approvals given to the first group, became counterproductive. This was not well received by Mr. Elijah Alier Ayom, who advised it should be done another way. I was a bit reserved because I wanted to be heard and make the people of Pinyudo feel there was a change in administration. Alier, my deputy Gabriel Gai Riak and myself had a good relationship, and we worked as one group for the betterment of unaccompanied minors particularly, along with the refugees.

Pinyudo Refugee Camp was established towards the end of 1987 after the fall of Pibor into the hands of the SPLA gallant forces. Dr. John was well ahead in anticipating the future of the SPLM/A, more than any other Southern Sudanese leader. He considered the mobilising of children, who would become the backbone of the Movement. He instructed axis or sector commanders to implement mobilisation of children in their command areas. Some complied but some didn't. Commanders Dr. Riek Machar Teny, Daniel Awet Akot and Kuol Manyang Juuk among others, heeded succinctly to the call of the Chairman. They started to collect the children in accordance with the Chairman's instructions and began to send them to Ethiopia. The first batch of the children arrived at Pinyudo in late 1987, as mentioned earlier. The second group came in 1988.

Plans to transport more children to Pinyudo were interrupted by an unfortunate incident. A transport boat which was overloaded with children, was travelling along the Nile from Bentiu to Bor. It capsized and 60 out of 76 children on board, tragically lost their lives. Upon learning the news of this fateful incident, people ceased sending children over. Also, news of the death rates among those who had safely reached the destination, was obtained by the parents of those loved ones. From the time of inception, Pinyudo received no direct support from the UNHCR. Starting a refugee camp is always hard . The Red Cross thankfully tried their best to maintain the children. Basic necessities such as shelter and food were insufficient for the camp inhabitants. As expected, some children were too young to cope with such rough living conditions. Some became home sick and hence could not survive or afford to resist the challenges. As time went by, the situation in the camp became manageable and improvements were made. Families begun to settle into Pinyudo. Food supplies and medical services became more sufficient and covered the needs of the camp residents. The Pinyudo camp managers started to exert more effort in delivering a better service to the camp community.

Mr. Pieng Deng and Elijah Alier Ayom offered the kids gentle and loving hands. The major challenge the kids were confronted with, was the construction of their dormitories and classrooms. There was neither a planned construction budget nor the manpower to carry out the job. Children were amassed at Pinyudo when they were ill prepared to receive them. Teachers who responded to the call of Dr. John, instructed the kids to collect heavy logs for the construction of the shelters and classrooms. It was an amazing sight to see them carrying the big and heavy logs. One log would be carried by five kids or more. It reminds you of aunt's style of carrying their foray.

Comrade Pieng and his group should be praised 100% for the tough job in the establishment. Without their dedication, the Pinyudo Refugee

Camp wouldn't have been in the way I found it in November 1989. When I took over from comrade Pieng, the construction season was underway. The Red Army were preparing to construct their roughly grass thatched premises. Teachers and the refugee community were making themselves ready to support the unaccompanied minors. The boys would divide themselves into groups depending on the assignment. A group for cutting wood logs, another for fetching grass, another for getting ropes for thatching and so on. These assignments would take a good few days and were carried out in the camps outside Pinyudo, which were established as assembling areas. All materials collected would be transported on foot to Pinyudo, and that's when the camp community would start to support the Red Army. I as the Chairman of the camp, participated in gathering the grass for school number six. It indicated the beginning of the construction process. After gathering the materials at the school compound, a construction date was set and the community would begin construction in all schools according to the sectors. Women would do the cooking and the men would thatch the roofs with the minors.

From an administration perspective, some of the teachers led by Ustaz Garang Deng Jurkuch, were assigned and given enough money to buy 20 bulls from the Itang Refugee Camp's auctioneering market. These bulls found their way to Pinyudo long before construction began. Twenty bulls were equivalent to the number of schools. The bulls were slaughtered at the beginning of the construction process, to raise the morale of the unaccompanied minors. Construction was eventually completed and the schools opened. My son, who is currently a medical doctor by profession, started schooling that year in 1990. The Pinyudo Refugee Centre was educating around 17,000 pupils. This demonstrates the magnitude of work that we had been implementing. Before my commitment to support the Red Army, they composed songs against me and the head teacher Mr. Mecheak Ajang Alaak, for wrongly received information. During the time comrade Pieng and Alier Ayom were in charge and when the health conditions were not favouring school children, the UNHCR was duty bound to improve their feeding by supplying high nourishing flour, full of proteins. They started feeding on this flour, which was easy to prepare and was consumed quickly. For whatever reason, maybe the improved ed health condition of the unaccompanied minors and before I could even come to Pinyudo, the UNHCR abstained from supplying that food item. With my bad luck, the suspension was executed right upon my arrival. It made the unaccompanied minors believe it was me who stopped provision of flour, when I was completely innocent. The song was composed as follows, "Jurkuch Barach was behind the reason for their pounding and Ajang Alaak is the instigator. Means I was instigated by Ustaz Ajang to stop the supplies of nourishing flour. And both of us forced them for pounding cereals for their feeding".

Upon the establishment of the Pinyudo Refugee Camp there wasn't a single wheel mills machine, which was required to grind the grains for the whole community. So, everybody in the camp was forced into pounding, a traditional manual style of grinding maize or sorghum for feeding and survival. When I came in, the Red Army were still pounding in spite of the improvement to the living conditions of the camp inhabitants. After acquainting myself with the general situation of the camp (particularly understanding the unaccompanied minors), the management team created a programme to satisfy their needs. Food supplies in the camp were already in abundance. We thought of engaging them in the field of sports. Many playgrounds were cleared to enable them to play a variety of sports, e.g. football, basketball and volleyball in addition to field games and athletics. We ensured all types of balls were available to the schools and the camp. One of the main sport centres at Pinyudo, was graded and courts added for basketball and volleyball. One of our first priorities, was to establish an internal Pinyudo inter-school competition, to engage the boys. We then aimed to organise an inter-refugee sport's competition, amongst the three camps of Pinyudo, Itang and Dima in addition to the Bonga Military Training Centre and Bilpam SPLA general headquarter.

The inter-sports competition for the refugee centres, was not a new thing to me. A similar competition had been organised previously, when I was at the Bonga Training Centre. This was a successful competition, attended by Itang and Pinyudo plus the host Bonga, in September 1989. An event which was organised by Itang, was much bigger than the one conducted by Bonga. It was attended by the Pinyudo, Dima and Bonga Training Centre's along with the Bilpam SPLA headquarters plus Itang itself. This time it was Pinyudo's turn to organise an event. For the last two competitions, Pinyudo took the lead with the most number of medals. Pinyudo was lucky to be populated with young men and was expected to be dominant in every game. Preparations in all the camps intensified. Sport activities in the refugee centres, elevated the morale of the fighters on the war front. Our teams at each level, were rated higher than the Itang teams, who were our main challenge. The competition at Pinyudo was scheduled for October 1990, when the rainfall was generally less. When the time came, the sports delegates arrived at Pinyudo and the camp was full with players and spectators. Commander Majak da' Agoot of Bonga and the Itang refugee administration's Chairman Taban Deng Gai, were heading their delegations. Some other senior dignitaries such as Pagan Amum Okich, also came to share the occasion. At the conclusion of the competition, the Pinyudo Refugee Camp was declared the winner, followed by Itang and Bonga.

We came up with this sports strategy because we wanted to divert the Red Army's attention from thinking about the missing dear parents and relatives. Also, so they didn't believe they were snatched from their parents and relatives, to lead this miserable life for no good reason. At the Red Army level, schools were functioning well. An example of this was 1ˢᵗ Lt. Mayen Ngor Atem, who took the lead in trying to diversify the crop production at Pinyudo for the children. He taught them how to produce their food colourfully, without relying on UN supplies. Colourfully, means fresh crop production from their local farms. The UNHCR was falling short of supplying fresh vegetables to the camp's inhabitants. Up to this day, the Red Army still recognise and remember Ustaz Mayen Ngor for what he provided to them at Pinyudo.

Some critics of John Garang de Mabior, take Pinyudo as an example of trouble and not beneficial to the kids at Pinyudo, but it was a blessing in disguise. Jesh Ahmer, or the Red Army, or unaccompanied minors, or finally the Lost Boys, when they went to Kenya, are now different people who are responsibly managing their own affairs. Some of them have participated in the war of liberation and are now senior officers in the SPLA's army. Many furthered their education and have become PhD holders and lecturers in various universities. Some also went on to become successful in business. Others moved to America, Australia and Europe are rearing their families and taking good care of their parents. What else is a person born on earth to do? It is rather to take the lead in national affairs and to take care of your children and parents, no more. If John Garang did not courageously make that decision, most of those kids would be living primitive and backward lives, with no benefit to the nation and others.

I chatted briefly with Dr. John at the Pinyudo training centre and wished him all the best in his endeavour to capture and control Western Equatoria. Soon after he left Ethiopia for his new destination. Operation 'Jungle Storm' was already prepared and waiting for him to kick start the operation. All equipment was ready, for the stage of the war front. As soon as he arrived, the frontal forces were already in position, close to the frontal lines. The target in mind was the whole of Western Equatoria, made up of Maridi, Yambio and Tambura. The secret in military success, is always centred in the deceit. The enemy believed that Yei town was the target. The SPLA activity was sighted and sensed by the enemy in Yei. What was puzzling about the SPLA manoeuvres and movements, was how they ferried their heavy war machinery across many rivers in Southern Sudan. They were not using the known roads that connect the town centres. The enemy was certain that the SPLA were either in or around Yei town. Mortar shells had been tactfully and deceitfully dropped on Yei town, capable of holding the enemy down while the real SPLA fighting forces were already around Maridi and Yambio towns. All Southern Sudanese in Yei were rebels, just waiting for the slightest act to occur so they could flee the town. Those few shells thrown into Yei town, were enough to make 119 vehicles leave the town and instantly reported to the nearby SPLA forces.

Dr. John Garang knew what he was doing, he therefore went ahead with his initial plan and captured the towns of Maridi, Yambio and Tambura. They were confronted by the enemy forces with only little resistance. The defeated forces had no alternative but to track the road across the border to DRC Congo and the Central African Republic. One prominent Southern Sudanese member among those forces and who hailed from the area was Commander Samuel Abu John Kabashi. Dr. John Garang wrote to him requesting his return to Yambio when he learned of his departure with the enemy forces. Commander Samuel Abu John heeded to his call and returned to the town immediately after discovering Dr. John's presence among the SPLA forces that had overrun the town. Both men knew each other during the Southern Sudanese first struggle Anya-nya one (1955-1972) and that is why he returned with confidence believing his life would be spared while in the hands of John Garang. Samuel Abu John was a heavyweight and with services much sort-after by Dr. John and the Movement. He was later appointed in 1992 as an overall administrator for the whole of Azandi land.

Dr. John Garang de Mabior decided to return to Ethiopia after the triumphs and victories he scored against the enemy forces in Western Equatoria. He had captured small and major towns in Western Equatoria, leaving it clear of enemy forces. His triumphant return to Western Ethiopia was marred with a heavy reception from the refugee community in Pinyudo, albeit his arrival being late at night. A messenger came to Pinyudo informing us of his presence at the nearby Pinyudo military training centre. There was nothing we could do at this late hour of the night to see him. Dr. John's request of us, was to line up on the side of the road going into Gambella early the following morning, to wave him off. I wanted to see Dr. John and convince him to hold a rally in the camp before he could leave, but the messenger stiffly opposed this idea. We then quickly passed the information to the Pinyudo population, alerting them of Dr. John's presence in the nearby military training centre, and explaining he would not have time to meet. Therefore, if you wanted to wave him off before he leaves for Gambella, please stand by the side of the road. The following morning, there was a strong crowd who attended, full of jubilant people who came out and stood alongside the mentioned road, waving and singing revolutionary songs. The women's ululation was heard loudly by the Pinyudo population as his long convoy (composed of 119 newly obtained vehicles that came from Yei, plus those ones from his headquarters) were passing by. All wished he could stay longer in Pinyudo, but we looked forward to the time when we could meet again. It was not only the people of Pinyudo who came to welcome and thank the triumphant Dr. John Garang de Mabior, but amazingly the roadside parade was carried out by many others as he passed through their areas.

After Dr. John had passed through Pinyudo with the large convoy of vehicles, I thought the Pinyudo administration may be privileged with one, if not two of the vehicles, due to the uniqueness of the event. Especially considering Pinyudo was mainly populated with unaccompanied minors, who were thought to be the future back-bone of the

Movement. They would soon be able to participate in the current war of liberation, along with contributing to the management and development of the country on completing their education.

With these ideas in mind, I wanted to pay Dr. John a visit at the Zinc military headquarters, east of Gambella, to discuss things further. I packed my belongings and left for Gambella, hoping to be honoured with the chance to meet with him. After being granted permission, I began by congratulating him for the triumph of the SPLA in Western Equatoria. I then outlined the reason for my visit. "I am requesting for your esteemed authority, to be provided with a vehicle for the Pinyudo Refugee Camp. The camp is mainly inhabited by more than 17,000 unaccompanied minors. If a situation arises, where a minor becomes sick or injured and needs to be evacuated to a nearby hospital for medical treatment, we would be confronted with the issue of no means of transport. We would very much be at risk of losing the dear life of the injured boy or girl. Since you have some extra vehicles under your higher authority, we would be extremely thankful if you could donate one vehicle to the Pinyudo Refugee Camp. This would enable us carry out our duties without failure." Dr. John appreciated the request I put forward to him and understood the need for a vehicle. He promised to release one for our camp at Pinyudo, and indeed, a vehicle and a driver were released to the relief of us all. The vehicle first had to be sent to Addis Ababa for a full maintenance check, before it could be returned to Pinyudo in full working condition. With a vehicle on hand, we were able to do our business and move around much easier.

There were two different scenarios currently affecting Sudan and Ethiopia both countries were facing internal problems. Whilst the SPLA was rapidly gaining ground on the war front in Sudan, the Ethiopian government was facing the opposite problem. In 1990, the Ethiopian government lost Kurmuk and Geizan towns on the same day to the

Ethiopian People Revolutionary Defence Forces (EPRDF). Of course, any loss to the Ethiopian government bears the same impact on the SPLM/A, in other words, it means an equal loss to the SPLA/M. Surely, the SPLA/M could not survive in Ethiopia without Mangistu's regime, however this was proved wrong in the years to come. As we were celebrating our victories in Western Ethiopia, we were mindful of the future of Mangistu's regime in Addis Ababa.

In 1990 after the victorious return of Dr. John to Western Ethiopia, he organised another large force to launch another offensive against the enemy garrison towns in the Northern Upper Nile, mainly in the areas of Malut, Jalhak, Maban and Renk town at the border of Northern Sudan. Commander Dr. Riek Machar Teny was to come from Bentiu with his forces to Malut. While Commander Martin Manyiel Ayuel and Commander Dr. Lam Akol Ajawin, were to move with the forces from the border town of Pagak to Maban. The plan was, one of those two commanders would proceed after capturing Maban to seize Sudan Kurumuk in South-Eastern Sudan. Meanwhile Dr. John's headquarters coming from Western Equatoria, under Commander Oyay Deng Ajak, were to move onto Malakal. Dr. Riek Machar managed to control the strategic towns of Malut and Jalhak, which gave a serious warning to the inhabitants of Renk town.

The scenario of affairs was completely different in Maban. Our forces pushed the enemy to one corner, but the covering force did not hold ground against the enemy rescuing force, who were advancing from Gofa. The Maban operation failed and did not live up to expectations. On the other side, Commander Oyay Deng only threw a few mortar shells at Malakal from a distance, which left no considerable impact. Some booties captured from the enemy at Malut and Jalhak were brought to the rear. I remember one lorry that was in good working condition was moving between Itang and Gambella, and in rare cases to the Pinyudo Refugee

Camp. We came to the end of the Northern Upper Nile's operation at the end of 1990, because the rainy season was about to commence. No real military operations can be conducted during the rainy season, across the whole of Southern Sudan. If there was a critical need to do so, it might occur in some parts of the greater Equatorial region but only if the terrain permits.

Management of Food Distribution at the Pinyudo Refugee Camp

Food distribution of UNCHR supplied rations to the camp inhabitants, was carried out twice a month. There were no problems encountered with this process, but there were challenges around the distribution of eatable oil, due to its cash value at nearby markets. It was used as a source of currency, so one can purchase items the UNHCR could not afford to provide e.g. protein foods and clothing. Another item many were interested in acquiring were quails and used clothes. The refugees wanted these items for personal use and for their market value, to generate cash. The UNHCR was also very keen to provide health services to the refugees. There was a hospital well-stocked with different medicines, which sufficiently covered their patient requirements. The only shortage was qualified medical personnel, as there was only two South Sudanese doctors attending to more than 80,000 people living in the camp. Hence some serious cases were referred to Gambella for more comprehensive medical treatment. The SPLM/A contributed herds of up to 400 cattle to the unaccompanied minors, as a source of milk for the children who were sick and required a better diet.

In 1989-1991, Pinyudo's refugee administration (besides the UNHCR), was run effectively by the following four people;

1. Mr. Jurkuch Barach Jurkuch----------------------------------Chairman
2. Mr. Gabriel Gai Riak Makol----------------------Deputy Chairman
3. Mr. Elijah Alier Ayom--------------------Stores and Food Controller
4. Mr. Rin Tueny Mabor------------------------------------Camp Security

Along with the managers above, the school management was led by Mecheak Ajang Alaak, Director of education. The teachers at the Pinyudo schools, were being paid a monthly salary by Friends in the West (NGO). Teaching had now become of value and interest, unlike the days when it was a voluntary job when the camp was first established. This was a situation where everybody was in terrible need, including the SPLM/A leaders whose families were also refugees. So a commander did not obsess about his family conditions while executing his duties, it was decided the camp administration should shoulder full responsibility over the families of the members of Politico-Military High Command, in the respective camp where they were residing. The family of the permanent member of Politico-Military High Command, had to be paid 500 Birr (Ethiopian currency) per month, which was the equivalent to $200 USD. Meanwhile, the family of alternate member of Politico-Military High Command was given 300 Birr per a month, in addition to their regular food rations received from the distribution centres. In our case as managers of Pinyudo, we thought of providing our families with 150 Birr a month. We were not informed of what amounts the other camp managers, my friends Taban Deng Gai of Itang and Dr. Atem Nathan Riak of Dima, had requested for their families. The question that is surely lingering in the minds of readers, is how did they acquire that amount of money (birr)? The answer would be, from the UNHCR food stuffs itself. We would allocate a few cartons of oil at the time of distribution and send them to the Gambella Markets for a private sale. The Refugee camp managers were viewed by their colleagues to be the equivalent to the oil rich Kings of the Arab Peninsula (Arabs of the Gulf). At Pinyudo we had the Women's Union, who would oversee all aspects of the women's affairs. These women would be assigned to take care of our guests, when visiting Pinyudo.

On one occasion, a Senior Commander came to visit and we felt privileged to have him in our camp. We accorded him the high respect he deserved, by slaughtering a bull for him from the Movement's dairy. We exchanged the bull with a heifer, to comply with the dairy rules. This exchange was misreported to Dr. John by one of our members. They had claimed the Pinyudo administration were violating the dairy rules and regulations, by slaughtering bulls for the reception of dignitaries. I received a message via radio communication from the Chairman Dr. John Garang, rebuking me for that act and advising to abstain from that behaviour. He stated the dairy was for the Red Army and no one was permitted to trade as they pleased. As punishment, the Pinyudo administration were sentenced to buy 20 head of cattle to increase the numbers in the dairy. I tried to explain to Dr. John that we followed the regular procedure of exchanging bulls with heifers, which is a system practiced by cattle owners in every cattle camp. This was to no avail, as the reprimand had occurred and the punishment of buying 20 heads of cattle had already been implemented.

When I took over from comrade Pieng Deng, he advised there was a group of recruits called Titbaay who were being trained at Pinyudo. These recruits were chiefs from different parts of the south, who came to Ethiopia to be trained and at the completion of training, will return to their home areas to protect themselves from the notorious enemies of the Arab herders. The majority of them were from the Bahr el Gazal Region. Three months passed and their graduation date was set, but it had to be conducted in conjunction with the Manyangdit group who were trained at Itang. A few days passed and Dr. John came to Pinyudo for the graduation of the two agroups, Manyangdit and Titbaay. Comrade Taban Deng Gai attended the ceremony with Dr. John, to support the people of his area who completed the training. The Chairman addressed attendees after I made a brief introduction. The ceremony was very colourful, with people dancing who had achieved their long-awaited objective. They were later given their armament, khaki and boots. A truck arrived to transport them to Pochalla and from there they proceeded on foot to their different home areas. That special occasion was recorded on video camera, by comrade Mou Manasseh Malak. I did not get wind of this video until after 10 years, when I visited Egypt as the SPLM representative to Egypt and the Middle East.

Another case to cite as success of the Pinyudo management was the buying of school uniforms for the unaccompanied minors. With meagre resources available, we were able to purchase roles of material to be made into school uniforms. This was accomplished in Addis Ababa, by the SPLM representative after obtaining enough cash to purchase the materials and execute the job. After it was dispatched to Pinyudo, some tailors were identified and sent to purposely implement that project. As they commenced their assignment, the security situation began to deteriorate in Ethiopia. Rebels of EPRDF were steadily capturing one town after another in the northwestern parts of Ethiopia. President Mangistu Hailemariam had no alternative but to flee the country on May 4, 1991. Following this, things did not change for the better and instead rebels were rapidly advancing towards the capital city of Addis Ababa. SPLM/A members of Politico Military High Command, Commanders Salva Kiir Mayardit, Dr. Riek Machar and Dr. Lam Akol were in Gambella, closely monitoring the situation. They had instructed us in Pinyudo to generate a force to be dispatched to Gore town which was very close to Metu city. Meanwhile comrade Taban Deng Gai of the Itang refugee administration, was also instructed to send forces to Damadollo town, north of

Gambella under the command of Commander Majak da' Agoot da' Atem, hoping they would do their best to protect the SPLM/A interests in the western region of Illababur. The two forces from Itang and Pinyudo, were deployed to their designated locations in April 1991, shortly before Mangistu could flee the country.

Mid May, Ethiopian forces in the western regions of Ethiopia fled to Gambella. Our forces under General Majak were dispersed by the advancing EPRDF forces and Majak reported himself to Gambella with only six men. It was an unimaginable disaster that most of Commander Majak's forces did not report to any of the SPLA's nearby camps. Dr. Mabior Juach da' Aweer and Clement Nyilma Katinya among many others, did not survive the unforgiving war front. The Pinyudo forces in Gore town, were in a different situation to those forces under Commander Majak. They were advised by the host community to leave the area before it was too late. They therefore all reported to Pinyudo before we decided to evacuate the camp in June 1991. Gambella fell into the hands of the rebels on May 26, which also meant the fall of the Itang Refugee Camp. The head of the camp administration Mr. Taban Deng Gai ordered an announcement to be made on the loud speaker, to inform the population to leave the centre immediately and meet in Jokou, inside the Sudanese border.

As expected, it was a disorganised evacuation. Some who were not ready to follow that particular route, crossed the Baro River and joined us at the Pinyudo Refugee Camp. The SPLA forces at the Bonga Training Centre, left Bonga and came to Abobo where surveillance guards had been deployed under the command of Captain Rin Tweny Mabor, to inspect the route and determine whether EPRDF forces were likely to attack us at Pinyudo. His other purpose while in Abobo town was to monitor the bridge for advancing EPRDF forces who could potentially dislodge us in the camp. If this scenario played out, Captain Rin would give the orders to demolish the bridge. Disappointingly, the forces went ahead and destroyed the bridge anyway to the surprise of Commander Salva Kiir Mayardit and the rest in the camp, when the news of the Abobo's town bridge being destroyed was received.

What prompted Captain Rin to make the decision to destroy the bridge, was some agricultural work that was happening in the area. The Ethiopian government had a big agricultural scheme along the Abobo/Gambella road. Cultivation in the farm was ongoing as the rain started to fall. Tractors working on the farm, were making sounds while ploughing the land or shining spotlights late in the evening, which could not be differentiated by the men assigned to the bridge at Abobo. The force was alarmed one day by the sound of tractors operating and the commander had to order his men to blow the bridge in anticipation of the EPRDF enemy was advancing. The bridge destruction which was carried out by our own forces in the area we were being hosted, became a shameful and regrettable mistake to the Movement's leadership, the Pinyudo refugees and the population inhabiting the region of Illababur. Abobo bridge was the only line of transport for goods and people to Pinyudo. When it was smashed to the ground, the impact was immediately felt by many. This shameful act occurred when there was no government or effective political leadership in Ethiopia, to inspect the area. The UNHCR administration was then expected to transport relief supplies to the refugees at the Pinyudo camp. It occurred during the interim period when the EPRDF were assuming power from the old administration of a socialist system, under President Mangistu Hailemariam. Commander Salva who was the only senior member of Politico Military High Command present, escaped direct blame from the host country Ethiopia and the UNHCR, when we evacuated the refugees to Pochalla (Sudan). But surely, the scales of indirect blame were channelled against the Movement.

It was mentioned previously that all Itang refugees had to report to

Jokou, to regroup and decide what best action to take. Some refugees from the refugee camp who did not wish to follow that route, opted to cross the Baro river and emerged at the Pinyudo camp. Among them were Commander Lual Diing Wal, an Alternate Member of Politico-Military High Command, Captain Atem Garang Deng de Kuek, Justice Captain Michael Makuei Lueth Makuei and Maker Lual Kuol among many others. With Commander Lual Diing at Pinyudo, we now had two senior members of Politico-Military High Command. What would happen next as all Southern Sudanese refugees were now in Pinyudo? The appropriate strategy to take, was to withdraw to South Sudan and the nearest town to the border was Pochalla.

South Sudanese Refugee Withdrawal from Ethiopia / June 1991

Our people had now all converged at the Pinyudo Refugee Camp. There was a complete regime change in Ethiopia. Those who assumed power in Addis Ababa on May 28, 1991, were the ones we had been fighting just a few days prior. If we stay as refugees as we are now, we were not certain whether the new regime may decide to victimize the innocent South Sudanese refugees (women and children) living in the camp. If we leave for Sudan during the terrible conditions of the rainy season, how would we find shelter and food in a new area? What is the UNHCR's opinion or position on the Pinyudo Refugee Camp? Do they want the refugees to leave for anywhere of their choice or do they need them to remain in Ethiopia? Surely the UNHCR on the contrary wanted refugees to remain in Ethiopia, but then what was the guarantee of our survival and safety for that matter? There was no one in contact with the members of the new regime, to communicate to us their opinions, even from the UNHCR. Even if they were in contact with them, would we really be in a position to believe what they told us? These queries and others were points of discussion for our meeting, to decide whether we leave for Sudan or not. The majority of the decision making group were clear in their minds, that we should leave for South Sudan and let all hell break loose. It is Sudan where we belong and we should return to, like the way it was handled by both refugees of Itang and Dima. Let us now organise the evacuation and march out of Pinyudo.

Pinyudo was organised or settled into sectors. The first sectors to begin the move were sector one and sector two, followed by sector three and four. The order of movement should be completed within four days. These groups would follow the route to the Gilo crossing and from there move onto Pochalla. The second group was the unaccompanied minors and the cattle camp, estimated to be 400 heads of cattle. They would have to cross the Gilo River at Ushamlom, 3km south of Pinyudo town. The reason we preferred them to take this route, was due to the proximity of Pinyudo to Pochalla, which was a maximum of two days on foot (60km). The soldiers or people with arms, were asked to remain behind until all the refugees had left the camp. We had learned some lessons from what occurred at Itang. We did not want to replicate that scenario at the Pinyudo Refugee Camp, which was an unorganised and disorderly evacuation. The refugees, as stated above, began to move sector by sector on June 26, 1991 and the move was completed by June 30.

What happened to those who possessed SPLA vehicles at the Pinyudo camp? It was decided that all refugees were of equal status and they should march together on foot. I let my family follow the order of the march and we walked on foot to the Gilo crossing post, about 40kms from Pinyudo. This was to show leadership to the rest of the refugees. The distance from the Gilo crossing point to Pochalla is estimated to be 70kms. However, I wasn't sure whether those orders were respected and implemented to the letter, by those who were lucky to have SPLA vehicles in Pinyudo. My runner Machar Madut Machar (a gentleman I very much respect), managed to locate a donkey to help carry our family belongings. As the head of Pinyudo's administration, I had to ensure all refugees had left Pinyudo for the Gilo crossing point and were heading to Pochalla town. Commander Salva Kiir being the most senior, had to remain behind with the forces in Pinyudo. It was an easy decision to evacuate, but it was very difficult to maintain the people at Pochalla town. Some frustrated refugees were coming back to either the Gilo crossing point or Pinyudo itself in search of food, as there was nothing in Pochalla. At the Gilo crossing, we advised families that opted to stay on the eastern right hand side of the river, to cross to the western left hand side, for safety purposes. I advised there was a possibility that the enemy forces may be coming in hot pursuit. If there is anything difficult to manage on earth, it must be people when they are hungry. It was a stiff challenge to convince the families and the unaccompanied minors to return to Pochalla, after the starvation they had experienced there.

After ensuring all refugees had left, I took a vehicle on July 3, 1991 and came to the Gilo crossing point. My family had already arrived at Pochalla, and had been transported by a lorry truck. My friend, comrade Gier Chuang da' Aluong and I, took a lorry from the Gilo crossing the next day. It was loaded to the brim. We knew the lorry wouldn't make it to Pochalla due to heavy rain. On the way, the lorry (like many others) got stuck and we had to abandon it and walk until dark. It was a miserable night, but we started again the following morning until we arrived at Pochalla in that evening. It was a huge disappointment for those who had attempted to transport their belongings by road from Pinyudo to Gilo. Many vehicles were stuck along the way and nobody dared to return, still until this date.

The enemy (EPRDF), then started to put pressure on our forces from behind. Commander Majak, the man assigned to confront them, was being pressured from behind. He advised the refugees at the Gilo crossing via radio communication, to cross to the western side of the river. They did not however heed this advice. They didn't have the means to ferry enough people across the river, as they only had two canoes. Disasters however don't surface in singles, they come en mass. To make matters worse, one canoe capsized while crossing with seven people on board and sank never to be recovered. The remaining canoe was not enough to ferry the huge number of people. The worst part was, that many of the SPLA fighters were not endowed with the art of swimming, while the unforgiving enemy was so close.

Commander of the forces, Commander Majak, suddenly appeared on the riverbank uncovering the disaster. It was known that once you sight Commander Majak, it means the worst as the enemy was already there with him. He allowed Commander Salva Kiir Mayardit, to cross to the other side of the river. At that busy time when all were preparing to cross, the enemy bombarded the area with mortar shells. My Goodness, the panic that followed when people started to jump into the river. Most of those who jumped into the river ended up in a disastrous situation, but those who could swim did manage to cross, but without their rifles or accessories. Many comrades from the Nuba Mountains could not survive the mayhem. They unfortunately perished in the waters of the Gilo River. One of the female officers I could remember who did not survive the mayhem, was 2nd Lt Female Officer Anip Marial Dot and sadly many others.

However, there was a surprising thing that occurred during the crossing event. Two young soldiers from the Nuba Mountains fortunately did survive, by God almighty's miracle. One was shot and injured in the jaw while the other was safe. The two hid in a secret place, where the enemy could not find them nor the local people of the area. The duo managed to spend three months in the area. The healthy soldier would search for raw food in the farms of the nearby local community. They would chew the maize while it was raw and waited for the rivers water to subside, until the wound of the other soldier healed completely. Their colleagues believed the two soldiers had died long ago, when they surfaced in October 1991 after we sent a force to control Gilo River. They hid from our force until they could confirm that the force across the river, was in fact their own colleagues. Commander of the force, Captain Gabriel Mathiang Aluong Padunyiel, provided them with an escort to take them to Pochalla, to the elation of the entire town. They could have been killed by the local people, had it not been for God's miracle. The force under Captain Mathiang Aluong which was sent to the Gilo River crossing, did not stay long in that area. They were fought and chased by the Ethiopian forces, and they eventually reported back to Pochalla.

Commander Salva with his forces arrived in Pochalla after walking for a day and a half, from Gilo. Jungle life is no joke. They were completely exhausted and emaciated when we met them on arrival, almost dying of hunger. We were bound by duty to take on this responsibility in Pochalla town, and rescue the situation. We slaughtered a bull and sufficient food was prepared and served, even though it was late at night.

Commander Salva as a senior member in the leadership of the Movement, was being monitored very closely by the Chairman of the Movement Dr. John Garang and upon his arrival, a hired plane was sent to fly him to the Kenyan border town of Loggichogio. Pochalla was over crowded with almost 50,000 refugees who had just arrived from Ethiopia. The refugees had their movements restricted by the Pochalla local administration, so they weren't hit by the many anti-personnel land-mines which were planted long ago by the warring forces of the SPLA and Sudanese government. Unaccompanied minors were settled at Gorkur, a suburb south of Pochalla town. That area had been earmarked for units of police, prisons and wildlife services. Our cattle camp was allocated across the Akobo River inside the Ethiopian border. The main challenge haunting everyone was the issue of food supplies.

The only NGO operating in Pochalla was the International Committee of the Red Cross (ICRC), which does not usually supply relief items. They had a large hospital in Loggichogio town in northern Kenya. With the new arrival of refugees to the area, they took up the challenge of settling them in. They had light aircraft as means of transportation for their staff. The aircraft could transport only 15 bags of 50kg maize per trip, into Pochalla town for the use of the unaccompanied minors. It was not enough to cover the huge numbers of school children (the unaccompanied minors).

The air strip in the town was not long enough to receive larger aeroplanes, so we started extension works. There were a few challenges before we could execute the plan. The area towards the end of the air strip was on low and wet land, that needed to be excavated to remove wet soil and replace it with dry soil. This meant heavy machines were required to implement the work. The other challenge was the presence of land mines that had been planted 7 years ago, by both the government of the Sudan and the SPLA forces. Many of the land mines had already been removed in the settlement areas without issue, so this wasn't too much of a hindrance.

It seemed the refugees coming from Pinyudo were finally about to encounter some good luck. When they arrived in Pochalla, they discovered the only active anti-personnel land mine was detonated by a cow a day before their arrival. I felt the level of contamination around Pochalla was high, but all if not most of the land mines were spoiled. The reason for this, was when anyone started building a residence within the town, they would encounter between 1-3 land mines in that small locality. We concluded that because Pochalla receives a good portion of annual rain, the grounds would stay wet enough to rust any metal that was planted. Secondly, Pochalla lies in a low land that receives a lot of water from the high land of Ethiopia and retains it for a long time. With these conditions, plus the lengthy time spent underground we were confident the threat was minimal. The fear and threat of land mines around Pochalla began to wither away as days passed without any incidences. People had confidently started to settle in different corners of the town.

However, when those returning from Sudan began to settle in Pochalla, they encountered three serious issues below;

1. Anti-personnel land mines, planted around the town
2. Hunger & starvation
3. The Sudanese air-force bombardment

The issue I would first like to address, is the Sudanese air force-bombardment. The two other issues will be narrated in the below paragraphs. The refugee population who were living in Ethiopia, did not experience the bombs being dropped by the fighter planes. It was in the afternoon when the Antonov bomber surfaced and unleashed the bombing of the town, killing and injuring scores of people. Those returnees from Sudanese community, had become timid and fearful. None had ever experienced such a horrible bombardment nor heard an Antonov airplanes before, said one returnee. What has been Happenings on the war front have developed to this next level, said one experienced soldier. The bombing continued for a while. We lacked the means of air defence to deter the Antonov bomber. After ICRC assumed responsibility to provide food supplies to the returnees in Pochalla town, Antonov raids ceased for reasons unknown. Some believed the Sudanese government was advised not to bombard the camp due to the presence of ICRC staff in town. It is also prohibited internationally to kill unarmed people, as the inhabitants of Pochalla were civilians who had just returned from neighbouring Ethiopia. It was therefore concluded that the Antonov attacks were brought to an end, after the interference of the ICRC Organisation.

The SPLA forces that came with us from Ethiopia were large in number. There weren't enough food supplies available in Pochalla, to feed such a huge force. This was a large concern for many people, including Commander Salva Kiir, who suggested they should be ordered to leave Pochalla as soon as possible. We breathed a deep sigh of relief the day they were seen departing Pochalla.

The hunger situation and lack of food, was still looming to the inhabitants of Pochalla. There were plans that the ICRC would begin to drop food supplies. In order for this to occur, an air dropping zone was the first thing to be cleared by the returnee population. We were advised this programme would commence on August 1, 1991, the following day. Due to the intense levels of hunger and desperate need for food, it felt like the food drop was still so far out of reach. Indeed, at about 11:00am on the promised date, two huge airplanes appeared in the sky hovering over Pochalla town. We sent men who would collect bags of food from the dropping zone. The first drop consisted of around 600 bags (30 metric tons) of maize. Another drop followed in the afternoon and the hungry faces which overwhelmed the town's inhabitants, started to disappear. Distribution centres were sufficiently supplied with food items ready to be distributed. Within a week, all the food stores were filled to the brim. It must be mentioned that other important food items e.g. eatable oil, sugar, salt and so on were transported into Pochalla via light planes. In addition to food supplies, other camp necessities were also provided, such as tents, plastic sheets, blankets, mosquito nets, quails and used clothes. All known kitchen equipment was made available to every family. Other materials to aid people in being self-sufficient like fishing nets, were also provided, knowing the local rivers were well stocked with a range of fish.

In no time at all, we observed the wide smiles appear on the faces of the people in Pochalla. What a difference it had made.

The ICRC Organisation was required to provide food supplies to the returnees in Pochalla for six months, until they became self-reliant. I must mention, the ICRC planes flying to Pochalla on a daily basis were also transporting to Loggichogio in northern Kenya, the returnees who did not wish to stay in Pochalla. The process of air lifting to Loki was causing unnecessary rifts between the relatives of those travellers. We received many calls daily via radio from all over Southern Sudan, requesting relatives to be airlifted to Loki. From there they would seek their way back to Southern Sudan. It became a point of hostility should we fail to transport these relatives, for reasons out of our control. We did not have any authority over the pilots and could not dictate terms, but instead it depended on the pilots goodwill and whether they would accommodate any proposals.

The community that inhabits Pochalla (Anyuaks), are hardworking people, all of them being farmers. At certain stages in their life they reared cattle along with subsistence farming. They decided to abandon cattle rearing when it became a source of trouble. The neighbouring Murle community would conduct raids, taking the cattle and killing the owners. Therefore, they had to abandon cattle rearing and concentrate mainly on subsistence farming. Anyuak people would start their cultivation at the beginning of the rainy season around April and May, and begin to harvest crops in July or August every year. When the rains began, fish would come in abundance from the rivers. So, they were fishing and cultivating at the same time. When the harvest concluded, the products are sowed and stored in their local stores. The second cultivation season would then commence, with harvest planned for November. Throughout this time, the Anyuak people would be fishing along the rivers and tributaries for diet diversification. When it came to the dry season the white-eared cob games would flock to the area to spend the dry season around Pochalla. This would provide another valuable source of protein for the population. In fact, I was told by a person who knows the Anyuak community very well that, the lactating mothers(unlike the cattle owning societies) they aimed to win their babies at the time when the white-eared cobs were in the area. This information, in order to be confirmed as correct, needs verification from the natives of the Anyuak community. Throughout the year, there is no specific time when the Anyuak people would experience hunger or starvation. Their land is heavily endowed with many natural resources, not available in other communities . The land is so fertile that everything planted would germinate and produce. When the returnees landed in Pochalla in late June / early July of 1991, the first harvest was about to commence. They interacted with the local community and began to exchange their belongings for grains, that would maintain their families requirements when the ICRC food supplies had not yet arrived. Plausibly, that was why there were no deaths reported that were due to starvation, until ICRC's food supplies rescued the situation.

Everything became stabilised in the camp. Food distribution at the earmarked centres was running as planned. Schools at Gorkur were functioning well. Continuous visits from the international donor community, to ascertain conditions of the unaccompanied minors, did not stop. We did receive a visit from a senior American congress delegation. Also, a French delegation led by the then Minister of Humanitarian Affairs and International Relations, Mr. Bernard Kushner came to visit the unaccompanied minors. We were also privileged to receive a visit from a prominent South Sudanese American NBA basketball player, Mr. Manut Bol Nyuol. This was a real thrill for everyone and he was particularly interested in understanding and familiarising himself with the unaccompanied minor and their conditions. He assured them that changes for the better would be happening soon.

The new dropping zone for the unaccompanied minors at Gorkur, was cleared and began operating. The idea of establishing a dropping zone, was so the unaccompanied minors no longer had to transport their rations on foot from Pochalla to Gorkur, which was a 3-5km walk. The dropping of food items wasn't without risk, with a few lives being lost, but this was only when mismanagement occurred. On one occasion, the management of the camp and the ICRC field managers, flocked to the dropping zone on a cloudy day in September 1991, to witness the dropping process. The pilot unexpectedly misjudged the dropping zone and the load was unleashed directly where we were standing. We ran away from the area at a speed which would have matched, or been equivalent to one of the world's best 100m runners. I was so scared that I thought my days were over. When I looked back after running a short distance, I heard the loud thud of a heavy load hitting the ground, after which I felt safe. We escaped unhurt, but I vividly remembered that incident for some time. A similar incident occurred a month later, and this unfortunately took away lives of three dear returnees. The pilot of the plane had again misjudged the dropping zone, but this time he fell short and the loads hit the roof of a grass thatched hut, killing two people inside and a disabled person within the vicinity. According to an eyewitness, the disabled person could have escaped without injury, but was unable to due to his disability. We as the management of the camp, placed a compensation case with the ICRC Organisation for the three lives lost. Until Pochalla was vacated in March 1992 due to the enemy offences, we failed to obtain a positive result.

As life was booming in town, alarm bells were ringing in relation to the Ethiopian Anyuak youths, for reasons no one could explain. They mobilised themselves in large numbers, heading towards Pochalla and ready to launch an attack on the town. The Sudanese Anyuak brothers advised them not to execute their plan, but they did not adhere to their advice. They were adamant to the extent, of mentioning the D-day for the execution of their plan. However, we the inhabitants of the town had no alternative except to prepare our defence of our children and territory, so long we were on Sudanese soil. We dug trenches and fox holes. A force was dispatched to Gorkur to defend the unaccompanied minors, while others remained in town. On the morning of the D-day, October 5, 1991, they arrived marching to attack Gorkur where they were confronted by the tough force of the SPLA. Many of them were killed and others ran away in disarray, back to the bush. After the fight at Gorkur, the assigned group to attack the main area of Pochalla, were still on their way. They started shooting at our forces, when daylight was about to break. They suffered the same fate as the first group, who couldn't resist the SPLA firepower, and they were scattered in the bush. The remnants were horribly managed, and we could trace their route back to Gambella, from where their journey had commenced. The challenge of the Anyuak youths from Ethiopia, was militarily resolved on the battlefield and life in town returned to normal.

While in Pochalla, one of the major events of the year occurred in Nasir on August 28, 1991. It was announced over the BBC radio by Commanders Dr. Riek Machar Teny, Dr. Lam Akol Ajawin and Gordon Kong Chol, that the Chairman of the SPLM and Commander in Chief of the SPLA, Dr. John Garang de Mabior, had been overthrown. The declaration made by the three commanders brought sharp division along tribal lines, among the southern population wherever they were. Dr. Riek Machar hailed from the Nuer tribe while Dr. John Garang descended from the Dinka ethnic group. We tried our best to inform the camp residents that it didn't concern us in Pochalla, so long as it was a political move which would be addressed and resolved by the Movement's leadership. The returnees listened to our advice and Pochalla remained calm and stable until the enemy launched a surprised attack in March 1992. The coup of Dr. Riek Machar will be discussed later in my story.

As mentioned earlier, the ICRC organisation would supply those who returned to the camp with relief items for six months only, ending in February 1992. Since most of the returnees hailed from Bor in the Jonglei Province, four members from the administration were selected and sent to Bor to acquaint themselves with the situation and the living conditions. The four people were transported by air from Pochalla to Loki. A convoy that composed of four trucks, left Loki for Kapoeta with the aim of arriving that same day. This however was a daydream. We found out there was a heavy downpour on the way. We spent the night at the border town of Narus, which was 36km from Loki. We commenced our journey early the following morning, and arrived at Kapoeta that evening. It was unusual for rains to be that heavy in the south and in October particularly. Our mission in Torit town was to discuss the condition of the returnees in Pochalla with the Jonglei Military Commander in Charge, Commander Kuol Manyang Juuk and the administration of the Sudan Relief and Rehabilitation Association (SRRA) in Kapoeta.

We advised that the ICRC were due to cease their support of the returnees in Pochalla, in the coming months. What would we do with those returnees? Would we take them to Bor? At this point in time, they could not provide any satisfactory answers to our questions, because the Bor area of Jonglei had recently been completely devastated by the White Army, under the Command of Dr. Riek Machar. They advised us to return to Pochalla, until they could decide on the best course of action. Since we did not reach Torit town, we failed to exchange views with Commander Kuol Manyang. We had to return to Loki and from there, take a flight back to Pochalla. We had to explain the situation we had encountered in Kapoeta to the returnees. The Nuer White Army of Dr. Riek Machar had invaded and devastated the whole Bor district. Many had been killed and they left with livestock, children and women to the Nuer area. On top of everything, the whole Bor population had deserted Jonglei for Equatoria.

A trip was organised again for the former team to visit Bor to witness it for themselves, after the Nuer massacre. We arrived in Bor town on January 4, 1992. We toured south Bor on the next day then returned to Bor town. We could not visit north Bor because of the floods that controlled the area. The looming floods had denied me seeing my dear mother, who I last saw in 1979. She later perished with her grandson Jurkuch Deu Barach, during those difficult circumstances. We met with the local authority and discussed the reasons for our visit. We explained we wanted to ascertain for ourselves, the living conditions of our people back home and seek advice on whether the Bor returnees living in Pochalla could safely return home. The local authority answered by saying, if anyone decides to return to the devastation you have just witnessed, it would be their own personal decision and we would not accept responsibility. We then packed and left Bor on January 6, heading for Torit, Kapoeta and finally Loggichogio. We could see the Bor people were still tracking the way to Eastern Equatoria, hoping to settle in the SPLA controlled or liberated areas. We returned to Pochalla with certainty that no one would be going back to Bor, which the displaced people had to consider. We reported on what we had seen for ourselves. The prosperous life our people used to lead in Bor, had been destroyed and replaced with devastating hunger.

Life in Pochalla was conducive to the extent that a person could select certain foods to eat during the day. White-eared cob flocked to the Pochalla area, in what is known by wildlife experts as seasonal migration. The backward South Sudanese community was and still is killing them for meat, when they should be preserved for tourism, hoping to generate income for the country. We knew Pochalla was a liberated town, so interested people would stay around depending on their ability to produce their own food without depending on the ICRC or UN food supplies. The ICRC organisation was preparing to supply non-food items to be used by those ready to settle around Pochalla. The site for settlement was already selected and surveyed.

A month came and went after we had returned from Bor. A certain incident occurred on the afternoon of March 3, 1992. An unidentified airplane appeared and hovered over the town for some time, then left in the direction of Ethiopia. Everyone in the town was puzzled as to the identity of the aircraft? And what was its intention? Was it a surveillance aircraft sent from Khartoum to survey the area for military purposes? Was the Khartoum Government ready to launch an attack on Pochalla town? And if so, what is the likelihood that they would be able to do so ? Was this in consideration to the possible routes of approach to Pochalla?

Geographically, Pochalla is located at the border of Ethiopia. If it was to be attacked and captured by the Khartoum enemy, then an approach route to Pochalla would either be from Bor, Pibor and then Pochalla. But Bor and Pibor were under firm control of the SPLA/M. The other approach route to Pochalla is from Akobo, but that force would have to pass through Pibor and then proceed to Pochalla, knowing there's no direct road from Akobo to Pochalla. However, Akobo and Pibor were under full control of the SPLA. The third available approach route to Pochalla is from Juba city to Torit, Kapoeta, Boma towards the junction of Pibor/Boma and from there to Pochalla. But this route might also not be possible, because those towns were all firmly manned by the SPLA forces. The attacking forces would have a difficult task controlling and passing through all of those towns, on the way to Pochalla. So, we were still very concerned, what was the intent of the surveillance plane.

Time proved us wrong because our analysis was based on considering the approach routes from the Sudanese side. We later discovered the enemy's approach route to attack Pochalla, came through Ethiopia using the road that was constructed by Dr. John Garang de Mabior almost six years ago. Also the enemy were in fact none other than the forces of EPRDF, who forced the Movement (SPLM/A) out of Ethiopia the year prior. The enemy forces who were targeting Pochalla passed nonstop through Pinyudo, on March 5, 1992. We didn't anticipate our enemy to approach via Ethiopian land. We ignored any potential danger coming from that direction, and had not sent any patrols to the Gilo crossing point. It was out of good luck that an Anyuak from South Sudan who was in Pinyudo town when the enemy passed through, came to Pochalla at 2:00pm and alerted Captain Gilo Agada Akuei. Captain Gilo immediately passed the information to Alternate Commander Malony Akou Nai, advising enemy forces were coming to Pochalla from the Ethiopian side of the border.

The forces were quickly prepared and took position on the eastern front of the town. This occurred on Sunday March 8, 1992. The enemy forces were now just a few kilometres away from the town. After an hour of reaching their position, the confrontation started at 3:00pm. The Ethiopian army were attacking in waves, one after another. The SPLA forces were repulsing them, as they advanced. Our men had managed to capture two wounded Ethiopian soldiers, in front of our defensive lines. At first, we thought that our men were going to gain the ground, but the Ethiopians were persistent in their fighting. There could be no comparison in terms of armament, between the Ethiopians and our forces. They were using tanks and heavy artillery, while our forces were using only personal AKM rifles. The battle continued unabatedly for five hours. Our forces started to leave their positions, when darkness started to fall. I remember Alternate Commander Malony Akou Nai, my family and I were the last to vacate the town exactly 8:00pm. The fall of Pochalla into the hands of the Sudanese armed forces, was announced the following day which was misleading and contrary to what had actually taken place on the ground. We forgot to evacuate the two wounded Ethiopian soldiers, even when the sun was still up. That could have been an undisputable fact to show the world that those who fought and captured Pochalla were Ethiopian forces, not the Sudanese as it was claimed.

We regrettably went and regrouped on the Oboth river side. It was a very uncomforting sight to see children unprepared to stay in such conditions. We gathered the displaced community and marched them southwards to Boma. I was not wanting to continue with the displaced assignment that I had been tasked with since November 1989. I then passed this responsibility to Captain Atem Garang Deng de Kuek, to lead the displaced community to Boma town. He accomplished this mission admirably. The displaced community then proceeded to Kapoeta and from there, to different locations of their choice in the Southern parts of the country.

Commander Atali Odol Cham, who hails from the area, remained without official assignment. Commander of the SPLA forces Alternate Commander Malony Akou, Captain Gilo Agada Akuei, Captain Michael Makuei Lueth, myself and many others remained around Pochalla town with a small force. The enemy after firmly controlling Pochalla, was organising itself to move to Pibor with the aim of capturing it. They were going to use local South Sudanese militia men from the Anyuak and Murle communities, to reclaim Pibor from the SPLA. They indeed departed Pochalla and clashed with the forces of Alternate Commander Malony Akou, shortly after I had left them on my way to Boma. Our force could not stand their ground against the enemy heading towards Pibor. They dislodged a small SPLA force at the Okello military base, under the command of Captain Joseph Mayen Akoon Abit and then proceeded to Pibor town. Commander Salva Kiir Mayardit requested I come to Boma with the returnees of Kapoeta town, where they were expected to reside. As I was already in Boma waiting for transport to

Kapoeta, Commander Salva Kiir Mayardit had instructed SPLA forces in and around Pibor to regroup in Pibor town then withdraw and move to Boma, where he already was. The reason was Bor, west of Pibor, was attacked and captured by the enemy and Pochalla in the east had fallen into enemy hands also. Therefore, the two enemy forces were going to converge onto Pibor making the SPLA forces extremely vulnerable. It was a wise decision to regroup in one defensive locality to form a cohesive and formidable unit, capable of deterring any potential enemy forces approaching.

The National Islamic Front, that had assumed power in Khartoum three years prior, wanted to give a bloody nose to the SPLA/M for exploiting sharp divisions that had recently occurred. The enemy forces advancing to Bor from Malakal did not face any confrontation, instead they were being warmly received and offered a heroic welcoming by the forces of Nasir SPLM/A of Dr. Riek Machar and Dr. Lam Akol Ajawin. The enemy had passed through all Nasir-faction controlled areas, targeting spots held by the SPLM/A mainstream. They were moving by land and by barge on river Nile to Bor, after a safe passage was guaranteed in the areas mentioned above. Bor town was captured by the forces moving by barges, along the river Nile. The mission of that huge force travelling via barge, was to open the river route from Malakal to Bor which had been blocked by the SPLA since 1985. They met little resistance from the SPLA forces under the command of Commander Bior Asoud Ajang Duot as they sailed to Bor town. Commander Bior was also controlling SPLA forces on land, under the overall command of Commander William Nyuon Bany and Commander Dim Deng. Commander Bior Asoud advanced to the Ayod area, to stop the advancing enemy forces on land. This mission was unsuccessful as the enemy rolled back Commander Bior's forces to the Bor area. This enemy force moving by land was avoiding direct confrontation with the SPLA forces.

Streamlined as they were, they could avoid possible areas where they could clash with the SPLA forces. Hence, they managed to enter Bor after it was controlled by the forces travelling by barges.

It is worth mentioning that the Khartoum government made a plan that year in 1992, to recapture all the areas lost to the SPLA/M in an operation code named 'Saf el Obour' which meant 'Crossing Summer'. The areas they had lost in greater Upper Nile, Greater Bahr el Gazal and greater Equatorial regions must be retaken, except those under control of the Nasir Faction. Many military convoys were simultaneously launched to seize them from the SPLM/A, in the beginning of dry season of 1992. During the implementation of that complex and ambitious plan, they managed to recapture Pochalla and Bor in March. Pibor and Boma were the next target in the greater Upper Nile region. Meanwhile other convoys advancing to retake Torit and Kapoeta in eastern Equatoria were already underway. There was another convoy heading to Western Equatoria, but it had to commence from Wau town.

Before the fall of Pochalla into the hands of the Ethiopian forces, a wise decision to evacuate the unaccompanied minors to Narus town in the Kapoeta area, was made at the right time. They commenced movement at the end of February 1992 in a well-organised journey, accompanied by their teachers and staff to guide them on the long and tiresome journey on foot, to Eastern Equatoria. Their journey was smooth in the areas around the Upper Nile Region, but this changed the moment they arrived in the hostile community of Taposa, where they began to lose some of their colleagues. We as their management team, were so grateful to the ICRC organisation for the sound guidance they provided to the unaccompanied minors on the way to Narus town. The overall plan of moving the unaccompanied minors to Narus town, originated during a meeting of the Movement's leadership. They had to look for the safest possible area to construct schools and run their education, without disturbances from the Sudanese government army or their allies, who had now been fighting with the SPLA/M for nine years. The area of Narus became like a safe-haven to the unaccompanied minors and the returnees who had come back to Sudan from Ethiopia.

Nasir Declaration – August 28, 1991

As mentioned previously, the Nasir coup d'état conspired by three Alternate Members of Politico Military High Command of the SPLM/A, will be discussed in a separate chapter. As soon as we returned from Ethiopia to Sudan (Pochalla town), the rough and difficult life faced in the beginning of the settlement started to stabilise. Relief supplies were flowing regularly and the unaccompanied minor's schools started to function well. But when the Movement's leadership began to focus on how to recover from the upheavals of the collapse of the system in Ethiopia, we were then shocked on August 28, 1991, by a declaration announced by three Commanders, Dr. Riek Machar Teny, Dr. Lam Akol Ajawin and the Illiterate Gordon Kong Chol (who happened to have climbed the Movement leadership's ladder through an agreement reached between the SPLM/A and Anya-nya 11 in 1988).

They announced over the BBC radio programme "Focus on Africa", they had overthrown John Garang de Mabior from the SPLM/A leadership. They then stated the many reasons that led them to this decision. Some reasons mentioned in the statement were the lack of democracy in the (SPLM) Movement and the liberation of the South from Northern Sudan.

What made the Nasir declaration so puzzling and disappointing to those who sincerely loved the SPLM/A Movement, was the situation in which the Movement had found itself in. The socialist government in Ethiopia, which was the Movement's only source of military support, had just collapsed. According to analysis in our circles in Pochalla town, declaring changes to the

Movement's leadership meant weakness in the lines of the Movement and therefore, the Movement's long-awaited target of liberating Sudan would not be achieved in the near future. The Nasir action, meant division in the ranks and files of the SPLM/A and it didn't take long before skirmishes occurred among southern people. This was the basis of fear that the objective was out of sight and would not be realised soon. Let me illustrate the key points brought forward by the two doctors as causes or reasons for declaring the August coup d'etat;

1. Lack of Democracy in the Sudan People's Liberation Movement (SPLM/A):

Democracy, in my opinion, is always exercised by sovereign nations that enjoy their own system of governance. The leadership of these states can choose any of the world known systems of rule e.g. capitalism, socialism or monarchy. In a capitalist system, democracy is adopted by that nation as a way of rule and therefore parties form to contest elections after a pre-determined amount of years, in order to choose their rulers and members of parliament. This system operates only in a sovereign country, as mentioned above. It is illogical to talk about democracy in a guerrilla movement where things are in disarray. For instance, SPLM/A members of Politico-Military High Command were leading their units across different war fronts. This alone would subject the Movement's leadership to be in a very awkward military situation should the chairman call zonal commanders for a meeting to discuss political issues. This could not occur due to the unavailability of transport on one hand and on the other hand due to the demanding security situation that faced commanders in their zonal headquarters.

Lack of democracy as claimed by the two doctors, was just a pseudonym reason for rising to power. A guerrilla movement under any condition, cannot successfully exercise democracy in their administrative systems. It has never happened in the history of guerrilla movement, to have heard or read about a democratic system of rule. Dr. Riek Machar and Dr. Lam Akol did not mean what they claimed, in their failed coup declaration. They broke away from the SPLM/A, and I didn't hear about them putting any democratic policies into practice in their guerrilla (SSIM/A) movement. The two Doctors instead of challenging the main enemy that made them pick up arms, turned their guns against the Movement with full support from the Sudanese Government when their coup d'état yielded no tangible fruits. Either we lead the SPLM/A Movement or else the house falls on us all. In other words, no liberation of South Sudan unless the liberation of the whole Sudan, as Dr. John and his group claim it.

2. Liberation of the South from Northern Sudan
On the August 28 declaration, Dr Riek Machar stated openly that the SPLM/A should be fighting for the self-independence of the south or separation from the whole country. To them, Dr. John Garang was fighting the wrong war. Southerners should not in any sense be wasting their time and energy to fight for liberation from the whole country. Southerners were generally obsessed with achieving separation of the South as an independent entity. That was the aim of the first struggle by Anya-nya (1) that took 17 years and ended with the signing of the Addis Ababa agreement on March 3, 1972. When the war broke out in Bor on May 16, 1983 this was followed by the formation of the SPLM/A Movement. Southerners expected those leaders to name it the South Sudan Liberation Movement (SSLM) and South Sudan Liberation Army (SSLA). But they were surprised to learn the names were Sudan People's Liberation Movement (SPLM) and Sudan People's Liberation Army (SPLA). Southerners were very disappointed with the naming, as their minds were totally geared towards the liberation of the South.

Dr. John Garang de Mabior and his group faced a lot of real challenges during the establishment days. Southerners who were still in the government controlled areas and had not yet joined the Movement, fell short of understanding those challenges.

Dr. John Garang rebelled with members of battalions 105 and 104 in Bor, Pibor, Pochalla and Ayod. They went to Ethiopia where they were warmly received by the socialist government of President Mengistu Hailemariam and established the SPLM/A Movement in August 1983. One of the challenges faced by Dr. John and his group, was that they rebelled against the pro-western or capitalist government of President Jaffer Mohamad Nimeiri. Those who condemned the naming of the Movement were failing to understand the complexity of the then ongoing regional politics. The Ethiopian government were fighting the separatist forces of Eritrea and Tigrinya, who mainly received their military support from Sudan. If John Garang was not considerate of this dimension and made the mistake of naming the Movement as SSLM/A, he wouldn't have been welcomed and warmly received by the Ethiopian government. This is because they were fighting the separatists in the northern part of the country, which would have led to the loss of the cause of the southern people. Other regional neighbouring countries Kenya, Uganda and Zaire were friendly to the western world, hence none of them would have been quick to support the southern cause. It was also unthinkable for the Movement's leadership to rebel against the capitalist system and expect backup from other capitalist governments in the region. That was why a socialist system of governance should lead the Movement, which would gain military support from the Ethiopian government. Within a brief period, the SPLM/A was able to acquire strong support from Ethiopia, Libya and many other socialist systems in the region and world at large.

In my opinion, Dr. John Garang de Mabior was well ahead in his thinking and ideas concerning the southern problem, compared to other southern leaders. He articulated that the way of rule in Sudan was unfair, to convince people in the marginalised regions. The make-up of Sudanese society varies in terms of ethnicity and religious affiliation. If we take it in terms of religious affiliation, the majority of Sudanese are Muslims. But on ethnical terms, the majority are of African background. Therefore, if you want to use religion as the basis for selecting leaders, then this policy would isolate non-Muslims from the top leadership of the country, causing potential instability. Non-Muslims, although the minority, would pick up arms and fight against the system which happened in the first struggle of Anya-nya (1). The African majority would eventually object to the rule of a few immigrant Arab Muslims and vice-versa. Therefore Dr. John Garang wanted Sudan to be administered on the new basis of equality. Religious and ethnical domination should be disregarded, in order for the country to be ruled based on abilities and capabilities. He wanted to fight for the whole country and eradicate marginalisation. This was contrary to the southern opinion of fighting to liberate the south. Dr John tried to assure the southerners, that the enemy you will fight while liberating the south is the same enemy you will confront while fighting for the whole of Sudan. So, let us fight together until you reach where you believe is the last point of your Southern Sudan. He mentioned that he would continue pursuing the war in the north with those who joined the Movement from Northern Sudan. But if no Northern Sudanese joined the Movement, Dr. John said he would be mad to continue the war in the north without enough manpower to support him. This means he would return and join hands with those contended in the liberated southern part of the country. He thought he would successfully kill two birds with one stone. He would have liberated the South using manpower from the marginalised areas of Northern Sudan if that was the style to be applied.

If Dr. John had centred his ideas only around the southern liberation, he would have followed suit of the Anya-nya 1 liberation struggle. The whole country would converge their forces against the south, as what happened previously in the first southern struggle. After considering the possibility of liberating the whole country, they successfully rallied the marginalised majority of Sudan, to back the SPLM/A Movement. People from marginalised areas of Sudan began to make sense of Dr. John Garang's claims. Even though he came from the southern part of the country, marginalisation could not only occur in Southern Sudan alone, but also in the Western, Eastern and far Northern Sudan. Therefore all the Sudanese from the areas mentioned above joined the Movement in great numbers, to fight with their southern brothers for the removal of minority rulers in Khartoum. The SPLM/A started to receive a huge influx of fighters from the Nuba Mountains, Southern Blue Nile and Southern Darfur, although relatively few in numbers. I will not forget to mention the intellectuals from the centre, east and far north of the country that also joined the SPLM/A Movement, right from inception.

John Garang's policy of fighting to liberate the whole of Sudan, made him gain not only supporters but also fighters from different corners. This disapproved the idea of fighting for the liberation of the south. It is worth mentioning that fighting to liberate the whole country, needed less manpower and resources from the south. Marginalised people from the marginalised areas, all along were the recruits of the minority clique regime in Khartoum used to fighting the Southern liberation struggle. Dr. John Garang's tactic this time, was to rob the Khartoum elites of the manpower they were using to challenge the southern liberation movements. Manpower from Southern Kurdufan, Southern Blue Nile and Southern Darfur had then joined hands with their brothers in the south to fight one common enemy, which was none other than the Khartoum Government. The southern based Movement (SPLM/A) was able for the first time in their liberation struggle, to reach Southern Darfur, Southern Kurdufan, Southern Blue Nile and as far east as Homishkureb and Kassella city. The war zone this time was broader and wider than previous one. . As a result, the enemy forces were reasonably scattered and the war was successfully taken to the enemy fields, causing panic to the population in the areas under control of the Khartoum government. The people in those areas had then started to experience the repercussion of war, the way their brothers in the southern parts had previously felt.

Southern Sudanese who opposed the strategy adopted by Dr. John Garang of fighting to liberate the whole country, were falling short to understand what occurred to the first southern struggle from 1955-1972. The Sudanese government or Northern Sudan had multiple resources in their control plus the formidable wealth of the Arab world behind them. This made them a gigantic body the South alone couldn't confront them and expect to win. It is like placing a thin man in a boxing ring and expecting him to beat the powerful world champion, Mohamad Ali. You would never expect the thin man to succeed and win the fight. Similarly, South Sudan, no matter what military tactic, would never alone succeed in achieving victory against the Sudan.

Hence, it was duly important to adopt high level tactics to challenge the Sudanese government on the war front. One of those tactics was to declare war on the whole country by mobilising people from the marginalised areas of the Sudan, in the way Dr. John had done. Logically, the population in those areas would be hostile towards the central government and as a result pick up arms and support the Southern SPLM/A Movement. Secondly, they would have to mobilise resources to support the Movement and their fighters. John Garang's tactic of fighting for the whole country was yielding more fruits than singling out the south. With this strategy in place, South Sudan was humbly requested by the Islamists to be prepared for its own independence in the years to come. It wouldn't be achievable if southerners only fought for the liberation of Southern Sudan. In the end, the two doctors who were uncomfortable with policies of Dr. John Garang, did return to the Movement after having spent a good eleven years being part of the unfruitful struggle against the SPLM/A, but not the Khartoum Government.

Was the Nasir Declaration Meant for the Southern Independence?

I would like to discuss the following questions to pinpoint why Doctor Riek had decided to declare his creeping coup d'état;

1. Why did Dr. Riek Machar turn his guns against the southern people?
2. After the coup declaration, why did Dr. Riek Machar cooperate with the Khartoum NIF government when he intended to liberate the south from the whole country?
3. Was it a plan by the coup leaders to fight against the SPLM/A to weaken it in the interest of NIF?
4. Did Dr. Riek Machar carefully consider the repercussion of his coup d'état?
5. I will further elaborate on each of the questions above.

1. Why did Dr. Riek Machar Teny turn his guns against southern people?

South Sudanese are Africans who inhabit the southern parts of Sudan. Most of them adopted the Christian faith unlike other African tribes in the north who adopted the Islamic religion. Some Northern Sudanese tribes do deceitfully believe themselves as Arabs. Those Northern Sudanese inherited political power from the British colonialists when they left the country in 1956. They were consumed by Arabism and the Islamic ideology and they began to overlook and undermine Southern Sudanese in the system of governance and in their social lives. Southerners were no longer included in the national government's services and if they were to be considered, they were ranked in the junior government positions. In addition to this, there were different salaries paid to Southern Sudanese and their Northern Sudanese counterparts, conducting the same job. This was only corrected after a long struggle. Considering southerners in political positions, was another difficult task. There were political positions that were prohibited for Southern Sudanese to assume, no matter how qualified that person was, e.g. Presidency, Defence, Foreign Affairs just to mention a few. The distrustful relationship between the Northern and Southern Sudanese created doubt and a lack of confidence on whether they can live together comfortably in one country. Southerners could not endure the imbalanced treatment and were becoming aggravated, leading to a rebellion in August 1955. They expressed their desire to have their own sovereign nation in the southern part of the country. Their endeavours over a 17 year period did not yield fruits and as a result they signed a peace agreement with the northern government in 1972. One of the reasons why their struggle did not achieve results, was due to the convergence of other regions in the Sudan, against the south. In order Not to be bitten twice, in one hole Dr. John Garang de Mabior, though interested to fight for liberation of the south, did not need to repeat the mistake committed by Anya-nya (1) leaders. He came in with new tactics to fight for the liberation of the whole country, which I believe the two doctors failed to understand.

Nasir coup plotters, Commander Dr. Riek Machar Teny and Commander Dr. Lam Akol Ajawin had very high ambitions to liberate the south and wanted to lead the SPLM/A Movement by any means possible. At that stage, the Movement was at the peak of her strength. Despite that, they were being haunted by the recent crumble of the Ethiopian government, which was the only dynamic source of the SPLM/A military strength. All Southern Sudanese refugees were forced to evacuate back to the bordering towns of the Southern Sudan with Ethiopia. At that moment, the two doctors wrongly executed their unjustified plan at a very unfavourable time. In my opinion, they were encouraged to take that decision by the fall of Mengistus regime in May 1991.

The atmosphere was conducive enough for the ambitious doctors to declare their coup against the leadership of the most capable southern leader, John Garang de Mabior. Instead of fighting the main enemy, they formerly took up arms to challenge and from which they wanted to liberate the South, they turned their guns against the fellow South Sudanese in a very surprising and astonishing manner. Commander of the coup Dr. Riek Machar Teny, started to mobilise what is now known as the White Army composed of Nuer citizens and Anya-nya 11 forces, who also originated from the same Nuer community, to attack neighbouring Dinka communities. The two coup plotters who were among the highly educated South Sudanese PhD holders and were perceived to be future leaders of the south, shocked all South Sudanese when they turned tribal leaders. Sorrowfully after the declaration of the coup, SPLM/A members who were thought to be standing up for their word (liberation of Southern Sudan) against the Arabs of Khartoum turned their guns at their brothers.

It was daring and conflicting that the White Army plus Anya-nya (11), in full knowledge and capacity of Dr. Riek and Dr. Lam Akol, marched to Bor and committed a massacre on the Bor people known as 'The Bor Massacre'. Tens of thousands of innocent people were killed and children and women were taken away to the Nuer areas for the first time in the history of the two tribes. Hundreds of thousands of cattle, owned by the Bor citizens, were driven away to Nuer land. It was total devastation. Those who escaped or survived the massacre, migrated to Eastern Equatoria where many children and old aged people perished at Ame,

Aswa and Atempi in displaced camps due to a poor and unbalanced diet.

Dr. Riek Machar had puzzled the Dinka people of the Upper Nile region. They could not anticipate whether he intended to rule the south without Bor, Pigi and Ngok Dinka people of Lual Yak. It is unprocedural for a leader to disregard or target sections of people from those he wants to lead. Some analysts assumed Dr. Riek saw no differences between Dr. John Garang who he wished to overthrow and the Bor community as people he could lead, and that is why he aimed at their annihilation. But then, this community was contributing immensely in the affairs of the southern people and that was witnessed in the first struggle of Anya-nya (1) and also in the present struggle of the SPLM/A he opted to lead. If Dr. John Garang de Mabior had descended from them, this should not have been seen as an excuse or reason for them to be exterminated.

2. After the coup declaration, why did Dr. Riek Machar cooperate with the Khartoum NIF government when he intended to liberate the south from the whole country?

After the coup declaration, Dr. Riek Machar started to dispatch emissaries to Khartoum, seeking means of support should they be attacked by the Torit mainstream. I don't understand the justification that prompted Nasir coup makers to behave that way. It shows that Nasir coup planners were not driving their main objective of separation, because you wouldn't declare liberation of the south from the Sudan government and request support from that same government as well. It seems Dr. Riek Machar had ill intention that he wanted to fight a war of attrition against the SPLM/A Movement for the benefit of those who we southerners, picked up arms to liberate ourselves from.

The other puzzling point, is why did he start making military offences against the SPLM/A mainstream when the Torit faction, hadn't yet launched any military offences against them? To answer this query,

Dr. Riek Machar came up with the idea of liquidating the SPLM/A Movement for the benefit of the NIF Administration in Khartoum. I believe he expected the Torit faction leader to immediately succumb and yield into acceptance of being overthrown, which is not common in a guerrilla movement where leadership is not stationed to a known locality. Therefore, Dr. Riek chose destruction of the SPLM/A Movement in return for failing to achieve his objective of leading the entire movement.

If Nasir Faction was ready for the purpose declared on August 28, 1991, he should have established his own faction and targeted the Khartoum government as the main enemy, rather than turning their guns on their own people. Dr. Riek Machar did not fight the main enemy for good, 11 years after the coup d'état declaration, until he re-joined the Movement in 2002. Instead of lingering in the bush opposing the real known enemy of the southern people, he and Dr. Lam Akol Ajawin, with no shame, decided to make a full board in the enemy headquarters, Khartoum city. This occurred when they failed to manage their factions, a task or responsibility they believed Dr. John Garang fell short to address.

3. Was it a plan by the coup leaders to fight against the SPLM/A to weaken it in the interest of the NIF?

This may not have been the real purpose of the Nasir faction. It came because of their failed endeavours to fight against the Torit faction. They might have wrongly believed Dr. John was no longer popular or capable to lead the Movement after the collapse of the world communist systems that followed after the fall of Mengistu's regime in Ethiopia. They believed those events were conducive for them to change the present leadership and take command of the SPLM/A Movement, which turned out to be a nightmare since Dr. John was still at the height of his popularity and the mainstream were standing against the Nasir coup planners calling "John Garang Must Go". The Movement in the whole of Equatoria, Bahr el Gazal and some parts of Upper Nile Region, then stood firm against the Nasir slogan of "John Garang Must Go".

Leaders of the Nasir faction faced stiff challenges, and they were frustrated to be confined to the Nuer areas of the Upper Nile Region. Their faction had quickly witnessed the disintegration between Dr. Riek Machar and Dr. Lam Akol, making each lead his own faction based on tribal support. Dr. Riek Machar named his sub-faction as South Sudan Independent Movement/Army (SSIM/A), meanwhile the other wing of Dr. Lam Akol named his faction as South Sudan Democratic Movement/Army (SSDM/A). This happened after many unsuccessful attempts on the battlefield, fighting against the mainstream of the SPLM/A. After the division, Dr. Riek took Nasir town as his headquarters since the announcement of the coup in 1991.

When the Nasir faction could not produce tangible military back up in support of Khartoum, the NIF decided to occupy Nasir town and other areas under control of the Nasir faction leaving their leader, Dr. Riek Machar Teny, with no alternative but to surrender and sign an undignified and humiliating peace agreement in 1996 with NIF. He reported himself to Khartoum as an Assistant President of the Republic. With that development, the SPLM/A mainstream was left alone in the bush, to continue with the war of liberation under the historical leadership of Dr. John Garang de Mabior.

To conclude here, the Nasir faction fought the SPLM/A mainstream when they failed to control them under the indisputable leadership of Dr. John Garang de Mabior. Imagine, the men who broke away from the SPLM/A Movement to liberate the South from the North, have paradoxically signed agreement with NIF Government and became part and parcel of it. There was a serious lack of principles, vision and honesty, followed and adhered to on the side of Nasir Faction.

4. Did Dr. Riek Machar carefully consider the repercussion of his coup d'état?

I would assume they were 100% knowledgeable of the expected coup outcomes. There's no way to execute a coup in the bush where things are not under control and expect it will succeed. The Chairman of the SPLM/A Movement, who Dr. Riek and Dr. Lam Akol wanted to remove from leadership, was a distance away in Torit. There was no miracle solution for controlling the chairman of the Movement at that far end. For the coup to then succeed, the two plotters should have got hold of the chairman before declaring the coup. They knew the coup would automatically fail. That led them to instead naming it a 'creeping revolution'. They also knew that the coup would weaken the SPLM/A Movement. The Movement would not be cohesive and strong again, since it might begin to fight itself and leave the common enemy, the Sudan NIF Government, to enjoy our internal differences and self-destruction.

It was obvious that the enemy benefited from the Movement's internal differences and started to regain areas long lost to the SPLM/A Movement. The Nasir faction had already united their ranks with Khartoum and started to launch unending waves of attacks on the mainstream in support of the NIF Government. The strong SPLM/A Movement at the beginning of 1992, lost most of the towns it had captured from the Sudanese government since 1985. The Nasir faction at that time, gave a heroic welcoming to the Sudan NIF forces when passing through the areas under their control. By then the enemy of the Sudan Government armed forces, would only begin to release their bullets when they were coming to contact with the SPLM/A mainstream forces in the areas they manned.

Nasir faction leaders could not synchronize the coup dance right from the time of declaration. The detained non-Nuer officers and soldiers who were not in support of their coup d'état, were prosecuted at the initial stages. Dr. Riek Machar Teny proved he was not in control of the situation when he was unable to stop the killing of those innocent officers. All he could do when informed about the cold blood killing of non-Nuer officers, was roll tears down the cheeks from his eyes. Many comrades had miserably loss their lives in that incident, including intimate Riek loyalists. General Hakim Gabriel Aluong Kang was the last killed in Waat in the presence of Dr. Riek and his British wife Ann Macon, in early March 1992. This occurred when Dr. Riek Machar was visiting the Twic East and Duk areas, to set the leadership hierarchy in the small town of Panyagor. Members of the Nasir faction had then gathered at Panyagor to address the challenging question of leadership.

I myself, could not understand the reasons why Dr. Riek Machar chose to conduct his Movement's leadership conference at Panyagor Village instead of holding it in Nasir town. Some analysts speculated that Dr. Riek and the Nasir faction wanted to prove to the SPLM/A mainstream and Dinka Bor people in particular, that the area had changed hands and become Nasir controlled land. A huge army from the Nasir faction was dispatched to Bor, to control and keep it for the Nasir faction leadership conference being held at Panyagor village. Members of the Nasir faction, in addition to those who recently broke away from the SPLM/A mainstream e.g. William Nyuon Bany Machar, Kerbino Kuanyin Bol, Arok Thon Arok, Joseph Oduho and many others gathered at Panyagor village in March 1993. Dr. Riek was confirmed as leader of the Nasir faction, deputised by Kerbino Kuanyin Bol, William Nyuon Bany, Arok Thon Arok and Dr. Lam Akol.

However, the leadership formation process did not run smoothly and to the logical expectations. A sudden surfacing of the SPLA mainstream forces under the command of General Kuol Manyang Juuk, made Dr. Riek and his faction's group run away at Panyagor in disarray back to the Nasir controlled areas. In that battle of Panyagor on March 27, 1993, a South Sudanese political veteran Joseph Oduho and Commander Kuach Kang among many others, were left dead on the battle ground. SPLM/A mainstream force commanders, Bior (Asoud) Ajang Duot, Biar Atem Ajang, George Athor Deng Dut and William Deng Garang Bany were in hot pursuit to the Nasir faction men. To them, it was illogical for the man who devastated the area and committed the Bor massacre to come and prevail over them in Bor land. That battle brought an end to the presence of the Nasir faction in Bor. Commander Kuol Manyang Juuk, with his mainstream forces, remained in full control of Bor until the end of the war in 2005. They could only launch military operations in the nearby Nasir faction's counties which were close to the Bor area, and sometimes they repulsed counter offences in an attempt to control Bor again. It was a very hard dream for the Nasir faction forces to realise.

To conclude, the Nasir declaration was a set back to the aspirations of the Sudanese in general and Southern Sudanese in particular. The SPLM/A were planning on bringing the war to an end in 1991-1992, with the capture of the South Sudan Capital City in Juba that year. The light near the end of the tunnel, could not be achieved as expected because of the storm that came against a sailors wish. Dr. Riek and Dr. Lam were the storm of 1991 that disrupted the smooth sailing of the SPLM/A ship and delayed freedom of the marginalised people of Sudan because of their petty claims. If the two plotters rebelled because Dr. John was claiming to liberate the whole country, then that is not a satisfying reason. The Northern Sudanese Arabs were surely still in different cities and towns in the Southern Region. And to dislodge them from the south ultimately required unity from our people to achieve that goal. In my opinion, the enemy a person confronts whilst aiming to liberate the south, is the same enemy that person would fight when aiming to liberate the whole country. Hence the objective was one and the same for the marginalised people of the Sudan.

As mentioned above, it was strategic to target the whole of Sudan rather than singling out the southern part of the country. The reason is, you would have to mobilise the people from the other marginalised areas so you can fight the enemy together, as long as the enemy is the same. It would be entirely different if solely fighting for the liberation of the south. The minority clique regimes that have been dominating everything in Khartoum, would unite the other marginalised people of Sudan against the south, as it happened in the first struggle of the southern people from 1955-72, which would make the task a nightmare to achieve. I don't concur with the idea of southerners targeting the liberation of the south alone, even though it was an overall objective to achieve. John Garang was wiser and more tactful than others and his strategy made the southerners achieve their long awaited objective in 2011.

The other claim of the Nasir declaration was the "non application of democratic policy at different levels in the SPLM/A Movement". This claim was also a non-issue. In the first place, there is no applicable democracy in a military system that people can refer to worldwide. Experience would indicate, that army doctrine in the sovereign states is founded utterly on discipline and control. There can't be more intelligent people in one army, as they claim. The two plotters were aware of that. They were indeed leading and managing their armies on the war front, but without consultation or participation in decision making from any of their subordinates. I might be falling short in understanding the democracy intended by Dr. Riek Machar in his declaration that he used as pretext to oust Dr. John Garang in his coup d'état. I did not succeed in understanding from Dr Riek or Dr Lam, the type of democracy that was circulating in their minds. The SPLM/A was a guerrilla movement that was struggling to find a foot hole in Sudan's political leadership.

Conditions to challenge the government of Sudan on the war front, were not conducive to survival, let alone the application of democracy principles. The duo had managed to break away from the SPLM/A Movement after declaring the coup, but to everyone's best knowledge they could not practice democracy in the management of their factions. Management of the Nasir faction ironically, became a stiff challenge to their leadership, with no application of democracy which is a system of plural rule in democratic nations, but not in guerrilla movements.

In a guerrilla liberation movement, there are priorities which usually remain as essential sources for survival. Those are centred in the provision of military equipment and other military supplies. Without them there can be no effective operations, and a guerrilla movement is not able to confront the government forces they are struggling against. The SPLM/A Movement became known in the world and indeed became more stable in the war simply because of their availability. Non-application of democracy in the Movement didn't do much harm to the organisation. Nor was the visibly tough and tight discipline applied by John Garang de Mabior, which was not a hindrance to the war achievements in the field of operations.

Dr. John and the SPLM/A had captured towns one after another over the past eight years from 1983-91, despite the fact that he was not a democrat, according to the claim. The SPLM/A started experiencing setbacks in 1992, only when the two Drs. turned their own guns against the Movement. Yes, I would agree that is some sense with the Doctors, that John Garang was a dictator. However, that was his prerogative in that situation. If Dr. John was successfully leading the SPLM/A Movement on the war front despite him being a dictator, then why object to his administration when all were seeing the light at the end of the tunnel, which was the liberation of the south. That alone could be considered by others as a malicious and jealous act, against the successful leader of the time. John Garang was not only successful on the war front but he also kept the Movement well united from the time of inception from 1983 to 1991. After all, southerners did rebel in the first place to fight injustices mounted against the south by the minority clique in Khartoum, but they did not rebel to come and apply democracy in the bush. The failed coup attempt subjected the Movement to wasting unnecessary time and energy, and became a point of contempt for the two doctors.

For any move a person or group want to execute at any time, there must be a desire to achieve. If that aim is to liberate the south or change of political dispensation in the whole Sudan, there must undoubtedly be means to execute this process. In this regard, the SPLM/A Movement and its' leader Dr. John Garang, had enough capable manpower to achieve that target. That said, the target must also be achievable. The able leader Dr. John Garang de Mabior, from the time of the Movement's inception, had been providing different military hardware and equipment to the SPLA officers, non-commissioned officers (NCOs) and men to confront the enemy on the war front. This process happened continually over the last eight years, before the Nasir coup in 1991. Again, I would stand in support of those who would oppose Dr. John Garang, if he fell short in the provision of military needs and equipment to the SPLM/A Movement. The core of success in the guerrilla movement, generally lies in the provision of different military necessities. I would therefore stand against those who oppose any leader who successfully supplies the military needs of his guerrilla movement, just for the sake of opposition.

To conclude, the SPLM/A Movement was fiercely confronting many enemies at one time, which included; the government of Sudan, the Nasir faction and the uncontrolled southern militia men in the Upper Nile, Bahr el Gazal and Equatorial Regions of the Southern Sudan. Despite all that, the SPLM/A under the command of John Garang, was emerging victorious. It defeated and destroyed Sudan's NIF army and its military capability as well as restraining different southern militia organisations in the regions of the south, as mentioned earlier. Restraining the militia bandits here, meant they were not the Movement's targets or enemies. They were being fought only when they touched the Movement's sensitive nerves that could not be endured. On seeing preciseness and excellent performance in the field of operations, the Nasir faction of Dr. Riek Machar and Dr. Lam Akol thought it would be a simple task to manage a guerrilla movement and that it could easily be performed by any commander of the SPLM/A, in the same manner as Dr. John. The two leaders became jealous of Dr. John, and the declaration of "John Garang must go" ensued right afterwards. They were faced with the challenges of leading a guerrilla movement when they took the leadership of the SPLM/A Nasir faction. In this context, you have to consider many aspects in order to perform successful guerrilla leadership, e.g. 1/ commitment of the community which a leader originates from, to the cause of the people, that alone keeps cohesiveness of the command, 2/ internal political relationships of the leader with political counterparts in that particular country and 3/ the leader's political relationship with the leaders of the neighbouring countries and international community, that matters greatly in this context.

Dr. John Garang de Mabior had a contemporary vision in running the Movement's affairs, far above the rest. He won the confidence of the Ethiopian government and its' leader Mengistu Hailemariam and the confidence of leaders in other neighbouring countries, without exception. That's why it didn't take him long to achieve the support needed in terms of military equipment, from the time of the Movement's inception.

There were unnecessary atrocities committed by the SPLM/A Nasir faction, against the officers and non-commissioned officers considered to have been opposed to the Nasir declaration. The killing unfortunately did not exclude wives and children. I will mention their names for history records, but I have not yet obtained the names and numbers of those who perished at the hands of the mainstream or Torit faction, for me to be fair in this acknowledgement. There surely would have been similar atrocities committed by the mainstream, the way it occurred in Nasir. I will have to make sure their names are also included in this book, when they are availed.

Here is the list of those who perished in Nasir and other areas under control of Nasir faction;

1. Alt. Commander Peter Panhom Thanypieny
2. Alt. Commander; Manyiel Kueth Makuei
3. Alt. Commander; James Lem Kuany
4. Alt. Commander; Maguet Dhal Malou
5. Alt. Commander; John Lat Manyok
6. Alt. Commander; Hakim Gabriel Aluong
7. Alt. Commander; Daniel Chol Riak
8. Alt. Commander; Kuoreng Akoi Yaak
9. Capt. Mach Riak
10. Capt. Magong Deng Ayiom
11. Capt. Kuer Duot Adohr
12. Capt. Kuol Deng Kuol
13. Capt. Aguer Bior Duot
14. Capt. Deng Mabior Deng
15. Capt. Bior Reech Gak
16. Capt. Awuol Chan Awuol
17. Capt. Wuor Jook Abyei
18. Capt. Michael Manyuon Anyang
19. Capt. Ater Jeroboam Machuor Kulang
20. Capt. Bior Pager
21. 1st Lt. Duot Bul Duot
22. 1st Lt. Paul Puor Wuor

23. 1st Lt. Ajak Manyang Jok
24. 1st Lt. Ayuen Buoi Ayom
25. 1st Lt. Louis Daniel Chol Riak
26. 1st Lt. Ajith Arok Juach Achol
27. 2nd Lt. Abit Lueth Jok
28. 2nd Lt. Dau Garang Dau
29. 2nd Lt. Biar Ajak Jok
30. 2ndLt. Biar Ajak Yoel Biar
31. 2nd Lt. Nyok Majak

And here is a list of women and children who had lost their lives in Nuer areas:
1. Adit Guot Ajak
2. Alek Chol Majok
3. Aruaal Garang Akuein
4. Achol Atem Kuer
5. Deng Garang Abit (Child)
6. Chol Deng Duot (Child)
7. Nyandeng Khot Deng Acuoth
8. Abuk Garang Ayur Bul
9. Achuei Nyuon Abui
10. Kuer Duot Bul Duot (Child)
11. Bul Duot Bul Duot (Child)
12. Bul Kuer Bul Duot (Child)

As mentioned above, here is the list of the Nuer members eliminated by the SPLM/A mainstream in cold blood in Lakes State and other South Sudan areas in 1991. I am so grateful to the Honourable Kwong Downhier and General James Koang Chol for this wonderful contribution.

1. A/Cdr Peter Kailech Toang
2. A/Cdr Daniel Gatwech Kuany
3. A/Cdr Peter Reath Koat
4. Capt. John Jok Reath
5. Capt. John Gatchai Thach
6. Capt. Diu Wang Lam
7. Capt. Gatwech Chang Jiel
8. Capt. Bor Dul Wethour
9. Capt. Jikeny Puot Yuot
10. Capt. Biel Gai Yang
11. Capt. Bol Chuol Gai
12. Capt. Charles Kuot Chatim
13. 1st Lt. Gatjang Kulang Pakur
14. 1st Lt. Jekow Biel
15. 1st Lt. Wang Gai
16. 2nd Lt. Mawar Ruot Diu
17. 2nd Lt. Koang Baguor Tuorkuny
18. 2nd Lt. Panyuan Madhier Yak
19. 2nd Lt. Gatluak Deng Jong
20. 2nd Lt. Tuach Riek
21. 2nd Lt. Ruon Thon Lith
22. 2nd Lt. Kuol Matil
23. 2nd Lt. Thony Gai
24. 2nd Lt. Madibo Koang
25. Gatwech Majok
26. S/M. Jual Tuach Yaat
27. Civilian. Gatyur Degay Biem
28. Civilian. Maley Lony Biem
29. Civilian. Gieng Lony Biem

The Fall of Kapoeta Town into the Hands of Khartoum Government on May 28, 1992

After the SPLA had withdrawn its forces from the Pibor area, the enemy marched into the town without firing a single bullet. It was unbelievable that the SPLA would relinquish Pibor to Khartoum, as easily as it happened. The act of the SPLA withdrawal from Pibor, motivated them and sharpened their appetite to gain more areas, without losing martyrs in the process. Hence, they moved more forces from Bor to Pibor towards the last week of April in 1992. The force which arrived in Pibor was the convoy aimed at capturing Kapoeta town in eastern Equatoria. This convoy faced the challenge of crossing the Kengen river when they started to move to Kapoeta. In the second week of May 1992, they overcame the Kengen river obstacle and crossed it after a hard labour. Commander Salva Kiir and his operational command officers in Boma became uncertain of the enemy intentions. Whether they intended to capture Boma or will they proceed to Kapoeta? Only time will tell exactly what the intentions of our enemy were.

In the first week of May, I left Boma for Kapoeta, then intended to proceed to Narus where the unaccompanied minors and the returnees were expected to stay. I arrived at Kapoeta in two minds. I considered returning to the military service where I would be reassigned to lead forces on the war front. However I had been appointed to refugee management three years prior and I had not yet been officially relieved from that assignment. It could therefore be seen by the SPLM/A top leadership to be disrespectful if I decided to abandon the job I'd been entrusted to implement. During the few days spent in Kapoeta, all I could think about was which decision to take. While I was considering my options, the enemy that caused havoc and instability to the SPLA/M forces in Boma had just bypassed it to the south, and was heading in the direction of Kapoeta. There was a sigh of relief in Boma, but fear and high alert in Kapoeta where members of my family were residing. The man in charge of the force in the town, Commander James Wani Igga, called an urgent meeting as soon as he heard of the new development about the enemy's movement and intentions. The meeting was attended solely by officers, and the commander requested the assistance of an officer to lead the forces to Kerkomoge, north of Kapoeta town, to prevent the advancing enemy forces. There was no hesitation when I raised my hand to affirm that I was willing to lead the force. The force was at Rwehito, under the command of Captain Majok Anyieth and they needed a senior officer to be in charge. The following morning, I received orders to prepare myself and a vehicle would be arranged to transport me that evening, to join the forces in Rwehito.

I arrived at Rwehito the evening of May 25, 1992. A radio message from Commander James Wani Igga ordering me to immediately leave Rwehito for Kerkomoge, was received by my radio operator and handed to me. I had no alternative but to implement the orders and departed with my forces on May 26, 1992. We walked for the entire night until we arrived at the targeted area. The ground was elevated and we stopped to erect the radio for communication. We attempted to find the possible site easy to locate the enemy position, but unfortunately we received word that the enemy convoy was using a different route altogether from the one we had followed. And there was no way we could confront the enemy in broad day light. They were well equipped and greater in numbers with around 3000 plus troops. I was ill-equipped with only 500 officers and men, thought by my commanders to be sufficient in preventing that huge and well-equipped enemy force. After realising that the enemy was using a different route, we decided to turn back to Rwehito using a parallel route with the aim of encountering them before they hit Kapoeta. The enemy, despite the fact they had heavy machinery, also walked the entire day to Rwehito where they spent the night. My force and I walked day and night until we arrived at Peringa village in the morning of May 28, 1992. This time the enemy was using vehicles and tanks on their move to Kapoeta, ready for action. The first enemy convoy managed to escap our ambush, but not the second. We fought for an hour but did not manage to stop them. I thought the second group had the better machinery. As we were fighting, they started to shell the town. After they realised the SPLA forces had ceased fighting, they packed up and resumed their journey to catch up with their frontline.

The battle and the fall of Kapoeta town, commenced exactly at 3:00pm. The enemy forces captured the town after one complete hour of fierce fighting. The forces defending the town withdrew to the south-eastern direction of Bonio. Many people fleeing Kapoeta were killed by the hostile community of Taposa around the town, especially the community of Khormashi, falling to the western side of Kapoeta. Commander James Wani Igga's headquarters, according to information I received afterwards from officers, fell into the ambush while fleeing the town. They fought back earnestly opening the way for others to pass through to the junction of Kapoeta, Torit, Kimatong and Chukudum road. My force and I converged at the mentioned junction where Commander James Wani was heading. At this junction, all who tracked this road were present which included my family, however my daughter only 17 months old, was missing. It was reported that, she was taken by a truck bringing relief food from Kenya to Kapoeta for displaced people living in the town. The young girl was received by passengers who were already on the truck. The moment her mother was about to climb onboard, the driver pulled away leaving her to fall on her stomach when she was five months pregnant. Thankfully no serious injuries were sustained, and the unborn child survived. My daughter went to Narus and from there to Nairobi/Kenya, under the care of family friends, Dr. Dau Aleer Abit and his wife Dr. Sitona Abd Allah Othman.

Reasons Leading to the Fall of Kapoeta, into the Hands of the Enemy

I would like to enlighten the readers on potential reasons for the fall of Kapoeta town. Firstly, Kapoeta was considered as a rear base by the leadership of the Movement and therefore no strong permanent force was earmarked for its defence. When the enemy convoy started moving from Bor, it was rumoured they were aiming to recapture Boma from the SPLA/M. Hence the forces collected from different places to defend Boma, were quickly dispatched. Commander Salva Kiir made sure the forces coming from Pibor and Kapoeta converged at Boma to aid in its defence. It was to the surprise of those at Boma town that the expected enemy did bypass them when heading towards Kapoeta. It became another headache for the SPLA/M operational command, on how to quickly rush those forces back to Kapoeta considering the approximate distance of 150kms between the two towns.

Secondly, meagre means of transportation hampered quick transport of the SPLA forces to the targeted town of Kapoeta. Thirdly, the enemy was a mechanised army using trucks in their mobility, unlike the SPLA that was at times moving on foot. Now, it became a marathon race to Kapoeta between the rivalling forces of the SPLA on one hand and government forces on the other. The former wanted to quickly reach Kapoeta to entrench itself in the town to repulse the enemy, while the latter wanted to go to the town before the former could make proper defences. In my opinion, the SPLA could have been in a better position defence wise, if my force was allowed to remain in town to build up their defences. This would have included digging trenches, setting up communications and making fox holes around town. Also, we could have contaminated the defensive frontage with anti-personnel land mines that could have scared the enemy when nearing our defences. With the Movement's lack of transport facilities, the enemy reached Kapoeta before the SPLA had the chance to build up its defences. Moreover, other forces who were deployed to defend the town, were still travelling from Boma to Kapoeta when the town fell. Therefore, the fall of Kapoeta was a consequential result of poor preparation to defend the town on the side of the SPLA.

The SPLA forces whom the enemy dislodged from town, withdrew to the south-east of Kapoeta and took a defensive position at Bonio. We also took a defensive position on the western side of Kapoeta, making sure the road to Torit was not passable. The enemy inside the town was completely sieged. In the middle of June 1992, the enemy decided to open the route to Torit in the west and the route to the Kenyan border south east of Kapoeta. As expected, moving two convoys out of town simultaneously was an impossibility. They therefore decided to open the route to Narus town to the Kenyan border. Commander Majak da' Agoot da' Atem had a huge and formidable force at Bonio, just 15kms south-east of the town. The enemy forces that came to Kapoeta didn't encounter a fierce battle even when they captured the town. Therefore, we all hoped to teach them a lesson they wouldn't forget and at the same time give them a bloody nose at the SPLA defensive position at Bonio.

The battle of Bonio began at 1:00pm and continued unabatedly for three hours after which government forces had to retreat to Kapoeta, leaving behind a great loss in manpower and equipment. The enemy underestimated the strength of the SPLA because of the easy victories they scored when capturing, Pochalla, Bor, Pibor and Kapoeta towns. With their defeat at Bonio, they started to believe the SPLA was a force to be reckoned with. The news of the government defeat at Bonio was circulated via radio and it was coupled with the news that SPLA forces had managed to enter Juba City on June 6, 1992. According to the Chairman's radio message to all units, he explained that the SPLA forces entered Juba and stayed for more than 10 hours forcing the enemy to withdraw to the northern side of the town. The news of the SPLA entering Juba, were celebrated all over the SPLM/A held areas. On the western side of Kapoeta we relaxed, knowing the enemy would not make it to Torit through this route. Therefore we were ordered to move to Torit to support the SPLA forces fighting the enemy earmarked for recapturing Torit town along the Juba/Torit road.

We started moving towards Torit, where we met Commander Kuol Manyang Juuk and Commander James Wani Igga who had left us a few days prior. Torit was nothing but a ghost town, as its inhabitants had evacuated in anticipation of the advancing enemy forces from Juba. Both Commanders advised us to proceed to the ambush site of Khor-Doleb. Upon arrival, we were received by Alternate Commander Kon Anyieth Mabil and many others who were manning the ambush site. He provided a short briefing on the general situation on the frontage and where the enemy was positioned. We were then deployed into the ambush site. We were allocated an area to cover to the left, meanwhile Captain Dhieu Warbek Ayuel was assigned to the right-hand side of the ambush area. The forces deployed on either side of the ambush area, were to stop the enemy flanking our forces either from either the north or south. The enemy convoy started moving from the nearby dry stream of Khor el Ingelizy, heading towards the ambush site of Khor Doleb. The enemy needed to cover a distance of 10-15kms within a two day period. They were 100% sure of the ambush laid ahead of them, and therefore they were extra cautious with every step they took. On our side, we were also attentive to every move they made as they were advancing towards the ambush site.

Knowing your enemy will soon arrive, is a terrible psychological test to endure. We hoped they would arrive as quickly as possible so the battle could commence. For our enemy, they would be expecting an ambush to be laid at any minute. That is probably why they dragged their feet for the first day, as we impatiently waited until it became dark. They spent the night very close to the ambush site. Everyone among us was sure we would clash in the morning of the following day. At 10:00am precisely, the two armies met in a fierce battle that lasted 5 hours of continuous fighting. Our forces lost ground and we withdrew to a nearby location of Lera-Lera, 6kms away from Khor Doleb. The report we then received from the headquarters of the Commander in Chief Dr. John Garang de Mabior regarding the result, was that the enemy had suffered 67 killed in action with hundreds injured. The death tally on our side, was 8 killed in action and over 20 injured. The reason our casualties were so low compared to our enemy, was because we fought in the trenches and fox holes, while the enemy were fighting on open ground. The fact they succeeded in dislodging us, was due to their superior armaments. The SPLA was relatively less equipped, only having the determination to challenge that well equipped Sudanese army.

The Last Battle of Lera-lera Before the Enemy Captured Torit Town

The last ambush laid against the sweeping enemy troops, was at Lera-lera a few miles to the west of Torit town. We again dug ourselves into the ground, in the form of trenches and foxholes, waiting for the enemy forces to advance to our position. As a precaution, we destroyed the bridge at the edge of Lera-lera to prevent the enemy's machinery from crossing to our side (especially the tanks and armoured vehicles). The ambush was laid along a dry stream at a width of 2–3kms. Some anti-personnel land mines were planted at strategic points along the ambush site to prevent the enemy reaching the frontage. Anti-tank artillery and other heavy machine guns were placed at strategic positions to destroy enemy machinery. At this point in time, it felt like it was our last opportunity to prevent the government forces reaching Torit. We had to throw our whole weight behind the operation at Lera-lera, believing that perhaps it might succeed after many previous endeavours. This operation of 'Saf- el-Obour' started in December 1991. By then it was an ongoing unabated process over eight months. They were overcoming one ambush after another, giving them high hopes of reaching Torit. It was becoming almost impossible to stop them reaching the town, and it was confirmed on our side that the enemy was unpreventable. It was only a matter of time before the enemy forces would capture Torit. The enemy had to spend seven days recovering from the bruises they sustained during the last battle. Their casualties were evacuated to the rear bases and they replenished what had been lost.

The invading forces then started moving from nearby Khor-Doleb, where they dislodged us a week earlier. As mentioned previously, it would take the whole day to reach the ambush site. It so happened that we unknowingly exposed our ambush site when the enemy forces were approaching the frontage. There was a small cutting in the low land close to the ambush site, that made the enemy to be suspicious and they opened fire onto it to check whether SPLA forces were present. This act was reciprocated by our artillery men from behind, thinking that our forces had already clashed with the advancing enemy. One or two mortar shells were fired by our mortar group. They quickly stopped firing when they were informed by our people on the front line, that the enemy was still some distance away from the ambush site. At this stage, the enemy had surely detected the ambush site and stopped at the Lera-lera bridge that was destroyed a few days prior. The sun was at the last stages of setting when they arrived. We contacted our officers on the frontline, advising them not to commence fighting at this late hour, but to wait until the following day. Reason being, it would have been difficult to control the soldiers at night. The two forces spent the night separated by a distance of only 100 metres. The following morning, the fight was about to begin when we received information that some of the enemy forces were boarding trucks to return to where they came from. We could not exactly work out their intentions. However, the return of that force was when we committed a grave mistake that caused us the battle of Lera-lera.

Our forces waited for the enemy to start advancing, but it was all in vain. They were waiting for that force to return then advance to the flank then start the fighting in the frontage. That force started fighting in our headquarters. They were about to capture the commander of the SPLA forces in this operation, Commander Isaac Obote Mamur and myself who was his deputy, but we narrowly escaped their attempts. With the fight at the rear, it was echoed on the frontage with heavy confrontation between the two armies. Our men were engulfed in the middle and couldn't hold their ground. They decided to casually withdraw to the rear resulting in us losing some heavy artilleries. These heavy artilleries mounted on trucks, were stuck in the bush while escaping the battlefield and hence were seized by the enemy. We therefore lost the battle of Lera-lera, but due to our strong spirit we were still determined to prevent the enemy reaching Torit town.

We regrouped then were advised by the leadership of the Movement to get into the town, destroy the Keneti Bridge and start defending. We fully complied with this advice. The bridge was blown up and we attempted to build defences around the town. The forces managed as best as they could but were unable to cover the whole town. We met with the commander of the forces, to decide whether to remain or move out of town, leaving the enemy to enter. Commander Obote Mamur, was not present when we were deciding on the best course of action to take. The outcome was, we would leave the town to the enemy and besiege it from all directions, hampering their movement. Indeed, we withdrew on the night of July 14, 1992, to Kilio. It was an orderly and well organised military evacuation. Kilio town was an NCA area with many abandoned buildings without a roof. Commander Mamur came to visit and instructed us to move to Iputu town, which became our temporary command headquarters. One task force under the command of Captain Elijah Biar Kuol, was left to control Kilio. A government convoy managed to enter Torit on July 19, four days after we had withdrawn.

At the beginning of August, Commander Mamur was directed by the leadership of the Movement to visit all Latuka areas to inform people about the recent military developments and to mobilise the communities. I remained in Iputu as Head of Administration, until my force and I were instructed by Commander Isaac Mamur Mete to move to Langabu to control Juba Torit road. This was to curve enemy movement along that road. We started to travel from Iputu to Langabu, which is a two day walk from morning to evening. We spent a night at Longyiero village, then started again early the following morning, walking until we reached Langabu late in the evening. There was an enemy convoy expected to be travelling from Liriya to Khor el Inglezi, our main target. After resting for a day, I sent my deputy, Alternate Commander Dhieu Warabek Ayuel, with the force to execute the mission. The expected enemy convoy did not show up for the whole week. They finally arrived at late sunset, when our men had already abandoned the site and proceeded to Khor el Inglezi without a fight. I was outraged by the outcome of the ambush, which resulted in me handing out a punishment. I was not cajoled by their excuses and ordered them to attack Khor el Inglezi the following day. Our force lost one person in the battle of Khor el Inglezi and two were wounded.

After regrouping at the base in Langabu Village, I received a radio message from Commander Mamur Mete ordering me to move to Magwi town south of Langabu immediately. I was to receive my final instructions in Magwi. It took us 1.5 days to walk from Langabu to Magwi. Upon arrival, Commander Mamur addressed the forces and instructed us to proceed to the nearby town of Ame (a displaced centre by then). A truck arrived to transport us to our destination. We wondered why we were brought to Ame village, which was far from the war front. At Ame Junction, I was called to Pageri town by Commander Mamur, to accompany some journalists who had arrived from Europe, to Iputu. They had requested to interview myself about the general situation around Torit. We had just lost the town some few days prior. The journalists hoped to ascertain whether the SPLA/M was still a force to be reckoned with. Secondly, whether the SPLA still had forces around Torit town. We arrived in Iputu with the journalists accompanied by the Sudan Relief and Rehabilitation Association (SRRA) Secretary of Information, Mr. Chaat Paul Nul Bior. I was interviewed in front of the huge army at Iputu, assuring the journalists that the SPLA/M was still intact and capable of winning on the war front, showing the besieged enemy at Torit. After two days, we then returned to Pageri and I reported the results of the visit to my commander Mamur Mete.

While with the journalists in Itupu, our forces managed to shoot down an enemy helicopter flying to Juba from Torit. A Norwegian journalist who was among the group, opted to remain behind when we travelled back to Pageri. He wanted to take photos of the helicopter as part of a main news story. That journalist unfortunately met his fate when returning to Pageri on September 28, 1992, the same day Commander William Nyuon Bany Machar rebelled from the SPLM/A mainstream wing. The SPLM/A, after the split of 1991, had weakened, losing many towns they had gained some years back. As a result, the SPLA/M Commanders were squeezed to the southern parts of the Equatorial border. Therefore Pageri

town was hosting the following distinguished SPLM/A commanders;
1. Chairman of the SPLM Movement and Commander in Chief of the SPLA Dr. John Garang de Mabior
2. Deputy Chairman William Nyuon Bany Machar
3. Chief of General Staff of the SPLA, Commander Salva Kiir Mayardit
4. Commander James Wani Igga
5. Commander Yusuf Kowa Maki
6. Commander Kuol Manyang Juuk
7. Commander Lual Diing Wal
8. Commander Gallerio Modi Wuornyang

It was observed that Commander William Nyuon Bany started to disobey the instructions of the Chairman of the Movement and Commander in Chief of the SPLA. This non-complaint behaviour from the Deputy Chairman, began when he returned from the Abuja/Nigeria round of peace talks with the Sudanese government in June 1992.

Commander William Nyuon was appointed to lead the SPLM delegation peace talks in Abuja/Nigeria, with the Sudanese government delegation. When it was observed that Commander William Nyuon could create unnecessary instability in the Movement, delegations were sent to him so he could amicably resolve his grievances, if any. However, the man was so adamant and would not listen to their advice. My force was called to Ame junction as a precautionary measure to address this mayhem, should William decide to rebel. Commander William Nyuon then did decide to rebel from the Movement. He began marching out from Pageri town on September 28, 1992, in broad daylight. It was decided that he should not be confronted, while still in town. He was allowed to move out of the Pageri area and be fought along the way to Magwi town. At the Ame displaced centre, William Nyuon was confronted by the SPLA/M forces, but he managed to evade the ambush and proceeded to Magwi. Innocent relief workers travelling from Polataka to Magwi, fell victim of the ambush site including the Norwegian journalist. The journalist was not able to accomplish the mission he'd remained behind to implement. He had decided to come back to Pageri and met with relief workers along the way. However, they unfortunately fell into that fateful ambush site at Ame where they all perished. The rebel commander, William Nyuon managed to avoid all SPLA/M held areas, as he went through to Lapon Hill.

People within the Movement's circles believed that Commander William Nyuon Bany wasn't pursued forcefully enough on his way to Lapon Hill. After his arrival without real and effective confrontation, many analysts thought the Nasir rebellion favourers started to reign amongst the SPLM/A mainstream. Those who were assigned to pursue Commander William Nyuon, were not sincere in their efforts. William Nyuons movement out of Pageri was a well-coordinated affair with the Nasir faction and some elements within the SPLM/A mainstream. Commander William was well hidden around Lapon, waiting for a detached force sent from Nasir to reinforce him in Eastern Equatoria. This force arrived at Lapon Hill in the middle of October and with that, the brewing rebellion within the SPLM/A mainstream was blown wide open. Most, if not all sons of Eastern Equatoria, deserted the mainstream and joined William Nyuon and the Nasir faction force under the command of Commander Peter Bol Kong. Undecided Isaac Obote Mamur, Pierre Ohere Okeruk and a few others, were left in the cold and were following the events very closely, maybe because they could be in a position to join the victorious side afterwards. Indeed, William Nyuon's morale was boosted by the new reinforcement of some Eastern Equatorian's, who started supporting his move against the SPLM/A mainstream. He did not receive resistance around Torit, until he came to Iputu where the SPLM/A had a reasonable force. The attacking forces of William Nyuon overran Iputu town evicting the SPLA forces. It was difficult to defend when the suspected forces were within or among the existing force. Iputu was not well defended due to the presence of those opposing elements from Eastern Equatoria, who managed to desert their positions upon hearing the first bullet. Instead of shooting at the attacking force, they would opt to turn their guns against their own comrades who they were expected to be defending the town with.

We in Magwi, under the command of Commander Salva Kiir Mayardit, decided to send our defending forces to Iputu to either liberate it from the forces of William Nyuon or stop them before they could attack Magwi. Our forces followed the road to Iputu but the enemy, who were not mechanised, took a different route on the way to Magwi. The aggressing forces made a surprise attack on the morning of November 11, 1992, dislodging a small defending force that had remained with us and captured the town. It was indeed a very brief fire exchange with the enemy. I remember being left in one part of the town with my runners and Captain Rin Tweny Mabor, not anticipating the rest of the defending force had already fled. The hasty withdrawal from the town, meant heavy machine guns and long-range communication radios had been left in Magwi together with personal belongings from Commander Salva's headquarters. They regrouped at Panyikwara village, which was on the way to the Ame displaced camp. When we arrived at Panyikwara with Captain Rin Tweny Mabor, we noticed the whole force had been reorganised by Commander Salva Kiir Mayardit, ready for a march back to Magwi. We automatically fell onto the line. At exactly 3:00pm, we began the march towards Magwi aiming to attack and recapture it. The operation started at 7:00pm with our first target being the grass store containing food and ammunitions. The RPG gunner assigned to execute the plan was very accurate, only needing to fire only one RPG shell to destroy the store. The burning of the ammo store was a difficult sight to bear, by the occupying forces of William Nyuon.

Despite the considerable effort exerted by our forces, they were not able to capture the town. They did prove however, they were not to be underestimated. The following morning, our forces were ordered to return to Magwi together with the red army under the command of Captain Mach Paul Kuol Awar, who had been forced out of Iputu by the same aggressing Nasir faction force. A firm siege on the town was laid, to restrict their movement. The operational developments at Magwi town made the Movement's leadership reassess, and therefore additional forces were ordered from around Juba to reinforce us at Magwi. Juba City was under siege by the SPLA forces after the two failed attempts to capture it. The first attempt was on June 6, as mentioned earlier, and the second one was on July 6, 1992. The two endeavours failed simply because our artillery could not make its way through into Juba City.

While the SPLA mainstream forces were to converge around Magwi town, we had the serious challenge of controlling the enemy inside Magwi. The dates of November 12 and 13 of 1992, are days I will never forget. Our patrols were clashing with SPLA Nasir faction forces in every corner. In the military system, there is nothing more important than reinforcement. We had been relieved of the challenges faced from the Nasir faction, when Commander Pieng Deng Kuol arrived at the small corner we were squeezed to. The morale of the forces was high, as Commander Pieng was getting briefed by Commander Salva Kiir. Commanders of the forces, Pieng Deng, Wilson Deng Kuochrot, William Deng Garang Bany, Mach Paul Kuol, Kuol Mayen Mading and Dhieu Aleu Anyang all met with Commander Salva Kiir Mayardit to plan how to conduct Magwi's forth coming operation. Indeed, Magwi town suffered a tremendous attack on November 14, 15 and 16 of 1992, all to no avail. The enemy, the SPLA Nasir Faction forces, firmly held their ground inside the town.

It was then decided the enemy should not be allowed an opportunity to rest, hence, we will attack by night and shell by day. On November 19, 1992, William Nyuon decided to withdraw from Magwi following the route leading to Torit.

Withdrawal of the Nasir faction forces from Magwi town was a huge relief to the SPLM/A mainstream, for the simple reason they had disturbingly arrived in the Movement's backyard. The Movement then took Pageri town as the new headquarters. Due to the fact the population from Bor had taken refuge in three displaced centres of Ame, Atepi and Aswa, it was not permittable on the side of the Movement's leadership to allow those who chased them away from their home area, to follow and evict them again from Eastern Equatoria. Also, the areas of Eastern Equatoria were a safe haven to the families of the SPLA/M fighters without exception. Fighting in Eastern Equatoria by the forces of Nasir faction, was a highly sensitive matter to the SPLM/A mainstream which they thought would only ever happen over their dead bodies. It was a no-go zone to any aggressor including the Sudanese government forces themselves.

We then quickly moved into Magwi town and began to organise the forces. Commander Pieng Deng was assigned the responsibility of pursuing William Nyuon's forces out of Eastern Equatoria. This was not an easy task, since the Nasir faction had won the confidence of the majority of Eastern Equatoria, including the communities around Torit town. Therefore, the SPLA mainstream forces would fight the main enemy in front, and be fought by their enemies from the rear and sides. William Nyuon took the route to Iputu and from there to Kilio, avoiding entering Torit which was under the control of the Sudanese government forces. The main challenge our forces encountered was the evacuation of the wounded soldiers to the rear, for medical attention. During this process, one of the SPLA's senior commanders Jok Reng Maghot was ambushed and injured in the eye while escorting the wounded soldiers from Kilio to Magwi. Myself, as mentioned before, was responsible for logistics for the second time since joining the Movement in March 1984, and hence was addressing logistical issues. I quickly searched for means of transport, to take the wounded men and officers to Aswa Hospital, for further medical treatment.

The pursuit that was mounted on William Nyuon and his forces, was so effective they put up little resistance. The only exception was in some areas north of Torit, particularly Loronyo and Lapon Hill where they managed to kill significant number of SPLA officers and men. In the last two battles, William Nyuon had narrowly escaped being captured. He finally reported himself with a few of his men to the enemy garrison town of Mugeri in January 1993. This brought an end to the disturbances his rebellion had caused to the SPLM/A mainstream in Eastern Equatoria.

Since the inception of the SPLM/A movement, there has never been - in my perspective - a tough and difficult year like 1992. The enemy (Khartoum government) was able to capture SPLM/A controlled towns and areas, one after another. Most of the SPLM/A gains in the Upper Nile and Eastern Equatorial regions which were acquired 9 years later, were quickly lost in secession to the enemy forces in a matter of four months. The only SPLM/A successes where they managed to stop the enemy, were achieved in the two fronts of Boo Bridge in Bahr el Gazal and Boma Plateau in the Upper Nile region. Commander James Hoth Mai with his forces, succeeded in defeating the enemy convoy purposely aimed at recapturing the Western Equatorial region from the SPLM/A forces. In the battle of Boo Bridge, the enemy was defeated, and they retreated to Wau town, leaving behind many men either dead or wounded, along with some heavy war machinery. The Western Equatorial region thankfully remained, after being firmly in control of the Movement SPLA/M.

The other victory against the NIF government in that year, was at the Boma Plateau. Commander Kuol Dem Kuol repulsed the attack mounted by the Sudanese government's army on Boma in June 1992. Their forces were beaten back to Pochalla after they suffered heavily, in terms of manpower and equipment. Two tanks were captured, and many dead bodies were found on the battle ground. The enemy suffered a third defeat at Bonio, when they attempted to open the route to Narus in June 1992 and in December 25 of the same year. Commander Majak da' Agoot beat them back to Kapoeta town, after they had suffered greatly. The three successes scored by the SPLM/A against the enemy forces made us walk with our heads held high, showing the year did not belong to Khartoum NIF alone, but to SPLM/A too. For me as a person, 1992 was also challenging year. It started at Pochalla when the enemy managed to evict us from town. Then came the Korkomege/Kapoeta losses, followed by the fall of Torit and concluding with William Nyuon capturing of Magwi, where I almost lost my dear life. Almighty God alone made me survive all the challenges of that year.

As I was comfortably carrying out my assigned logistics duties at Magwi under the command of Commander Salva Kiir Mayardit, I was ordered to report to the headquarters of Commander Kuol Manyang Juuk. I was then informed that I must take up a new assignment at the Ame displaced camp as the top administrator, replacing Mr. Maker Deng Malou. This came as a disappointment, since I was not ready to return to the same job I had been doing a year before. This was the reason I opted to lead the forces for Korkomege, to fight against the advancing enemy forces to Kapoeta in May 1992. Commander Kuol Manyang tried desperately to persuade me to accept the job, explaining it was a responsibility equal to facing the army on the war front, and more importantly, these are the people displaced from your own constituency and they need your service the way you did, in Pinyudo and Pochalla. I was left with no option other than to surrender to his pleadings and accept the challenge of running the administration in Ame.

After I took over the Ame displaced administration from Mr. Maker Deng Malou, I surveyed how to make changes to the old system and did my best to develop a new food distribution system. I changed the old guards, with the new ones. The new administration in addition to myself (the Chairman of the displaced camp), was composed of Mr. Maker Lual Kuol, Mr. Mayen Ngor Atem, Mr. Elijah Alier Ayom Aluong, Mr. Isaiah Chol Aruai Barach and many others. All in the camp were utterly emaciated and many of the children and elderly were dying in great numbers due to the poor diet provided. Relief food supplies composed of grains (sorghum or maize), oil, lentils or beans and salt, all in small quantities. Some non-food supplies e.g. blankets, used clothes and kitchen equipment, were provided by relief organisations. The food items supplied to the displaced people of Bor, did not match compare to what they had been accustomed to back home. They previously fed on milk, meat, fishes, butter and grains in large quantities. In Dinka and Nuer traditions, milk is the best food for children and the elderly. Subjecting them to feed only on relief items, was the main reason for their demise. Our policy as the new administration, was to make a difference from our predecessors. We changed the food distribution process, so that a group of five people deserved a bag of sorghum as well as a tin of oil, unlike the old system whereby everything was to be scaled with the cups. We were fortunate that food supplies became regular, sufficient and timely. Life at the Ame displaced camp, immediately improved for the better and it was sincerely reflected in the songs women sang, in praise of the new administration. Cases of death amongst camp inhabitants begun to reduce significantly. The number of people attending feeding centres, became minimal. The town life they have found themselves in, was completely different to the displaced Bor people, who had previously known country life. Some small cooperative shops were opened, which enabled camp inhabitants to buy essential commodities sourced from the nearby Ugandan markets.

Local dances, that the people of Bor are well known for, were commonly witnessed in the displaced camp. Marriages became a common activity to watch. All the practices mentioned above were indicators of a good life within the camp, which was what the administration had aspired to achieve.

However, we were faced with the challenge of providing the SPLM/A army with food, which was a bound responsibility of the community. The second lot of food rations for displaced people, had been drastically reduced after the first. We fell under the administration of the SRRA department, who dictated terms to us. They requested Ame contribute one third of their total rations to the SPLA army, which left only two thirds to the displaced population. Although the cut was unbearable, we still managed to fairly distribute an acceptable level to the displaced community. I tried to resist directives of the SRRA director, Mr. Mario Muor Muor, to reduce the amount to 150 instead of 300 cartons explaining that Ame's displaced camp was inhabited by a mainly rural population who were not knowledgeable on how to diversify their diet. My endeavours to help the situation fell on deaf ears as Mr. Mario, who was a man of his own decisions, could not adhere to such pleadings. You might have observed, there is no mention about Ame's contribution of sorghum to the SPLA army. This is because sorghum supplies in the camp were in abundance, unlike eatable oil which was supplied in small quantities, and therefore was a concern whenever a cut was made. Moreover, eatable oil was to be used for consumption and could also be sold for cash, unlike sorghum which was not found in any market in the vicinity of Uganda.

The other confrontation I experienced, was with the food monitors. They believed the style of food distribution we had adopted was not acceptable and distribution norms from displaced and refugee's centres worldwide, involved rationing by scale and weight. This is unlike the new style of providing it in blocks to the group to divide among themselves. If five people are allocated a bag of sorghum (50kgs) for a month, then it's issued unopened, which the monitors thought to have been a violation and illegal. It should have been opened then scaled in cups, to know how many cups each deserve. We could not heed to their opinion since the displaced people were happy with our style of distribution.

Christian Relief Services (CRS) NGO was the organisation in charge of food supplies to the three camps of Ame, Atepi and Aswa. Meanwhile the Norwegian People's Aid (NPA) was responsible for health services and other non-food items. NPA was running a hospital at Aswa which was considered a referral centre for serious cases that could not be addressed at the current level. This hospital was not only attending to the cases of displaced camps inhabitants but also treating the SPLA war wounded. So far, the SPLA was very active around Juba and Torit cities. My own young daughter, Aliei Jurkuch Barach, fell sick and was referred to Aswa for further medical treatment. From there she was referred to the Gulu Lashor hospital, but unfortunately the poor little girl only five months old, died of meningitis that had not been diagnosed prior.

This very sad news, was unfortunately broken to me by a European friend when we met unexpectantly at Ame. Such news in my culture (the Dinka Tribe) or in Africa generally, requires a special process to be conveyed firstly to the other family's close relatives, instead of being broken directly to the father of the diseased child that, I have sad news for you, the way that Khawaja was telling me. Of course, it was a question of culture. He was very unaware that it would hurt the feelings of the receiver but the Khawaja did his best. He let me know the death of my daughter, which otherwise may have taken days to be revealed. The news of the death of my little daughter, was coupled with the news of the death of my mother Abul de Mayen de Duot with her grandson Jurkuch Deu Barach Jurkuch. Their death had occurred at home some time back in 1993. I was then mourning the death of many family members. I was terribly saddened with this news, especially the death of my mother who I last saw in 1979. I had wished to see my dear mother alive, after such a long absence. We live as guests in this world and it would be difficult to design its affairs to your tone or liking, otherwise I would had wished to see my Mum, Abul-got de Mayen de Duot, before she could farewell this world.

Life at Ame became subsequently stable. It is worth mentioning that running such an administration is not as easy as others may imagine. Resources all over the area were very meagre. Whenever there was a distribution of food relief, you would witness many unregistered people flocking to the Ame displaced camp, expecting to get something from the administration, when they knew they weren't entitled to food rations. When they failed to get a carton or a tin of eatable oil, they would show their disappointment by abusing Ame's administration for not receiving food items like the registered camp members. Again, I would like to reiterate that eatable oil was the only relief item everyone required at home and was also for sale in the nearby markets of Uganda. Failing to grant this item alone to the needy people, would make you lose credibility in the eyes of friends and community members who would always hope to receive support from the camp's management. They believed food was available in large quantities only and the camp managers were denying them. Whenever distribution time drew near, you would feel sick not knowing how to appease the hovering, needy people.

I fell sick in February 1994 and had to be referred to Aswa hospital for further treatment. My health condition didn't improve and therefore I was referred again to the Gulu Lashore Hospital. It was discovered that I was suffering from hypertension (high blood pressure) and that was the reason why I was staggering while walking. I was very lucky, I must admit, and was on bed rest for more than a month which was a long time to correct my blood pressure. The doctor prescribed medicines to keep my pressure at the lowest level possible. Also, he advised me to avoid eating food that contained salt. Equally, I should avoid consuming fatty meat that may be a source of cholesterol, in order to maintain my dear life. I spent one month in Gulu undergoing medical treatment. My health condition improved to a satisfactory level, and I was discharged from Lashor Hospital with plenty of medicines to take daily, for the rest of my life. While in Gulu town in Northern Uganda, some unfavourable news about the Ame displaced camp was coming from Southern Sudan. Ame was attacked by bandits opposed to the SPLM/A, forcing displaced people to flee the area. What exactly happened at the Ame displaced camp? I will detail in the next paragraph.

Withdrawal of the Displaced People from Ame, Atepi and Aswa

Just as life in the Ame displaced camp became stable and was running smoothly, they were attacked by bandits who opposed to the SPLM/A, on night of March 6, 1994. Displaced people were forced to flee the area and head towards the southern border of Uganda. The population of Ame and Atepi looked for safer sanctuary and tracked the route of Owinykibul, Polataka and Pajwok all the way to Labone, a few kilometres away from the Ugandan border. Meanwhile, the Aswa inhabitants had to move and settle in the Mugali area very close to Nimule town. Whilst relief supplies could easily flow to Mugali inside the Sudanese border, it was a challenge for these supplies to be transported to Labone. There was no road from the small border town of Awan Alwi to Labone, inside Southern Sudan's border. The Ugandans were using an old ungraded road from Kitgum town to the border, which was used by small vehicles at times. Some bridges were not suitable for heavily loaded trucks. Work was required to open the route to Awan Alwi and a new road would need to be constructed to Labone, if food supplies were to be transported by land to Labone through Uganda.

The displaced population that travelled to Labone from inside Southern Sudan, were to get their supplies from Northern Uganda. Food supplies, although available, were not reaching the camp due to the road being un usable from northern Uganda. Therefore, hunger was looming in the camp. The displaced people who relied on relief food supplies, were experiencing unimaginable suffering. This was coupled with the heavy construction work that all camp inhabitants were subjected to. The displaced people who arrived at Labone were required to construct their lodging shelters for the accommodation of their families, which could not be underrated. The situation continued for two months, until the road construction was completed. Relief supplies started to flow regularly to the camp, and the Labone inhabitants breathed a deep sigh of relief. The Norwegian People's Aid (NPA) constructed a hospital that was addressing medical cases from the inhabitants of the Labone camp. Face Foundation had also constructed schools that were accommodating all school age children. Christian Relief Services (CRS) constructed huge stores and big Rabb Halls for food storage. Offices for local administration were also put in place by the camp administration. The busy stage of constructing Labone camp was over and life in the camp returned to normal, especially after the airstrip was laid which could receive small and relatively large aircrafts.

A short geographical description of Labone follows. It is located at southern most part of Southern Sudan and the community residing in this area are the Acholi tribe. We understand the Acholi people were divided by the colonialists into two; one parts in Northern Uganda and the other in the Sudan. The Acholis from this area were the host community to the displaced people of war, from other parts of Southern Sudan. Labone village is surrounded by mountains from the north to the south, and from east to west with the displaced camp situated towards the end of the Imatong ranges to the south. The land is dissected by many running streams. It is a gifted land, you can imagine. The weather is cooled with thick cloud filling the sky throughout the year, making rainfall very common and continuous for ten months a year. The land is so fertile, that anything planted will flourish. When the displaced population realised that the land of Labone can grow anything cultivated, they started to plant different crops in their small subsistence farms. They were able to obtain fresh food from their own backyard.

Life for the displaced people became distinctively stable, but there was a persistent problem of insecurity around the camp. The SPLA enemies were mounting offences against the Labone guards as well as the displaced people. Bandits of the Nasir faction conniving with locale outlaws, exerted consistent efforts to ensure the displaced people who were loyal to the SPLM/A mainstream, were dislodged from the Labone area. Therefore, a few skirmishes and running battles around the Labone displaced camp were unfortunately experienced. I would cite the first battle fought by SPLA against the Lord Resistant Army (LRA) on the outskirts of Labone at a place called Amisha on May 9, 1994, where my cousin Sergeant Yaak- Pager Akoi Jurkuch and two others were killed. I would also cite a major battle that was fought inside the Labone displaced camp on October 4, 1997, in which Alternate Commander Deng (Madoot) Leek Deng and 53 others were Killed by Equatorial defence forces.

Even though those battles were occurring, they were not posing a serious threat to the camp. The displaced people remained in Labone until the signing of the Comprehensive Peace Agreement (CPA) on January 9, 2005, which ended the long struggle for liberation that was fought between the north and south of Sudan. After the agreement was signed, the displaced population had to orderly abandon the camp and return to their respective states in Southern Sudan. As the displaced people left Labone, they wished a good future to the inhabitants of that gifted land.

The enemy forces that attacked the Ame displaced camp were not acting in isolation. They were coordinating their activities with the Khartoum government's army. Dr. Riek Machar, Commander William Nyuon Bany, and Dr. Lam Akol of the SPLM/A Nasir faction, were coordinating their activities with the Sudanese government against the SPLM/A mainstream. Sudanese armed forces were exerting efforts to push SPLA forces away from the sieged city of Juba. This was not a simple task for the government's forces to execute alone, without allied factions of the SPLM/A Nasir group and the Equatorial defence forces.

The strategy was to pinch the SPLM/A from behind and divert its attention away from Juba. A huge force earmarked to implement this project, was moving from Juba to Lobonok. They encountered strong SPLA forces on their way, near Rejaf town. This attempt occurred in the beginning of 1993. The enemy forces did manage to push SPLA forces to the Awiny Mountains, mid-way to Lobonok. Our men held their ground until the beginning of 1994, when another unfavourable condition emerged. Running streams in the area started to dry up, leaving our men with no water source. Water needed to be fetched from a distant location, near the disputed site. This subjected the SPLA forces to untold vulnerability. As a result, the SPLA forces had to abandon their strong defensive position at the Awiny Mountains. This event occurred in the first week of January 1994. SPLA forces, under Commander Oyay Deng Ajack, were driven to Aswa for the operation which took more than five months. In June 1994, they stood their ground across the Aswa River 15kms north of Nimule after the bridge had been demolished. The two forces remained facing each other for almost two years, when General Ogel was finally dislodged and chased away in 1996. The enemy did open another front of Magwi, Obbo, Palotaka and Pajwok and turned westward to Owinykibul and Pogei, in their endeavour to arrive at Nimule. It became an impossibility to reach, through the direct route of Aswa.

Again, the attempt of arriving at Nimule town through Magwi, Obbo, Palotaka and Pajwok, resulted in failure. They were given a bloody nose at Pogei and beaten back to Pajwok town, leaving behind many dead bodies including engineer Dr. Mohamoud Sharif.

On October 26, 1995, the SPLA forces launched a surprise and swift attack on the enemy position in Pajwok. It was captured and the SPLA continued capturing every outpost found on the way to Palotaka, and finally to Obbo that very same day. Every enemy defensive position encountered on the way to Magwi, was defeated. The enemy force at Owinykibul, destroyed their machinery after it made their escape impossible. The SPLA strong forces met little resistance at Magwi and proceeded to Ame Junction. From there they moved to Kit, cutting the main road that connects Juba with Nimule. There was a huge government force at Aswa under the command of Major General Ahmad Ogel, which was tasked with capturing Nimule from the SPLA forces. It seemed the enemy was encountered, when the SPLA forces stepped onto Juba-Nimule road. The government forces mounted a series of attacks in quick secession, with the hope of forcing the SPLA to retreat, but their endeavours did not materialise. Instead, the SPLA were steadily advancing towards Juba causing the government to change route to Lobonok. In order to bring an end to the continuous government rescue attempts, the SPLM/A leadership prepared a capable force to dislodge Major General Ahmad Ogel from his position at Aswa. In March 1996, the government position was finally assaulted and captured by the gallant SPLA forces under Commander Oyay Deng Ajak. They also evicted from the area, the arrogant Commander Ahmad Ogel, who then had no alternative but to track the road all the way to their headquarters in Juba. The SPLA now became the only master force manning the area around Aru Village and along the Juba-Nimule road.

SPLM/A First National Convention held in Chukudum April 1994

While at the Ame displaced camp in 1993, the SPLM/A planned to hold a convention to reshape its outdated structure. Most members of the Politico-Military High Command council were either detained or split. They formed their own factions and one prominent commander, William Nyuon Bany Machar, defected and joined the Nasir faction on September 28, 1992. There was a need for the SPLM/A mainstream to restructure and replenish the leadership.

The convention, which aimed to attract members from all areas under control of the SPLM/A mainstream, was firstly planned to be held at Pageri (known as Moli-Andero) which was a short distant east from the Juba-Nimule main road. Construction teams were formed to erect shelters at the proposed site. These teams were made up of residents from the three displaced camps of Ame, Atepi and Aswa. This important event was planned to take place towards the end of 1993, according to the preparatory committee led by the member of Politico-Military High Command, Commander Yusuf Kowa Maki. The members of the Secretariat Committee were;

1. Commander Elijah Malok Aleng de Mayen
2. Commander Pagan Amum Okich
3. Commander Yasir Saeed Arman
4. Commander Mario Muor Muor (SRRA) Secretary
5. Commander Abd el Aziz Adam el Hilu (Logistician)
6. Captain Michael Nyang Jok Alith
7. Captain Gabriel Alaak Garang Diing
8. Captain Isaiah Chol Aruai Barach
9. Captain Ayuel Bul Koach Atem

Discussion topics for the convention (among other things) were the following;
- Unity of the Sudan on a new basis
- Separation of South Sudan from the Sudan
- Progress on the war fronts

As the committee was preparing the event to be held in the Pageri area, some alarming signals were threatening the security situation. The enemy forces broke through our defensive lines around the Awiny mountains. There was no way the convention could be held in this area, and we had to decide on another venue which was more secure and safe. Chukudum town in Eastern Equatoria, was chosen as the new venue to host the first ever SPLM/A convention. Members of the convention who had already arrived in Pageri, were transported to the new proposed convention site of Chukudum. Transport was provided by the friendly government of Uganda. During the relocation process, a vehicle driven by a Ugandan soldier overturned at the border of Uganda and South Sudan, killing a score of people including Capt. Andrew Kuir Riek Kuol. I was nominated to attend the convention, and represent the Ame displaced camp. However, I was unable to attend due to my ongoing health condition.

The historic event successfully took place in April of 1994. Dr. John Garang de Mabior and his deputy, Commander Salva Kiir Mayardit were elected unopposed, to their respective positions of Chairman and Deputy Chairman of the Movement, for the first time in the history of the SPLM/A. All the SPLM/A structures were legitimised and would now be firmly followed when making decisions within the Movement circles. The two other important points, namely unity of Sudan on a new basis and the separation of the south from the Sudan, were brought to light. It was decided that the unity of Sudan on a new basis must be maintained, but people of Southern Sudan would be asked for their opinion over the unity of the country, if this failed to be achieved. The old system which the Movement had run, would be different.

When all dispersed from Chukudum, they knew new life was injected into the Movement and everyone was assured of their role to play in the implementation of the Movement's policies. What I would like to illustrate here is the election of Dr. John and Salva Kiir by the convention brought an end to any senior members of Politico-Military High Command who had deserted the Movement at any stage. If they requested a return to the SPLM/A, they would not be reinstated into his or her former position, no matter how senior they were and how much following they enjoyed among the southern population. The return of Commanders William Nyuon Bany and Kerbino Kuanyin Bol to the Movement in 1995 and 1997 respectively, did not permit them to return to their former positions. According to the Chukudum newly adopted policy, the Chairman of the Movement preferred to wait for the new leadership to sit and decide on whether the two Commanders would be reinstated into the ranks of the Movement. If they were to be reinstated, they would need to be considered by newly adopted structures, before allocating a position. The two commanders unfortunately passed on, before the status of their positions could be reconsidered or determined.

The only commander who managed to escape the system was Dr. Riek Machar Teny, who returned to the Movement in 2002 and was reinstated to his former position, after Commander Salva Kiir Mayardit and before Commander James Wani Igga. Commander Lam Akol Ajawin was unlucky not to receive the same treatment as Dr. Riek, when he returned to the Movement SPLM/A. He could not return to his former position after Commander Dr. Riek Machar. Commander Dr. Lam Akol believed his failure to be reinstated to his former position, was in the hands of the Chairman Dr. John Garang alone.

The issue in my opinion was that Dr. Riek Machar was reinstated due to his large following in the Nuer community. Meanwhile Dr. Lam Akol, though hailing from the Shiluk community, didn't conform to that consideration. When Dr. Riek Machar rebelled in 1991 against the SPLM Movement, the majority of the Nuer in the SPLA stood by him. Therefore, his return to the Movement was expected to draw back the large percentage of the population he took away in 1991. This situation was not the case for Dr. Lam Akol, as his followers were minimal. It was thought by the decision-making group, that his coming back will not add any significant weight to the Movement and therefore his claims to be reinstated were ignored.

The Family Travel from Gulu to Kakuma Refugee's Camp

While receiving treatment in Gulu, I received news that the Ame displaced camp was evacuated on March 6, 1994. I therefore decided to take my family to the Kakuma Refugee Camp in the northwest of Kenya. I believed it was wise to move the children to a safer place, where kids had the opportunity to enrol in schools and were supplied food by the United Nations High Commissioner for Refugees (UNHCR). My daughter Nyankiir Jurkuch Barach whom the family departed with in Kapoeta 1992, was in Kenya/Nairobi city with the family of my dear friend, Alternate Commander Dr. Dau Aleer Abit and his wife Dr. Sitona Abd el Allah Othman. I would ensure we passed via Nairobi to collect the young girl from the very caring and responsible family who had been looking after her. We would then proceed to Kakuma, and settle as refugees. I would then be free to participate effectively in the course of liberation, without hindrance.

We started our journey in the early morning of April 2, 1994, from Gulu where the family had been staying. We caught a bus heading to

Kampala and arrived at 5:00pm. We spent two days in Kampala preparing for our next journey to Nairobi/Kenya, where my young daughter was. It was not a simple task for a guerrilla man and his family, with no official documents, to cross the international borders of Uganda and Kenya. In addition to purchasing the bus tickets, we had to manoeuvre around and seek someone from the bus crew to facilitate us crossing into Kenya.

The journey commenced at 3:00pm and continued for the whole night, till morning. We had to briefly stop at a border checkpoint so we could illegally sneak into the Kenyan side of the border. At the checkpoint, we were fearful of being caught and denied entry to Kenya. We thanked God, that we finally managed to escape from the border checkpoint at Bussiya without hindrance and then continued our journey to Kisumu where we had dinner, then resumed our journey to Nairobi. My wife, Achol Juach Diing and I, found our beloved missing daughter, Nyankiir Jurkuch Barach, in the house of Dr. Dau Aleer. We introduced ourselves as her own and real missing parents and the two boys with us were her brothers.

I decided to remain behind in Nairobi but made the family proceed to the Kakuma Refugee Camp under the care of a brother and a friend Geu (Baboor) Ayuel Warabek, who was familiar with the camp. The family, as new arrivals to the camp, were briefly accommodated in the house of Geu Baboor. I later found them here, when I visited the camp. The family had the opportunity to construct their own accommodation shelters, after being provided with building materials by the camp administration. My son Yaak Jurkuch Barach joined Lodwar Primary School, leaving his siblings Ajang and Nyankiir with the family in the camp.

Life at the Kakuma Refugee Camp, was not in any sense the same as refuge life experienced in Western Ethiopia. The variance between the refugee life in the two countries, was that refugees in Ethiopia were masters of their own affairs. Refugees alone could deal and decide on their own issues without interference from the UNHCR and the country's administration. All the camp administrators would help with was the provision of relief items from the stores, when it was time for food distribution. This was not the situation in Northern Kenya where food distribution was planned and implemented by the camp administrators, surely, none of them were South Sudanese. In Western Ethiopia, refugees would construct their shelters on their own, using local construction materials. There was freedom of movement for a refugee, without restrictions from the Ethiopian administration. A refugee could at will travel to Addis Ababa without objection from the security personnel, a traveller may encounter on the way.

Relief items, though legally prohibited by law to be sold, would still find their way to the nearby markets of Gambella and other towns. The reason relief food items were finding their way to nearby markets without recognition from relief workers, was because relief food was in abundance. With that consideration, the refugee's financial situation was exceptional. Refugees by then, had the purchasing power competitive or equivalent to the local people or even better. Here in Northwest Kenya, there was no freedom of movement for the refugees. Construction materials were to be provided by the camp's administration to the camp inhabitants, the same way food rations were received. If a refugee from Kakuma wanted to travel to Lodwar or Loggichogio towns, they would have to prepare themselves not only for the bus fare pay, but also bribe money for police, so they can reach their destination safely. The difficulty was the many police checkpoints in all directions and their demand for payment would be the same.

In Kenya, a refugee is a person confirmed to the locality they are permitted to stay in, and should not be seen moving at free will unless there is a convincing reason. A refugee would be denied access to any direction, if he didn't otherwise have to comply with police interests. If you were thought to be undermining their authority, you could face violence or detention. Occasionally, if you encountered the police while travelling or walking in any of the town's streets, they would request your legal documents to verify. If considered authentic enough, they would then request a refugee to substantiate or support the document and compensate them with cash. Failure to do this, meant the end of your journey, with no return to where you even came from. A Kenyan police would be extremely delighted if they by chance met a fellow South Sudanese national or any foreigner. That would provide a good source of living for the day, for he would not be let to go without cash being handed over.

The reason Kenyan Police were adamant in seizing the South Sudanese, was because they knew the refugees would not be in possession of authentic and legal documents that would be shown upon request. This alone made them easy foray to thieve from, providing cash for living expenses. I must reiterate that it was not only South Sudanese refugees who were the target of the Kenyan police, but also refugees from other countries. The act of grabbing someone's property or money without any justifiable claim, was completely new to the South Sudanese. They hadn't previously experienced it at home nor in Ethiopia where we first took refuge. We came to the conclusion that in Kenya, a refugee has little or no social standing compared to a Kenyan citizen.

It should not be misconceived by the readers that the treatment subjected to the refugees in Kenya was a government policy. It was not at all. The Kenyan government was very friendly to the SPLM/A Movement. Our leaders were being accorded with diplomatic respect equivalent to that of the leaders of independent states. At times, the Chairman Dr. John Garang de Mabior would be received by having the red carpet rolled out when visiting Kenya. It is a practice always bestowed towards the head of a sovereign state. South Sudanese were enjoying their every right at the high government echelon. This was reflected at the time when the influx of South Sudanese first emerged at the border town of Loggichogio in May 1992. They were allocated land inside the Kenyan border near the town of Kakuma, which was established as a refugee camp to harbour more than 30,000 Sudanese refugees.

Refugees' worldwide are allocated land, inside the host country under the protection of the UNHCR. Hence South Sudanese were expected to be confined to the area provided by the host country and to receive services under the care of the UNHCR. However these refugees mentioned, were not ready to comply with the camp's rules and regulations. They wanted to visit different towns in Kenya for their own reasons but they were not permitted to be mobile. Being totally ignorant of how refugees live in a host country, the South Sudanese refugees would have been extremely irritated when questioned by the police about their identity. They were not aware the identification documents were required to be presented when requested by the police. They would see the police as an offending body when they were subjected to such questions, not understanding that police were executing their assigned duties. The South Sudanese allegations of police harassment on the road to Loki or Lodwar and in big cities such as Nairobi, Nakuru, Eldoret and others in my judgment, was of no substance. It was not only the refugees who would be asked to identify themselves, but also nationals would be questioned and asked to show their identification when necessary. My identity document was being requested so often by police at checkpoints, and I would show my SPLM ID card and be released without hindrance. There are official documents all people must possess in their own countries e.g. nationality certificate, personal ID card, birth certificate and a passport. You are expected to carry your passport when travelling outside of the country. This was often missing from the South Sudanese refugees living in Kenya and elsewhere, because some were rebel fighters fighting their own government so they wouldn't be expected to possess such documents. That fact alone was known to the Kenyan police, and they wanted to exploit it for their own benefit. The refugees were discouraged from travelling to other towns in Kenya, aiming to confine them to the Kakuma Refugee Camp. A refugee already under the care of the United Nations High Commissioner for Refugees (UNHCR), must obtain a travel document from the refugee administration to enable them get respect from the security personnel and police service when travelling. But that was not provided to the Sudanese refugees in Kenya.

The brutality experienced by South Sudanese refugees and other refugees living in Kenya, were not particularly meant for them alone. Instead, it was a way of life for every person living in Kenya, including nationals and foreigners. Robbery was common practice and was subjected to every Kenyan citizen. You could be easily robbed of your property in the streets of Nairobi and other cities in broad daylight. Your vehicle could be snatched at gun point in the street, never to be recovered. A house hold's belongings could be robbed from the family by night or day, but no criminals would be mentioned. Banks were robbed in the morning hours of the day by thieves, with no goods recovered. Any crime in Kenya could happen. No one should attribute blame to the Kenyan police for the tough action taken against criminals because it was necessary in that situation. South Sudanese and other refugees would have come under those repressive behaviours conditionally. This was the challenge the police hoped to end. This lifestyle drastically changed in 2002, when President Mwai Kibaki came to power through democratically conducted elections.

Job Opportunity with the Norwegian People's Aid (NPA) 1997-99

As I was shuttling between South Sudan and the Kakuma Refugee Camp where my family were residing, a job opportunity was presented with the Norwegian People's Aid (NPA) as an administrator at the Labone Displaced Camp. The NPA organisation was running two major relief services. The first being health services and the other supporting communities in the form of agricultural tools and knowledge, to fill the gaps due to the ongoing civil war. The NPA was a major food and health service provider outside the Operation Lifeline Sudan (OLS). It had established three big health facilities in Chukudum, Labone and Aswa, which was later relocated to Nimule when the area became insecure, and Yei after liberating it in 1998. The NPA organisation was rendering services to South Sudanese to their highest satisfaction. They were always readily available in the areas where other relief organisations could not reach, due to insecurity. That alone enabled the NPA to have a high level of respect amongst the South Sudanese.

The health coordinator who appointed me was Dr. Temesgen who hails from Ethiopia. The appointment opportunity received was so beneficial, that I was able to pull my family out of the Kakuma Refugee Camp to Eldoret, which provided better living and schooling for the children. I arrived to the Labone displaced camp to commence the new job. The inhabitants of the camp were the people I was managing three years prior at Ame. There were no challenges confronting me in the new position I had assumed at the NPA. The camp administrators and hospital staff were all former team workers. The only group I hadn't yet been acquainted with, was the international staff that descended from Ethiopia, Kenya and Uganda. We cooperated and respected each other as we implemented our assigned duties.

I spent only three months at the Labone displaced camp before being transferred to Nimule, as Chief Administrator for the health centre. In addition to the work in the compound where doctors and other international health workers lived, I would visit the hospital to inspect buildings and check other items that may need to be fixed in the health compound. It was a routine business that would take place on a daily basis. Stipend, in the form of salaries to the nurses and other health workers, would be paid at the end of every month. I would have to collect the income and up-keep money for the staff living in the compound from Nairobi, or else they would be brought by any visitor coming from Nairobi. In addition to the official assignment, I would also be implementing a coordination role in matters relating to the SPLA/M Movement. Being a senior SPLA officer, a due respect was usually accorded to me. This was especially shown by the young men rounded up by the army, who had deserted or abandoned their positions on the war front, preferring to stay in the displaced centres. The same process would apply for the health workers who would equally be rounded up like deserters, and they would require my presence to plea to the SPLA officer in charge to exempt them.

Feeling nostalgic towards the areas we had once lived in some years back, I was morally forced to pay a visit to Pageri, Aswa, Ame and more importantly to the former NPA compound at Choy. A former beautiful Choy compound was abandoned and became no-man's land. I could not believe my eyes when I saw it. The temporal structures built by the then Sudanese government and NPA, had disappeared completely with the semi concrete ones. Buildings were dilapidated. The view of the whole area showed me that, the only beautiful place on earth is where people do live in. The beautiful Pageri area along the Juba-Nimule road turned ugly in the absence of the inhabitants of the area, only two to three years prior. The invading forces of the Sudan government overran the whole area in 1994, from Moli up to Aswa where the SPLA forces managed to hold them back. Nimule town was within the reach of their long-range artillery. The NPA were receiving praises from the South Sudanese and the SPLM/A, because they used to stay with the people in the war front of Nimule, Mugali and other displaced camps, unlike other NGOs under the control of OLS. Those NGOs would always comply with OLS safety measures and surely had to distance themselves from the war front.

I stayed in Nimule for two years but was again referred back to Labone, before the end of 1999. My employment with NPA health service eventually ended there. I came back to live with the family at Eldoret, miserable without a job to do. Whilst in Eldoret, I was able to seize the opportunity of educating myself in computer technology. In the advanced world, office work cannot be performed without computer knowledge. There was no way one could find a job opportunity in a city like Nairobi without being computer literate, and hence it was a demand for me, under any condition, to implement it. I was promised by some NGOs to get employment with them in Southern Sudan or even in Nairobi city itself, should I become computer literate.

But all those efforts were later thwarted by the SPLM/A Movement. In February 2000, they asked me to be a representative of the Movement in Egypt and the Middle East, replacing Alternate Commander Arop Mayak Monytoach. This opportunity had diverted my plans. My focus and attention was to get a job that would enable me to provide a better education for my children and to keep the family away the unfavourable conditions of the Kakuma Refugee Camp. Free services from the UNHCR in terms of feeding and education were insufficient, and therefore we preferred to find a job and cater for one's own family. We also had to be mindful about the course of the southern Movement (SPLM/A), that had dealt away our time and energy for a good 17 years. We were questioning whether it was time for us to begin thinking about our families and forgetting the course of the southern people? What about the fighters who have forgotten about their families and are still engaged in battling the enemy? I then thought of forgetting my family for the bigger goal, being the liberation of Southern Sudanese people and hence, I had to succumb to the demand of going to Egypt as the Movement's representative.

Mr. Daniel Deng Athorbei was instructed to facilitate my journey to Egypt, for my new field of assignment. I had to acquire a travel document from the friendly country of Ethiopia. When the ticket was available, I left Kenya for Egypt on board an Egypt air flight on August 30, 2000. The Egyptian security personnel greeted me on arrival at the Cairo International Airport. I was immediately taken to a residential apartment where I met some South Sudanese who were managing the SPLM office. I was shown to the office the following morning. It only had two rooms, which could not accommodate the office staff and was ill-equipped. The staff were all students who had graduated from Egyptian universities and could not find their way back to Sudan because of war. They were above all, staunch supporters of the SPLM/A Movement. Every person there was working on a voluntarily basis. The office was lacking in resources to pay its own staff and they would therefore report to the office once the earning source was over and could report at their wish. Those I found in charge of the SPLM office hailed from different corners of the Sudan but the majority were from the South and Nuba Mountains. Among them were comrades Engineer Agoth Ngot (Maper) Riiny, Tangon Sebit, Omar Othoman, Rashid Ali and Omar Fur, just to mention a few. Permit fees from those wishing to visit Egypt from different parts of the world, were the only source of income that could be shared among the many operational staff in the office. Myself as the representative, was a host of the Egyptian government and therefore had to be paid dues for rent and upkeep from the presidency itself.

The office was situated at Miser el Jededah, a suburb far away from the Cairo city centre. At one point, the Egyptian authority thought to honour the SPLM/A by shifting the office to the city centre and upgrading it to a better building with capacity for more personnel. The new office was situated between Remsis and Ataba. It was relatively accommodative to our staff numbers. It was composed of three offices and a wide space sitting room. The communication system (landline telephone) was up to date but was restricted to internal communications, not outside Egypt. The new office was to be renovated before we could officially occupy it. After the renovation was complete, we were notified to officially move in by the concerned authority. As an SPLM/A political administration known to different Sudanese political parties, the Africans and international foreign services (embassies), we decided to have an official opening of the new office, so our location was well known to the diplomats and foreign representatives living in Egypt. The opening day came, and as we were preparing to receive the invited guests, a man strutting in a white police uniform emblazoned with stars, dropped into the office enquiring about the person in charge at the office. The police officer was a colonel sent from police headquarters to inform them of the name of the man in question. When he was given the name of Jurkuch Barach Jurkuch by the office's officials, he reported this to his commander. The commander in the head office then wanted to know the meaning of the name given to him by the colonel and he asked, what was the meaning of that name? The colonel explained it was like the traditional naming here in Egypt, "Hasab-allah Ismail Hasab-allah". As he was communicating this to his boss, and heard by the office staff, they were very amused by the colonel's interpretation of the meaning of the name "Jurkuch Barach Jurkuch", and to have that meaning in Arabic. They all laughed and communicated the whole affair to the Chairman Dr. John Garang and others before I could even learn about the new name given to me by the Egyptian colonel. I have become known by the name of Hasab-allah Ismail Hasab-allah. The new name became a code to be used by Dr. John Garang and his inner circles when he visited Egypt. He would tell those he preferred to accompany, that they would be visiting Hasab-allah's place. Anyway, the occasion went very smoothly after that and our office was visited by many delegates making our day very elegant, colourful and beautiful.

A week after my arrival in Cairo, it was arranged by the Egyptian authority that I should pay a visit to the presidency so I could be introduced to the top officials in the office. Whilst in the presidency, they asked me to present the accreditation letter which indicated my legal status as an official representative of the Movement in Egypt. The accreditation letter was disappointingly not in my possession. I was not aware that such a document needed to be presented to the higher authority of the host country. Those who were running the SPLM office in Kenya, I assumed, were not aware of such a procedure either. It was a diplomatic gap that showed we were just a guerrilla movement, not knowledgeable on many things in the field of diplomacy. The Egyptians took it well and assured me it was just procedural and will not make a difference in our working relationship. It is worth mentioning that ambassadors assigned to represent their nations in foreign countries, are usually received by the Head of State of the host country. That was not true in my case as I was just a representative of a guerrilla movement and therefore did not deserve to be introduced to the President of the Republic of Egypt. I returned to the office and continued with business as usual.

Egypt, as one of the leading Arab countries, had managed to create a special relationship with the SPLM/A Movement that took up arms against the government of Sudan. The support from the Egyptian government, though insignificant as it was, was viewed by Sudan and other Arab countries as a clear violation of the norms upon which the Arab League was created. Logically, Arab League member states should avoid close relationships with hostile body against one of their member states.

Although Egypt wasn't supporting the SPLM/A militarily, the Sudanese government was displeased with the assumed political ties.

What was the motivating reasons that prompted Egypt to permit itself to entertain the SPLM/A Movement? There were a number of reasons to cite here and in accordance with my perspective, the first reason was the river Nile. This is a lifeline to the Egyptian people and passes geographically through Southern Sudan. Consecutive Sudanese governments that came and went from power, didn't do much politically to end what Northern Sudanese called the 'southern problem', since the independence of Sudan on January 1, 1956. Should the people of the South, represented here by the SPLM/A, succeed in separating from Sudan, then they should not be seen tempering with Egypt's interest in the Nile. The second reason was that Egypt wanted to endear itself to the people of the South, to see that the war they were fighting against the Sudanese government was an internal issue. Therefore Sudan was not being supported by Egypt and all other Arab countries. Hence, the bitterness around the war would remain a Sudanese affair and excluded Egypt and other Arab state countries that were not buying northern ideas. The third reason was that Egypt, as a leading country in Africa, wanted to display justice in the Sudanese internal dispute, so they would not blindly support the north against the south, focusing on their own interests. I would like to highlight that Egypt had been big supporter of the Southern regional government, right upon the Addis Ababa Peace Agreement being signed in 1972, between Northern and Southern Sudan. The support provided, was in the field of education. Egypt accepted into their universities around 100 South Sudanese students every year. Many leading figures in the SPLM had graduated from Egyptian universities, myself included. This confirms the saying, if you want to help a person, give him a fishing net but not a fish. All in all, Egypt played a greater role in supporting the people of Southern Sudan and that was what they intended by keeping close political ties with the SPLM/A Movement during a difficult time by allowing the Movement a presence in itself.

Another Arab country who's contribution towards the Movement could not go unnoticed, is the Arab Democratic Socialist Republic of Libya. Libya, during the first days of the Movement's inception, made a significant impact in supplying the armaments to the SPLA/M in 1984. It was an open secret that President Moammar El Gadhafi of Libya had a sour political relationship with his counterpart, the Sudanese President Jaffar Mohamad Nimeiri. Gadhafi for so long had wanted the regime change in Khartoum. He found it was an opportunity to achieve his long-time dream when war broke out in the southern part of Sudan in 1983. He did not waste time in supplying arms to the Movement to implement his objective, when the SPLM/A delegation met with him in Tripoli. Those weapons became a strong foundation upon which the SPLA/M initiated the remarkable challenge to the government forces, in the first days of the Movement's establishment. It was after about a year when Jaffar Nimeiri's regime was sufficiently dealt with, in April 1985 in a popular mass uprising in Khartoum. It was a logical conclusion that President Jaffar Mohamad Nimeiri could not withstand the cleansing war in the southern part of the country and the strong popular uprising taking place in the capital city of Khartoum. He eventually succumbed to the reality of the situation when he returned from the United States of America. He was advised by Egypt's president Hosseini Mubarak, not to proceed to Khartoum since there was already a coup d'état in support of a mass uprising in his country.

President Moammar el Gadhafi's prime objective in supporting the SPLA/M, was just centred in the removal of President Jaffar Nimeiri from power in the Sudan. Since he had achieved that goal, he then started to advise Dr. John Garang de Mabior to cease the war against Sudan by agreeing with a new military junta in Khartoum, led by Lt General

Abd el Rahman Mohamad el Hassan Swar el Dhab. Of course, the southern revolution was not in any sense related to the regime change in Khartoum. John Garang adamantly refused to adhere to this advice and continued with the war of liberation in the south, demanding that a total change was required in the Sudan. In the end, the two had to part ways. Gadhafi ceased his military support to the SPLA/M and Garang proceeded with his war of liberation against the Sudan military junta and his collaborators. The situation remained the same for a year, until the elected government of Sadiq el Mahdi came to power in Khartoum in 1986.

After the opening ceremony of the SPLM office, the introduction process to the Sudanese parties in exile and diplomatic missions accredited to Egypt began to commence. We started with the Sudan National Democratic Alliance (NDA), which sat beside the SPLM, the Unionist Party under leadership of Moulana Mohamad Othman el Mirgani, the Sudan Communist Party, the Legitimate Command Council and finally the National UMA Party, which was outside the Sudan Democratic Alliance group. I was also introduced to other prominent Sudanese nationals. They were either politicians with no allies to any Sudanese known political parties, e.g. Farouk Abu Issa, or business people like Amin Akasha who originally descended from the north but spent most of his life in the south, mainly Juba town. Farouk Abu Issa was the head of the Union of the Arab's Advocates Association in Cairo city. Both Farouk and Amin agreed to support me during my time of need. Amin Akasha was formerly a member of the DUP Party but believed himself to be a full member of the SPLM/A to date, meanwhile Farouk Abu Issa was historically affiliated with the Sudanese Communist Party. He was the first Sudanese Minister of Foreign Affairs when Jaafar Mohamad Nimeiri assumed power by coup d'état on May 25, 1969. He fell out with General Nimeiri when Hashim el Atta attempted the coup d'état' against Jaffar Nimeiri that failed in July 19 & 22, 1971. Farouk then escaped to Egypt while his colleagues were rounded up and massacred in Khartoum. With the newly established National Democratic Alliance (NDA) in Sudan, Farouk Abu Issa wanted to seize the opportunity to resurface in the Sudanese political arena once again. Hence, he was a dedicated member of National Democratic Alliance (NDA), with its headquarters in Asmara.

By the way, I don't need to talk much about the South Sudanese nationals whom I found in Egypt. I knew many of them from long ago . I met many of them in the first few days of my arrival to Egypt. They were frequent and constant visitors to the SPLM office, together with members of the Nuba mountains and Ingasna hills. I had met them at one of their many social functions conducted in different parts of Cairo. Among the people I was with before the war, was Mr. Abdon Agaw Jok Nhial, before he left Egypt to resettle in Australia. Personally, I was pleased with the migration for those seeking political asylum abroad except for Mr. Abdon Agaw Jok. I believed Agaw was a rare cadre that should remain in the country to support the establishment of the Southern government and assist Sudan in achieving their independence. I had thought people migrating abroad, would end up staying indefinitely in the foreign land. I was completely wrong with this justification. It became a known fact that people can migrate and return to their homeland, should they wish to do so. Abdon Agaw Jok did indeed return to South Sudan and he is serving the government the way I believed he should. In fact, when I was in Egypt between 2000-2003, I never felt for one day that I was in a foreign land. At every occasion, I was being respected as a guest of honour. At times I would give lectures about the Movement's aims and objectives and so on and so forth.

It was routine for NDA members to meet once a month and sometimes an exceptional meeting would be called, if necessary. I left Egypt in late 1981 upon completion of my university study. This was at a time when the Sudanese population living in Egypt were mainly students and a tiny percentage compared to the Sudanese community living there at present. I was wondering why Sudanese people had been driven away (from both north and south) to this extent? In the light of my inquiries, I found out that the ruling elites of Muslim brotherhood were the only factor behind the Sudanese migration to Egypt and other countries around the world. Political opponents were scared of the unforgiving Islamic system reigning in the Sudan. Civil war in the south was at its peak, causing the economy to dwindle to its lowest level. I understood that areas where war was being intensively fought were surely affected, and therefore inhabitants of those states were justifiably excused to migrate from the country. However, it seemed the sickness that was affecting those states marred by civil war was also hitting those living in Khartoum itself. So, in the Sudan there was no safe haven for the politicians, businesspeople, moderate religious groups and other toiling citizens. Most of the Sudanese I found in Egypt had to win the daily bread for their households while serving in the houses of Egyptian families. This was completely unlike the life we had led when studying in Egypt. The opposite was true, in that we were employing Egyptian mates to serve us in our apartments. In the present conditions, Egypt turned out to be the springboard for the Sudanese wishing to migrate and go abroad for resettlement through the UN migration process. Many Sudanese found their way to the United States of America, Canada, Australia and Europe.

The other groups to meet and introduce myself to, were the diplomatic missions accredited to Egypt. I first met with the embassies of the USA and Britain. It seemed we had many things in common with those countries. The British were the Sudanese colonialists, who left the fate and future of the southern people under the control and leadership of the Arabs in the north. The moral support provided to the people of southern Sudan to repair the damage when they left Sudan, was incredible. Americans were no different in this regard. We were fighting Islamic fundamentalists in Khartoum, who were also enemies of the United States and the western world in general. American military diplomats were frequent visitors to the SPLM office. I was kept busy constantly relaying necessary information back and forth between the SPLM leadership and the embassies, as required.

The relationship with the western world had significantly improved for the better when the Islamists blasted two American embassies in Nairobi, Kenya and Dar salaam, Tanzania on August 7, 1998. They also destroyed and brought down the Twin Towers on September 11, 2001, in an unimaginable sight never previously witnessed by the world. American security was highly undermined by the terrorist act of high-jacking four American civilian airplanes and smashing two of them into the Twin Towers. The third plane hit the Pentagon, while passengers onboard on the fourth plane wrestled the high-jackers and crashed on a farm in Atlanta Georgia, before it could reach its possible target.

On the African side, we had frequent working relationships with the embassies of Ethiopia, Kenya, Uganda, Eretria and the Republic of South Africa. On the war front, we could succinctly observe contributions from Ethiopia, Eretria and Uganda when they faced the enemy side by side, with fellow SPLA fighters. The victories of 1995, 1996, 1997 and others to follow, wouldn't have been achieved without their helping hand. This was also reflected in the diplomatic field.

During my time, I participated in television and radio interviews. The interviews centred around the issues relating to the war front and aims and objectives of the Movement. Pro-Arabis's and Islamists interviewers would gear their questions towards unity of the country, not aware that Arabization and Islamification were the core sources of the Sudanese problems. The majority of the Sudanese are purely Africans and a good number of the Sudanese population are not Muslims either. Calling Sudanese holistically as Arabs, would affect the unity of the country. Likewise, calling them Muslims would also culminate in disagreement. The most appropriate term is to call them Sudanese, plain and simple, then among the Sudanese there are Muslims and non-Muslims. The paradox for all in the Arab and Islamic world, is that they are always pleased to call you in their name and their religion, and they would expect you to accept. Raising your eyebrows in objection to such an identity, would make you be seen as an anti-Arab or anti-Islam. Anyway, God the almighty was not silly in creating the world as colourful as it is now, and to unify it according to someone's best interest, would be a nightmare to obtain. The giants of the world; Americans, Russians and Chinese, would have tried their best to change the world to their liking, but the moment they tried to implement this, not find a single race in the world would support their philosophy.

One of the best journalists, Miss Asmaa el Husseini of the el Ahram daily newspaper, interviewed me on many occasions. She would invite me to attend many political functions she was attending. The Sudanese Ambassador to Egypt, Ahmad Abd el Haleem and I, participated in many debates on the Egyptian el Nile television, on the issues of war and peace in the Sudan and how best they can be peacefully addressed. As war intensified on the war front, peace negotiation efforts also intensified in Kenya. Islamists and fundamental Arabis, were seriously moved on July 22, 2002, when the two warring parties signed a memorandum of understanding at Machakos, Kenya. The agreed points were inter alia, that, people of the southern Sudan have the right to self-determination. This point to Muslim brotherhood, was like the whole world had risen up and could not understand how to sit down again. The following morning, representatives from the two Sudanese warring parties were invited to attend an important meeting in the office of the Egyptian Physicians Council, known in Egypt as the core of Islamists organisation. Sudanese Ambassador, Mr. Ahmad Abd el Haleem and myself, were in the meeting hall. We were both asked to deliver the views of his party.

I stated that Sudan was not ruled on an equal basis, there were elite Sudanese who lead and the low rank Sudanese would follow the masters. In other words, there were slaves and slave masters, in the composition of the Sudanese society. Most of the Sudanese population were true Africans, but the country was being identified as an Arab country with a serious religious domination by Muslims, over Christians. Unless those differences are abolished, we in the south would abide by the principles of the Machakos declaration. The Sudanese ambassador negated all that I had said and without being ashamed, called me a liar at the top of his voice. This led to the meeting organisers shutting him down, saying we were in an official meeting and there was no need for that depiction. The outcome of the meeting was that Egypt as a country and people, were not ready to have another country created along the Nile basin. Also, Egypt was not in a position to have another Israel in the south. This would include any other state created along the Nile that had political ties with the Jewish or Hebrew state. According to the Egyptian preference, they were adamantly concerned with Egypt's interests only, but not in fact aware that those interests were the fundamental reason behind the Sudanese instability. But anyway, it was not of their concern.

In a different context, I was subjected to many questions regarding the Nile waters, mainly what would happen to the Nile should South Sudan succeed in becoming a sovereign nation? Will the south be tempering with the water of the Nile e.g. building of dams along the Nile or diversion of the Nile for other directions of interest? My regular answer to such questions would explain that we would not build dams along the Nile, provided it would not interfere with the interest of the countries downstream nor divert the course of the Nile to our own interests. The reason is we don't irrigate agricultural schemes from the Nile, instead we depend very much on the rainwater for farming. Again, I was assuring the Egyptians that we cannot divert the course of the Nile to other directions, because there are so many tributaries that flow into the Nile and therefore rest assured that Egypt cannot be denied the Nile waters. Those answers were to diffuse the situation at the time. The questions from the Egyptians regarding the Nile waters, were mere fabrications and were politically motivated. They wanted the south to remain unified with the north, and accept being Arabs and adhere to Islam. According to their thinking, the Islamic religion must move into the interior of Africa through South Sudan. The Islamists in Sudan, Egypt and the whole Islamic world have one common objective which is that Islam should reign and be spread all over the world, either peacefully or forcefully. If that is the mission, then why should the south be standing against Islamic policy? In the end, Sudan and other Islamic countries of the world, have accepted that South Sudan should succeed. This would provide them with an opportunity to implement their arrogant Islamic and Arabic policies, without any objection or jeopardy.

Political meetings had intensified following the Machakos declaration of principles. The President of the United States of America, George W. Bush, had appointed Senator John Dan forth as his representative in Sudan, to bring the two warring parties to the negotiating table to find a peaceful solution to the longstanding problem. This had also coincided with the IGAD appointment of a Kenyan retired General, Lazaro Sambeyweo as the chief mediator between the Sudanese government and the SPLM/A. Senator John Dan forth started to shuttle between America and Africa. He was travelling to Kenya, Sudan and Egypt gathering opinions on the problem in Sudan, from concerned groups. I believe the solution to the southern problem we aspired to achieve, was reflected in the Machakos Declaration of Principles. The disputing ball was now thrown into the courtyard of Northern Sudan. They would either change the system of governance to let the country be ruled on equal basis, or else let the south succeed and forget about it.

Change of Venue and Two Chief Negotiators

General Lazaro Sambeyweo began to organise his office by initiating consultation with the two conflicting parties. He was advised to change the two chief negotiators, General Salva Kiir Mayardit from the SPLM/A and Dr. Gazi Salah el Din el Atabani from the Khartoum government. I can not specify the reasons why the two principal negotiators were changed, but what I am certain about is the two new principal negotiators were the top leaders of their own parties. They were, Dr John Garang de Mabior, Leader of the SPLM/A and Sheikh Ali Mohamad Othman Taha, Vice President of the Republic of the Sudan. It was designed so that the two chief negotiators would not have anyone to consult with or seek advice from. Sheikh Ali Othman Taha was fully mandated by his government, therefore their decisions would always be final. Again, the venue was also relocated to a resort situated on Lake Naivasha in Naivasha town, some 70kms northwest of Nairobi city. At first, when the two principal negotiators were called to the venue, they underrated the matter and thought they would return to their bases within a day or two. Ali Othman assured his circles in Khartoum of his quick return to the country, and likewise Dr. John did the same in Rumbek, when he was addressing his senior officer's conference. He thought he would continue with the conference in around 24hrs time. This was a misjudgement of the situation on both sides, as one whole month would elapse before they could temporarily return to their respective locations. They were required to stay in Naivasha until the end of the negotiations. Sheikh Ali Othman would visit Khartoum when there was a break or to attend religious functions with his family. Likewise, Dr. John would visit the war front only during matters of urgency, otherwise he would visit Nairobi where his family lived. This was the furthest point he could reach.

Mediators did not have time to waste. Topics to be discussed the following day, were prepared a day prior and would be the first items covered. People say, if you aim to walk a distance of one thousand miles, you must begin with one step. Indeed, it took two principals 1.5 years of non-stop peace negotiations until the Comprehensive Peace Agreement (CPA) to the Sudanese problem was finally initialled on January 9, 2005. I think the two principals were continuously receiving words of encouragement and appreciation from home and from the world leaders. The President of the United States, George W. Bush, took a leading role in advising the chief principles of the peace negotiations. Dr. John Garang and Ali Othman started to build confidence between themselves as they progressed in the hard negotiations. The United States Foreign Secretary, General Colin Powell, would frequently visit Kenya and Naivasha to acquaint himself with the progress of the peace negotiations. Signing of Comprehensive Peace Agreement (CPA) was a relief to all Sudanese people except the fighters of Western Sudan under the command of Abd el Wahid Ahmad el Nur, of the Sudan Liberation Movement Army (SLM/A) and those who wished South Sudan would not become an independent nation. Among the topics discussed were;

1. Governance
2. Security
3. Economy
4. Foreign Policy
5. The 3 areas of; Nuba Mountains, Southern Blue Nile and Abyei
   Considering the subjects mentioned above, you can grasp the

magnitude and dimension of the peace discussions. The approximate 1.5 years spent in peace negotiations, was tantamount to the size and the level of the war fought within the country.

The 9th of January 2005, was the day in which 1.5 years of continuous, difficult, hectic and meaningful peace negotiations were concluded. The long-awaited peace in the Sudan, was to be celebrated in the Kenyan Capital City of Nairobi. Nyayo National Stadium was the remarkable venue, where important dignitaries of the world were invited to share this joyous day with the Sudanese. The stadium was packed to the brim from the early hours of the date mentioned. Security personnel and the organising committee arranged the sitting. Planes hired from Khartoum transported many Sudanese according to their different states, to witness the signing of the peace agreement. The African President and world dignitaries invited to witness the ceremony, were in addition to President Omer Ahmad Hassen el Bashir, Sudan's former President General Jaffar Mohamed Nimeiri, the host President Mwai Kibaki and Kenyan former President, His Excellency Daniel arap Moi, Yoweri Kaguta Museveni of Uganda, Isaiah Afewerki of Eretria, President of the Republic of Somalia, Prime Minister Males Zenawi of Ethiopia, Secretary of Foreign Affairs Colin Powell of the United States of America, representative of the UN Secretary General, Arab League secretary Aamir Musa, representative from Troika countries Hon. Hilda Johnson, Secretary of the African Union and many other dignitaries.

Speeches were delivered from the host countries President, Mwai Kibaki, welcoming guests to this rare and formidable occasion. Following this, President Omer el Bashir passed on his regards to the two principals who made peace possible, followed by his deputy and one of the principals, Sheikh Ali Mohamad Othman Taha. He acknowledged the difficulty they faced, finding a peaceful solution to the Sudanese problem, hoping this peace would not be dishonoured by the Sudanese. Finally, he gave his regards to the world leaders who supported the Sudanese in reaching their goal. The last to speak on this occasion, was Dr. John Garang de Mabior who gave a long, articulated, touching and valuable speech. His point of difference from the other speakers, was that he concentrated on the issues of the implementation, saying we have brought peace on a silver platter, to the Sudanese people. It came after a long struggle. No single beloved Sudanese child would dare to die after this. The cost of not implementing this peace agreement, will be much higher than the cost of maintaining it. Hence, let us do our level best to keep it as a reward for those who fought and a reward for those who made it happen. The formidable day ended here, with the event vivid in the minds of those who attended and those who followed from both home and abroad.

My Mission and Residence in Egypt

While in Egypt, I performed regular duties at the SPLM office and I lived alone at my residential place in el Maadi. This was a suburb of Cairo, mainly inhabited by diplomats. I was thinking, if I had one of my wives by my side, the house would be complete. There was a potential risk of terrible marriage temptation, should I continue to lead this life alone. I was convinced beyond doubt, there was no sense in marrying a third wife in this world of economic challenges. I questioned what the requirements were, in bringing one wife from Kenya to Cairo. There were two challenges confronting me in this process. Firstly the aeroplane ticket and secondly the passport. Neither were easy to obtain. But there is an English proverb which says, "You never try, you never know". I had two people in my knowledge bank in Cairo, that I could approach regarding the aeroplane ticket. Those were none other than Mr. Amin Akasha and Ustaz Farouk Abu Issa, of the Arab lawyer's organisation.

For the second issue of the passport, I had many friends I was well acquainted with in the Sudanese police service. Among them was a brother and friend, Brigadier Riak Akon Riak, who was Police Chief Administrator in the port of Port Sudan. I wondered how possible would this be, since my wife Achol Juach Diing was not in Sudan and was also a wife of a rebel representing the Movement in Egypt. How could we struggle finding the legal means of identification, from a system that doesn't recognise either? If there was a leak of information to the authorities about this process, would it cause betrayal that might risk Riak's employment? These questions and many others were hovering in my mind. I then decided to be courageous, picked up a pen and wrote to Brigadier Riak Akon and said, "I am in Egypt as a representative of the SPLM/A Movement, all I need you to do is process a passport for my wife Achol Juach Diing, to enable her to travel to Cairo where I live. Remark that brother, I am staying alone in this city and I don't want to be tempted to marry another wife again, which could be possible if I continue to live alone. So please, rescue my situation brother". Riak Akon thankfully processed the passport immediately and it was dispatched to me. Upon receipt of the travel document, I had to contact the two friends Mr. Amin Akasha and Ustaz Farouk Abu Issa regarding the air-ticket which was thankfully provided. Our family was then immediately united in Cairo, in early 2002.

As the family was united, we were shocked by the sad news of our only daughter, Nyankiir Jurkuch Barach, being shot and killed by unknown robber when she was traveling from Eldoret to the Kakuma Refugee Camp to attend the head count. Brother Chaat Paul Nul Bior broke that sorrowful news to me. An armed man had stopped a Matatu bus with my children and others on board, aiming to steal passenger's properties. I wish he had done the robbing, however the driver did not heed his demand and continued driving the bus. The gunman didn't hesitate in showering the bus with live bullets and the innocent Nyankiir became the only victim of the mayhem. She bled till she passed away, on that long journey to Lodwar town. God the Almighty gives and takes and its name be glorified. Right upon hearing the unfortunate news of Nyankiir's death, the Egyptian government gave us two tickets and we immediately rushed to Kenya and proceeded to Kakuma, where we met with three brothers of the deceased. Final prayers were conducted in Kakuma with the rest of the family and we quickly had to return to Eldoret where the kids were. The return journey to Nairobi then Egypt, was successfully completed.

All South Sudanese residing in Egypt and the Sudanese in general, were extremely pleased with the peace negotiation progress taking place in Kenya. Peace was just around the corner, the Sudanese assumed. And indeed, peace was so near to be achieved. Whilst our focus and attention were geared towards that, I received a telephone call from the SPLM head office in Nairobi. They advised a team composed of twenty plus persons would be going to Hague in the Netherlands to attend a diplomatic training course and I was included among the group. In order to catch up with them, I had to quickly make the necessary visa arrangements in the Dutch Embassy in Egypt. Thankfully this process did not take long. I went to Dan-Hague as the last person of the team.

The group had already completed one week of training, but I did my best to catch up with them. The topic of the training was international relations among the world countries. International Pacts, e.g. North Atlantic Treaty Organisation (NATO), Warsaw Treaty (WT), African Union (AU), United Nations (UN), European Union (EU), Arab League (AL) and Asian's Union of Nations were thoroughly taught. We had to travel to Brussels and visited the UN's office of disarmament. It was a must that we paid a visit to Amsterdam and other historical places in the Netherlands. We were shown how their systems operate, particularly in Holland and other European nations. On the other hand, we found a huge Sudanese community that was eager to have time with us. Some people took the risk of a long drive from distant countries such as France and Italy, just to meet with the team. The training ended in a months' time and all had to disperse back to where we came from. It is worth mentioning that those who attended the training course, were not all from the Sudan or Africa, but also hailed from Great Britain, the United States of America and some other European countries. The common yardstick applied for their selection, was their commitment to the SPLM/A Movement.

Upon my arrival back in Cairo, I received a telephone call from a strange Sudanese person living in the United Arab Emirates. He introduced himself as Mohamad Ahmad Ibrahim, nicknamed as Mohamad Ardeb. He was eager to meet and exchange political ideas with the SPLM/A Leadership, especially Chairman Dr. John Garang de Mabior and his deputy General Salva Kiir Mayardit. He stated, the only way to achieve this was through the SPLM/A office in Egypt and the Middle East. Considering I was the head of that office, he opted to accomplish that through me. Splendid, I was more than happy to help, I replied to him. However, I also informed that I should be provided with an air ticket to Nairobi. He availed the ticket the following day, and I immediately travelled to Nairobi, our meeting venue. Dr. Dau Aleer Abit and I asked Ardeb if he could provide a gift in the form of a vehicle to the family of Dr. John. If so, that would be appreciated and Dr. Johns reception would be meaningful and respectable. He carefully heeded our advice and bought a V8 Toyota Landcruiser. It was a bit of luck that the Chairman was in either Nairobi or in the nearby town of Naivasha, where the peace negotiations were taking place. It was arranged that Mohamad Ardeb would meet with Dr. John on the morning of the appointed date.

His aim in meeting with the Chairman of the Movement was purely political. Ardeb was opposed to all systems that came and went in the Sudan and that's why he exiled to the United Arab Emirates, Dubai in particular. Although he was not a prominent political figure within the Sudanese national politics, we allowed him to meet the Chairman Dr. John Garang de Mabior, as long as he opposed the systems we had been fighting. After meeting with the Chairman, group photos were taken in remembrance of the two groups. Ardeb and his group left the Chairman's residence promising collaboration with the Movement during this peace time and afterwards. Another introductory meeting between General Salva Kiir and Ardeb was scheduled to take place in the Nairobi Hilton Hotel. This meeting was short and brief. We wanted the two to be introduced, since General Salva and Ardeb had not met prior. Ardeb and his family spent time in Nairobi, then moved to Asmara, Eritrea where he stayed until peace was finally initialled on January 9, 2005. It is worth mentioning that Mohamad Ardeb successfully played his political cards to his satisfaction. Contacting the SPLM/A Movement's leadership when peace was about to be signed, was relevant at this crucial time in his political life. Ardeb had no tangible political atmosphere back home to rely on, and therefore he was looking to springboard back to his country as a personality to be reckoned with, in the Sudanese political arena. He was then able to mount the van of peace with the returning SPLM/A members to the Sudan, and in recognition of his contribution, albeit brief, he was appointed as Khartoum North Deputy Mayor representing the SPLM/A.

There were other connections relating to prominent political and business personalities in the United Arab Emirates. One of those personalities was a businessman, Mr. Ahmad Ibrahim Lootah. Lootah owns a huge firm in Dubai. A good Samaritan hinted that I should contact him, as the head of the firm. He might be a good support to the Movement, if peace was around the corner. Lootah owners were interested in oil exploration, should the chance become available. The contact to the Lootah firm was conducted through the Samaritan, after which Ahmad Lootah with one of his advisors, paid a visit to where the chairman of the Movement was. The Chairman Dr. John Garang then met with the visiting team, and discussed areas of cooperation. I returned to Nairobi with Lootah's delegation, and then proceeded back to Dubai. Following Lootah's visit to South Sudan, the Movement's leadership were kindly asked to pay a visit to Dubai, in response to the visit they had paid to South Sudan. A three man delegation, led by Deng Alor Kuol, Dr. Dau Aleer Abit and myself were sent to Dubai to meet with senior staff members from the Lootah company. The delegation was accommodated in one of the best hotels in Dubai. A schedule to visit Lootah's companies was arranged. We visited the construction sites in the afternoon, in the unforgiving heat of the sun. I was born and lived in the hot African tropical weather, but the heat I experienced in the Arab peninsula was terribly alarming. I could not understand whether those living in the Gulf would be subjected to hell's punishment when judgement comes at the end of the world, as mentioned in the books of the prophets. Believe me, such heat was honestly unbearable. I was amazed when I saw people working under the scorching weather conditions. Our hosts prepared a working lunch for us. Seafood, which some of us were not fond of shewing, were among the dishes. Mr. Deng Alor Kuol opted to return to Kenya, leaving behind Dr. Dau and myself.

Behind in Dubai, we were able to meet with many Sudanese earning their living in the Gulf. Out of their contacts, we were privileged to meet with Prince Amir of Ajaman and his cabinet. Prince Amir was more concerned with political settlement, rather than the Sudanese. It was a touching issue for every Sudanese and we confirmed that it was only a matter of time before a solution to the chronic Sudanese problem would be found. And indeed, the Sudanese quagmire that took over twenty years of continuous fighting, finally ended after 18 months of non-stop negotiations. Two days was enough time for the two of us to spend in Dubai, before we returned to Nairobi. I was nominated to coordinate the SPLM/A's activities with the Lootah Commercial Firm, in addition to my diplomatic mission in Egypt and the middle-east. After that, I departed Kenya for Egypt - my final destination. The business at the SPLM/A consulate, was coming along splendidly. The United States Secretary, General Colin Powell, was constantly shuttling between America, Europe and Africa. I one day learnt of his visit to Kenya, specifically to inspect how the Sudanese peace process was progressing in Naivasha. I seized that as an opportunity to come to Kenya, to see things for myself. General Powell urged the Sudanese to grasp the opportunity to achieve peace, not only for their benefit but for the interest of the entire country. Peace was achieved at the end of 2004 but was officially celebrated in a buoyant ceremony attended by some of the world's highest ranked dignitaries. This event took place on January 9, 2005, at the Nyayo National Stadium in Nairobi, Kenya.

In coordination with the Lootah Company, I began to visit Dubai frequently. There wasn't a clear understanding between the head of the company and the Movement, to enable business to commence. The Lootah Company Manager was interested in oil exploration, as mentioned earlier. The Movement therefore decided to part ways with that company. I came back to Nairobi and became closer to Dr. Lual Achuek Lual Deng and Commander Kuol Manyang Juuk over the issues relating to future businesses. I was not ready to return to my duty station in Cairo for personal reasons. As I was deeply engaged in my personal affairs, I was involved in running some small businesses with some Kenyan nationals. Mr. Paul Konange and other business people were of great interest, with the hope to engage in business activities later in South Sudan. This was because peace was now around the corner, and the SPLM/A would be an outstanding body in the Sudanese political and business affairs, in their thinking, to endear themselves with. As a result, I rented an apartment in the suburb of Lavington in the most elegant part of Nairobi city.

My Appointment as Director of De-Mining Authority 24/8/2004

This position was held by Alternate Commander Aleu Ayany Aleu. The mine action programme surfaced for the first time in the areas held by the SPLM/A in 1997. This was when the international community agreed in Ottawa, Canada to ban production, use and transfer of anti-personnel land mines and destruction of their stockpiles in what was called the 'Ottawa Anti-Personnel Mine Ban Convention'. At this stage, although the SPLM/A were still a guerrilla movement fighting for liberation of the whole of Sudan from the ruling NIF Government, they managed to join the convention. The reason for banning production of the anti-personnel land mines, was due to the terrible way they maim their victims and the indiscriminate killing of innocent people, in addition to restricting movement of people and development in the contaminated areas. Mr. Aleu Ayany Aleu then established a non-government organisation which he named, Operation Save Innocent Lives (OSIL). He became the Director of OSIL NGO. The Sudan People's Liberation Movement/Army (SPLM/A), which was controlling Southern Sudan managed to establish mine action authority composing of the following departments;

1. Defence
2. Interior
3. Foreign Affairs
4. Health
5. Information

6. Education
7. Roads and Transport
8. Humanitarian Affairs and
9. Directorate of De-mining taking the role of secretariat.

Mr. Aleu, in addition to his position as the head of the OSIL organisation, was also assigned as the director of the newly established directorate of mine action in the SPLM/A. This duel responsibility, meant Mr. Aleu had to deal with all working international Non-Governmental Organisations (NGOs) and Indigenous Non-Governmental Organisations (INGO's) - OSIL included - conducting mine clearances in Southern Sudan. In executing the assigned responsibilities and duties, he greatly differed with some managers of working international NGOs. Mr. Aleu aimed to put the NGOs under his direct authority, which was encountered with resistance from the working NGOs. This rift didn't remain within Aleu's frame of authority but went beyond to other SPLM/A circles. The SPLM/A's top leadership were consulted to advise on the situation, but no tangible outcome would have brought harmony between the opposing sides of the NGOs and Mr. Aleu himself. Hence, a decision to remove Commander Aleu Ayany Aleu was reached and announced on August 24, 2004. The same decree that removed Commander Aleu Ayany Aleu, was the one used in appointing myself as his successor in the directorate of mine action. My assignment as the head of the SPLM office in Egypt came to a halt, as per the letter of this appointment.

The Composition of the De-Mining Directorate

There are five pillars which constitute the de-mining programme, which are outlined below;
1. **Mine Risk Education (MRE)**
2. **Mine Clearance (MC)**
3. **Victim Assistance (VA)**
4. **Stockpile Destruction**
5. **Advocacy.**

Every member state must commit to the above stated pillars, when conducting mine action activities in their territory. Following is a brief illustration of each of those five pillars;

1. Mine Risk Education (MRE)
This pillar educates communities on how to live in the anti-personnel landmine contaminated areas without harm or injury. It is a pledged responsibility from the working NGOs and mine action authority, to provide lessons to the population who reside in these conditions. Mine risk educators would educate those living in such areas, not to touch objects or metals they are unsure of. Instead, they are required to report such items to the authority. Again, they are warned to avoid the areas with signposts marked with red, clearly indicating danger. There are three colours that must be observed by the population. Signposts marked with red, indicate danger and therefore are a no-go zone, to be avoided at all cost. Signposts marked with yellow, indicate work of clearance is still in progress but not yet complete. Finally, signposts marked with white indicate it's a landmine free area and all are allowed to practice normal businesses in such areas.

2. Mines Clearance (MC)

Mine clearance is the main theme of mine action programme. All mine affected areas with anti-personnel landmines must be cleared of those unforgiving devices. Before conducting landmine removal from affected areas, a survey of contamination must first be completed and assessed. This process is technically known as 'landmine survey'. To determine the level of contamination, the survey team would either conduct a general or technical survey. The known contaminated areas would be recorded in a database, which would then determine which clearance method to use.

It is not an easy task to conduct a mine clearance programme. There must be NGO de-mining teams trained at competent institutions who are qualified for removing land mines in the affected zones. Medical personnel, who were well aware of the danger of landmine operations, must be equipped with medical accessories and address the de-mining teams on the possibility of unforeseen eventualities during the operation. De-mining personnel are classified as manual, canine and mechanical teams. Manual teams are always slower than dogs and mechanical de-mining teams. Mine Clearing Machines come in different sizes from the manufacturers (e.g. mine wolves, bozinas), that serve in the mine fields of the world's affected nations. Committed member states and other international community members, sponsor working international NGOs to clear those dangerous devices.

3. Victim Assistance (VA)

This pillar targets victims of land mines. It oversees the injured victims from the time of injury, to the time of hospital discharge. Victims of land mines and other vulnerabilities must be accorded with proper care from the concerned de-mining authority. Victims are supported in many ways, such as;

A. Rehabilitation centres for receiving discharged victims from hospitals to be established. A victim would spend time in the centre being rehabilitated and cautioned on how to cope with life after the injury. While staying in the rehabilitation centre, all life requirements must be made available to them and their family members.

B. Centres for production of prostheses and artificial limbs for the people with disabilities to be established. In these centres, victims are supported with artificial limbs and trained on how to walk while using them.

C. A small provision of cash to the victims or people with a disability to be provided. This would enable them to operate small shops to sustain and maintain themselves and their families.

D. Victims should be assisted by providing them with vocational knowledge. Provision of technical training in schools is vitally important. This would include;
   1. Carpentry Training Centre
   2. Plumbing Training Centre
   3. Construction and Brick Laying Training Centre
   4. Electrical Training Centre
   5. Mansion Training Centre

We do recognise that disability is not an inability, and therefore provision of such knowledge to people with a disability, should enable them to lead an independent life. Vulnerability and stigmatisation of the wounded should not be experienced, so long as they can be self-dependent in most aspects of life.

4. Stockpile Destruction

The Ottawa Mine Ban Convention directs member states to prohibit production, use and transfer of anti-personnel landmines and their destruction. Stores are to be completely emptied of landmine stocks. A country who has become a member state must set a timeline for destroying their stockpiles and report it to the UN for recognition. Member states may maintain very small quantities of anti-personnel landmines for training purposes.

5. Advocacy

This pillar ensures the committed member states worldwide, follow the rules and regulations of the antipersonnel mine ban convention through reports of landmines monitors and other non-government organisations. Independent monitors do closely keep track of each member state's commitment in relation to mine production, clearance and stockpile destruction and report it to the treaty members. Should there be any violation to the treaty agreement committed by any state member, it must be addressed in a forum convened by the state party members. No member state party is permitted to violate treaty norms in any sense.

My Assumption of Mine Action Directorate

Following my appointment as Director of Mine Action, there was no ceremonious handing over and takeover process that usually occurs when there is a change of guard in any administration. There was no independent or separate office established. Commander Aleu Ayany Aleu was conducting mine action operations in the premises of the OSIL organisation. He was the director of OSIL. The office equipment and a vehicle donated by UNMAS to the mine action directorate, were not received by the new administration. Directives from the SPLM/A leadership to release the equipment to the new administration, were defied. Things didn't go down smoothly between the Chairman of the Movement Dr. John Garang de Mabior and Nhial Deng Nhial on one side and Commander Aleu Ayany on the other. Commander Aleu was utterly disappointed with the recent development, accusing the Chairman of nepotism by appointing his hometown colleague to succeed him. This appointment rapidly got caught in political fire. The Movement's unity was given a serious test by those who sympathised with Aleu accusing the Chairman of favouring people from his home area.

When I took over the Directorate of Mine Action from Commander Aleu, I had to request new office equipment from the United Nations Mine Action Services (UNMAS). The UNMAS then happily provided us with sufficient office equipment and cash to rent a new office. A Toyota Land Cruiser vehicle was received sometime late in 2005 but could not be used in Kenya because it did not meet the legal requirements for registration. The vehicle was later placed with a temporary plate number for driving in Juba, South Sudan.

NGOs, international and indigenous working in South Sudan, had their head offices in Kenya. They all started to register with us. The United Nations Mine Action Services UNMAS acting as our counterpart, was and still in charge of all de-mining commercial companies and NGOs conducting mine clearance in South Sudan in collaboration with National Mine Action Authority. Being new in this field, I began to learn different fields of the mine action programme. The first experience encountered, was the first Mine Ban Convention held in 2004 in Nairobi, for the member state parties. The opening speech was delivered by Kenyan President, his Excellency Mwai Kibaki. It was attended by all member state countries and also by non-state actors of mine action. I represented the SPLM as a non-state actor but by then acted as a full member of the mine ban treaty. That alone gave the SPLM/A special respect among world countries, because it was still a guerrilla movement fighting for its own identity. The Sudan warring parties (Government of the Sudan and the Sudan People's Liberation Movement SPLM/A) were requested to hold a press conference to declare their position towards the convention and the peace process occurring in Naivasha town. Both parties committed themselves to peace and abiding with the treaty obligations. As mentioned earlier, the SPLM/A had committed itself to the convention since 1997 when landmines were completely banned from production, use, transfer and the destruction of their stockpiles.

After the first review conference on Mine Ban Convention, I learnt a lot about mine action activities and applied these terminologies as well. Introductions to the working NGOs and commercial demining companies, were a daily routine. The source of mine action support originated from UNMAS. The SPLM/A as a guerrilla movement could not successfully managed its own mine action programme, and therefore my office depended solely on international financial support. From the finances rendered to us by UNMAS, we rented an office in Lavington estate in Nairobi. Our administration began to get a grip on the operating NGOs and de-mining commercial companies. Inspection by management on de-mining units in the field, were felt by all. The NGOs and commercial companies conducting mine clearance in the south were the following:

1. Norwegian People's Aid (NPA)
2. Danish Demining Group (DDG)
3. Danish Church Aid (DCA)
4. Mechanical Chemical (MECHEM)
5. Mine Advisory Group (MAG)
6. HALO Trust
7. Operation Safe Innocent Lives (OSIL)
8. Sudan Integrated Landmines Information Response Initiative (SILIRI)

As a priority, clearance operations immediately commenced on the main roads near the Kenyan and Ugandan borders, leading right into the interior of Southern Sudan. The roads linking Nadipal, Narus and

Kapoeta were cleared and opened by MECHEM, a South African de-mining commercial company. The road was later extended from there to Torit and Juba. Meanwhile, the Nimule-Juba Road was cleared in 2004 and opened in 2005 by the HALO Trust. The same happened to the road linking Kaya, Yei and Juba city in the same years. The work on the main roads linking major towns in the south were completed in 2006/2007, providing easy access to all types of transport travelling in each destination. The challenge remained in the clearance of feeder roads, which linked small towns and villages with each other. Road rehabilitation started to emerge on the major roads, as removal of land mines is always aimed at the safe utilisation of the contaminated areas. Therefore, goods and other duty bound services began to flow without hindrance to the targeted destinations. Minefields in the inhabited locations were prioritised for clearance, so the land could be safely utilised by the owners.

Levels of landmine contamination showed the hatred between the warring parties was great. Subsistence farms for local people were mined as well as water points, boreholes, and lanes between villages. All the roads (major or feeder) were properly planted with anti-tanks and anti-personnel mines. Minefields, battlefields, defensive locations and the front areas between the two armies were highly mined with uncountable unexploded ordnance. With the present level of contaminations, we knew the task we faced was immense. I was able to visit every area where de-mining teams were operational. This was to witness the situation for myself and to encourage the de-miners to exert their best effort in combating those unforgiving devices.

When the Comprehensive Peace Agreement was signed in Nairobi on January 9, 2005, we had to relocate our office to Juba. However, this wasn't completed until the beginning of 2006. We agreed with our counterpart UNMAS, to jointly share one facility since the purpose of our objectives and operations were inseparable. During the visits I paid to Juba in 2005, I made sure land was put aside for future construction of an office for the

Mine Action Authority. Indeed, that land was approved by the government of the central Equatoria state. The most committed UNDP administration under the leadership of Qadeemtariq, provided us with pre-pap buildings which we occupied while construction was in progress of the permanent building we now occupy. There was no complication in requesting funds from the ministry of finance, so long as the monies were not misused. Funds were easily flowing from the ministry of finance and economic planning and the construction of the office was finalised in a short time. However, I must mention the UNMAS New York contributed further funds to finish the final touches, when the government funds were exhausted.

At the completion of the office's construction, we invited the Vice President Dr. Riek Machar Teny as the guest of honour for the opening ceremony in August 2009. We didn't want to let this big occasion pass unnoticed by any of the government's top men and dignitaries. The building was very large, comprising of 23 offices and conference rooms. It's been a pleasure to accommodate the Ministry of Higher Education in our building rent free, for the last two years. They were certainly appreciative. In my remarks in the opening ceremony of the building, I requested the Minister of Higher Education to look for their own new facility because two years was a generous offer, and their organisation was large . The Mine Action Authority compared to the Ministry of Higher Education was very small in size. Sharing a premise with them was becoming an obscuring factor, in our place where we wanted to shine. The Mine Action Authority's building was known to many people in Juba city as the Ministry of Higher Education. A feeling of envy was mounting and we, as management, decided to send them away so our status-quo remained. We were elevated high in the remarks of the Vice President and the Minister of Higher Education for a job well done. After the departure of the Ministry of Higher Education, we remained firmly prominent and proud in our compound.

Training at James Madison University (JMU), Virginia/USA

Being the Director of the Mine Action Directorate, I was nominated by UNMAS to attend a training course at James Madison University (JMU) in Virginia, USA in June 2005. I first had to travel to Geneva to attend inter-sessional meetings of the member state parties (MSP). My journey to Washington then started from Geneva to Amsterdam and from there to Heathrow, London. It was at midnight when we arrived with two other colleagues at the JMU compound, on June 23, 2005 from Angola. Training commenced after two days at JMU, when the expected number of participants had arrived . The trainees were drawn from the member states of affected countries, under the threat of anti-personnel mines and cluster munitions. The training sessions began at 8:00am and ended at 5:00pm. They were very comprehensive, educational and relevant to the member states attending . Lessons were taught in the classroom, then demonstrated and implemented in the field for the appropriate subjects. As training would progress, they would be punctuated with visits to locations of interest. Those would be historical and current locations in the history of the United States of America. Albeit, we did not succeed in visiting the White House although it was on the plan. The visit was cancelled at the last minute for reasons we could not anticipate. We concluded it was due to the very unfortunate incident that occurred in London on the very same day we were scheduled to visit the White House. The Islamist terrorists attacked the London underground railway and other locations, killing dozens of innocent people. Our lecturers took us straight to the freedom square, where names of the American freedom fighters who perished in America and other parts of the world, were displayed. From there, we went to the US Department of State, American Congress and the Pentagon. At midday, we were advised to go for lunch in the city centre using the underground metro on our own, then return to the meeting point for departure to the JMU compound, our last destination. Once all had returned to the meeting point, we started our journey back to the JMU compound at 5:00 pm.

Back in JMU, the university was on leave which made our lives easy in attending meals in the dining hall. Our day would start with breakfast, then into the classroom for 8:00am. Lunch was at midday then we returned to class at 2:00pm, and finishing at 6:00pm with supper. This was our routine, five days a week. As mentioned earlier, some subjects taught in the classroom would be demonstrated in the field. Hence, demolition of different types of landmines would be demonstrated to the participants at a chosen site. A newly manufactured de-mining machine and devices were demonstrated to the trainees, along with how to clear landmines in the minefields. This process continued for a full month, after which we finally graduated towards the end of July, 2005.

After the end of the JMU training in Virginia, I was bound for Africa and took a long flight to Nairobi from Washington, with two transits along the way . I spent only a day in Nairobi then proceeded to Rumbek, to attend an important workshop on de-mining scheduled for July 28, 2005. This workshop continued for two days after which we flew to Yei, to attend another 2-day workshop. Our flight arrived in Yei the morning of July 31 . In Yei, we arrived at our hotel accommodation . Towards the evening, things did not feel normal. Rumours of the whereabouts of the Movement's Chairman Dr. John Garang de Mabior, were not known. Speculation grew and it became no secret. Means of communication in Yei, and indeed in the South Sudan, were minimal. The select few people who were in the centre of events with real and correct information, didn't want to release it to the public for the fear of unknown. A group of senior officers (myself included), travelled to the residential house of the most senior SPLA officer in Yei, General Gier Chuong Aluong. This was to ascertain the facts about the rumours currently circulating in the mouths and ears of the town inhabitants. To no satisfaction, he was also unsure of what he was hearing. Gier himself was informed of the situation by Omega 15 (Bior Asoud-Ajang) in the afternoon of Sunday July 31st 2005, via radio contact. We were advised to return to our respective homes, until the following morning.

The speculation was that Dr. John Garang de Mabior left Entebbe for New Site on the Ugandan presidential helicopter in the evening of July 30, 2005, but had not reached the destination 24 hours later . The distance to New Site, was estimated to be less than one hour via helicopter. Everyone all over the south and in Yei in particular, lost hope that Dr. John would be found alive due to the following reasons;

1. The flight shouldn't have taken any longer than one hour
2. If they were forced to land for any reason, they could have communicated this to their headquarters or family members, which did not happen
3. After 24 hours they should have arrived at their destination, even if it meant walking by foot
4. Aircraft incidences are usually fateful, which confirms that Dr. John had already perished taking into consideration the helicopter had crashed and there was nowhere to recover him alive

In the evening of July 30, at the time he left Entebbe for New Site, Madam Rebecca de Mabior, Deng Dau Deng and other members of his headquarters travelled to the air strip to receive Dr. John at his expected arrival time. However, there was no sign of the helicopter. Madam Rebecca opted to return to the residential area because she didn't feel up to waiting at the air strip. She was later followed by those who remained behind, after the helicopter did not turn up and it started becoming dark.

Madam Rebecca together with those at New Site, began to enquire with those who the Chairman left at the departure point.

They confirmed his departure but were not aware he didn't reach his destination. People at New Site began contacting people along the expected route, attempting to ascertain facts about the Chairman's whereabouts, but with no convincing results.

The large SPLA/M force undergoing military training at New Cush, which is southwest of New Site, were contacted to find out whether they had seen a chopper flying over their area, heading in the direction of New Site. Unfortunately, no such sighting had taken place. They were then instructed to form a force to undertake a thorough search on the eastern valley on the road to Ngatinga, the following morning. The secret facts about the mission were revealed to the commander of the force, but not to the men. The search was implemented as planned, in the early morning of the 31st by the forces commanded by General Atem Agwang Atem. The site of the incident was eventually located. The body of Dr. John Garang de Mabior, along with the bodies of the other people on board the helicopter, were recovered and sent to New Site. This was the day we were travelling from Rumbek to Yei. News of the helicopter crash were highly concealed within the circles of the Movement. It was known to those who had the opportunity to listen to the media and the international broadcasting service houses e.g. BBC, Voice of America, CNN, Radio Detesch-Wella etc. It became a known secret to the majority of the Sudanese people after almost 24 hours of the Chairman's disappearance.

The following morning which was the 1st of August, all inhabitants of Yei gathered at the Yei River Hotel to hear the latest development on the fate of the Chairman Dr. John Garang. The most senior officers among all, were Gier Chuong Aluong and Garang Mabil Deng. They helplessly confirmed the death of Dr. John Garang de Mabior, on July 30, which was the day he went missing. All who gathered in the playground wept bitterly for the sudden demise of the leader of the Movement. That day was the darkest ever in the history of the SPLM/A, one would recall. All dispersed from there not certain of the Movement's future, following the death of their beloved Chairman. The group and I boarded a special plane heading to New Site, which was used as the headquarters of the SPLM/A Movement. I met with the wife of the late Chairman Dr. John, Madame Rebecca Nyandeng de Mabior, before being taken to see the remains of Dr. John. Senior members of the Movement including Deputy Chairman Salva Kiir Mayardit plus many other people from different corners of the world, started to flock to New Site to determine when and where the burial of Dr. John would take place. Above all, the central points to the Movement members was that the burial of the late chairman would be held after his successor was named and appointed. Ten senior members of the Movement met that evening and decided that Comrade Salva Kiir Mayardit, should be the new Chairman of the SPLM and Commander in Chief of the SPLA forces. A process thought to take a long time, was unexpectedly finalised within a brief period. This act demonstrated, the Southern Sudanese people were politically mature enough to run their own affairs. Some people believed the appointment of Dr. John's successor was going to be a tough process, due to the presence of the two ambitious 1991 coup planners - against Dr. John Garang. They were none other than Commander Dr. Riek Machar Teny and Commander Dr. Lam Akol Ajawin. The presence of the two gentlemen posed a real challenge. All those present at New Site, and other South Sudanese in the country and around the world, breathed a deep sigh of relief when they learned of the successful appointment of the new Movement leader, to succeed the late Dr. John.

The lingering questions in the mind of every concerned person regarding the death of the Chairman, were the following;

1. Was it a genuine accident or was it malice, to do away with the life of Dr. John Garang de Mabior?
2. Suppose it was an intentional ploy, who then was behind it?
3. What would have been the intentions of the killer/killers?
4. Who would become the next leader of the Movement, at this critical juncture?
5. Will the new leader follow in the footsteps of the late Dr. John?
6. Will the Khartoum administration have the will to cooperate with the new SPLM/A leader and respect the recently initialled Comprehensive Peace Agreement?

To discuss the questions above, I must begin with the first question which asks, **Was it a genuine accident or was it malice, to do away with the life of Dr. John Garang de Mabior?**

To begin with, no one was certain of the causes of the helicopter crash that claimed the life of the SPLM/A leader Dr. John Garang de Mabior. The helicopter assigned by the Ugandan President Yoweri Kaguta Museveni, to transport Dr. John Garang to his destination of New-Site, had departed Entebbe around 5:00pm. Dr. John Garang de Mabior and Yoweri Museveni became friends during school days in Tanzania, in the mid 1960's. It is known that Dr. John Garang with his colleagues, led an armed uprising in Bor on May 16, 1983. They indeed went to the bush and established the Sudan People's Liberation Movement/Army (SPLM/A) that same year. When Yoweri Museveni, who was also fighting in the bush, seized power in Uganda in 1986, they resumed their almost faded friendship. Hence, President Museveni became a staunch supporter of the SPLM/A Movement in addition to other friendly countries that I need not mention in this text. When Dr. John Garang went to Khartoum and assumed his official position as the first Vice President of the Republic of the Sudan. After three weeks in

Khartoum, he turned back to the south and proceeded to Uganda where he met his friend Museveni outside Kampala city, at his hometown of Mbarara. Dr. John boarded the presidential helicopter to Entebbe and from there to his last destination of New-Site. On the way, the helicopter crew could not evade the last obstacle to New-Site, which was the eastern range near Ngatinga. The chopper crashed, killing the Chairman of the SPLM and Commander in Chief of the SPLA, Dr. John Garang de Mabior, together with his four bodyguards and the crew on evening of July 30, 2005.

The SPLM/A representative to Uganda, General Riak Jeroboam Machuor Kulang, believes there was no malice in the death of the SPLM/A leader. He instead thinks it was a genuine accident due to weather conditions and the pilot's lack of geographical knowledge on the selected route. I for one, do blame those behind Dr. John's late departure at 5:00pm in July, the middle of the rainy season. Helicopters do fly low, but they cannot avoid clouds which hinder visibility during the rainy season. I believe this was the reason behind the chopper crash. General Riak thinks the pilot delayed the trip purposely, with the intention of spending the night at New-Site then returning to Entebbe the following day with a helicopter filled with gifts. This is in accordance with previous experiences, of those who went before him. He then blames the crash on the pilot for the late trip, but not any other politically motivated reasons.

I would like to write down the findings from the investigation team that was formed after the crash, and stated by General Gier Chuong. The findings were the crash was due to weather, human error and the c contradiction around the helicopter used by the late Dr. John Garang, on whether it was truly a presidential chopper used by President Yoweri Museveni or not? The black box (BTR) in the chopper was tempered with, spare parts used and the quality of services/maintenance was questionable.

Now to the second question, **"Suppose it was an intentional ploy, who then was behind it?"**

As mentioned earlier, no one was identified as planning to eliminate John Garang de Mabior during the incident that occurred on July 30, 2005. The investigation committee was led by justice Abel Alier Kuai Kut, a prominent South Sudanese who was the Vice President of the Republic of the Sudan and the first President of the High Executive Council of the southern government in 1972, after the Addis Ababa Peace Agreement. The investigation came out with no fingers being pointed against any person in the Sudanese government or against anyone in the region. However, many people believed the crash was not a mere accident, committed by the crew. The justification of those who held this idea, was that the chopper was a presidential chopper used by the President of the Republic of Uganda for normal trips. This meant it was well equipped with night vision devices that would sense danger from a distance and would send an alarm to the pilot before it could hit the object. Therefore, there must have been someone somewhere behind the crash. But Commander Riak Jeroboam blames the pilot for the late flight and that was the only factor behind the crash. Those of that opinion were not very far from the truth, because the black box equipment placed in the chopper was later found by the investigation team to have been damaged and it failed to record the reason behind the helicopter crash. Some people believe the chopper was changed at the last minute in Entebbe, and the helicopter that took John Garang was not the presidential chopper used by President Yoweri Kaguta Museveni. This allegation is being disputed by Commander Riak as a baseless allegation, meant only to confuse the public.

Here, we can conclude there was no political figure or ploy in Commander Riak's opinion that was behind the helicopter crash. If there was a reason to point a finger in any direction, it should be directed towards the pilot for unnecessarily delaying the trip until late in the evening, when clouds and rain were present . Also the assumed presidential chopper, hadn't been serviced in a long time. This could have ultimately resulted in the damage of the black box which therefore could not record the reason behind the chopper crash.

The third question demands, **"What would have been the intentions of the killer/killers?"**

According to what was discussed in the second question, it seems there was no political ploy in the death of Dr. John, only negligence on the side of the pilot, for reasons articulated above. However, the following is my personal opinion which does not rule out other opinions. There might have been a ploy against Dr. John Garang de Mabior, planned by those against him from the north and south, which were many. I therefore should not be wrongly misunderstood or judged of denying the planned elimination of Dr. John by those who were against him. Time may later reveal which opinion was true.

The fourth question is, **"Who will be the next leader of the Movement at this critical juncture?"**

By then, Dr. John had been deputised by General Salva Kiir Mayardit since 1992, when the man who was a deputy to Dr. John rebelled. William Nyuon Bany Machar decided to rebel against the Movement in Pageri on September 28, 1992. Dr. John was left with no option except appointing a deputy who would assist him in deciding upon the Movement's issues. General Salva Kiir Mayardit, was the third person in the Movement's hierarchy. As previously stated in the former chapters of this book, the historical members who led the formation of the Movement in 1983 were;

1. Colonel Dr. John Garang De Mabior / Chairman of the SPLM and Commander in Chief of the SPLA.
2. Lt. Col. Kerbino Kuanyin Bol / Deputy Chairman of the SPLM/A
3. Lt. Col. William Nyuon Bany / Chief of Staff
4. Major Salva Kiir Mayardit / Deputy Chief of Staff for Operations
5. Major Arok Thon Arok / Deputy Chief of Staff for Administration

This group later named themselves as permanent members of the Politico-Military High Command. Meanwhile, those who were promoted to the same office due to their performance in the field of operations, were given the name of Alternate Members of Politico-Military High Command. And they were as follow:

1. Major: John Kulang Puot / Member
2. Major: Nyachigak Ngacilok / Member
3. Lt Col. Dr. Riek Machar Teny / Member
4. Major: Dr. Lam Akol Ajawin / Member
5. Major: James Wani Igga / Member
6. Major: Yusif Kwoa Meki / Member
7. Lt. Col. Daniel Awet Akot / Member
8. Lt. Col. Martin Manyiel Ayuel / Member
9. Lt. Col. Kuol Manyang Juuk / Member
10. Lt. Col. Gallerio Modi Huronyang / Member
11. Lt. Col. Lual Diing Wal / Member
12. General, Gordon Kong Chol / Member

With the defection of Lt. Col. Kerbino Kuanyin Bol and Lt. Col. William Nyuon Bany, Major Salva Kiir became the second man in command of the SPLM/A until the signing of the Comprehensive Peace Agreement on January 9 2005. With the new development relating to the death of the leader, Dr. John, all members of High Command had to converge at New-Site to address the challenging leadership question of who will be the successor. All members of the Politico-Military High Command (mentioned above), were present except those who were far away. The most senior among the group were General Salva Kiir Mayardit, General Dr. Riek Machar Teny, General James Wani Igga, General Dr. Lam Akol Ajawin, General Daniel Awet Akot and General Kuol Manyang Juuk. Also, General Elijah Malok Aleng de Mayen and General Chagai Atem de Biar were senior people to be reckoned with at such tempting moments. The group entered the meeting hall, including General Elijah Malok. With an atmosphere of uncertainty surrounding the meeting hall, we were relieved when it was revealed that General Salva Kiir Mayardit had been chosen by the group to be the new Chairman of the SPLM and Commander in Chief of the SPLA forces. This occurred without hesitation or opposition from those attending. All at New-Site, without exception, did happily accept the outcome of the meeting, and congratulatory messages were written to the new leader of the Movement, Salva Kiir Mayardit, for his assumption of the new leadership position.

The next question is, **"Will the new leader follow in the footsteps of the late Dr. John?"**

The answer to this question will solely depend on the reader of the political and economic situation in the country under Salva Kiir's leadership. Each reader will have to focus on the prevailing developmental aspect and security situation in the new southern administration. Also, the relationship of South Sudan with the neighbouring countries and the world at large, must be evaluated. To correctly conclude whether General Salva Kiir will follow in the footsteps of Dr. John, a fair comparison between the two leaders must be completed.

Will the Khartoum administration have the will to cooperate with the new SPLM/A leader and respect the Comprehensive Peace Agreement (CPA)?

There's no doubt the Khartoum government did what pessimists didn't expect. They respected the CPA and accepted General Salva Kiir to be the first Vice President of the Republic and the President of the southern interim government for the coming interim period leading to a referendum. Thank God the prayers of hundreds of thousands of Sudanese people were answered, and we were not again bound to a devastating war. The Islamists didn't want to return to an open war with the south, at least for then. They preferred to disturb southern administration by fighting a proxy war and instigate their southern supporters to initiate it. This was what occurred in Malakal town when the marauding Gabriel Tang Gienya of Anyanya 11, broke out on several occasions and fought against the SPLA forces. This was echoed in many towns in the south where selfish and arrogant Khartoum supporters were found. These behaviours on the side of Khartoum were clear indicators that the Khartoum government, which had signed the CPA with the SPLM/A, was not genuinely interested in achieving peace. Though Khartoum was not sincere in the implementation of the CPA, they could not come out openly against it. It is a known fact, the consequences of undermining the CPA would have been unimaginably sky rocketing. Hence, they opted to continue with the peace until the referendum that led to the separation of the south from the north was finally achieved.

The Burial of Dr. John Garang de Mabior in Juba, August 6, 2005

There was much speculation around where Dr. John Garang de Mabior's burial would take place. His family decided he should be buried in his home village of Wangkulei. Other decision makers from Jonglei State, felt he should be buried in the capital city of Jonglei (Bor town). The SPLM/A leadership disregarded those suggestions and finally decided he should be buried in the capital city of the Southern Sudan, that is Juba, claiming Dr John was the leader of the Southern Movement and therefore, deserved to be laid to rest in Juba city. Laying him to rest in Bor town, or Wangkulei, would localise him as the leader of the southern people, they argued. The family and the Jonglei State leaders were convinced by southern leaders and complied with their opinion that he should be rested in Juba city.

Since Dr. John was the leader of the Sudan People's Liberation Movement (SPLM) and Sudan People's Liberation Army (SPLA) this meant his body would be toured in the liberated areas under his command. The first leg of the tour commenced in Kurmuk town, in the Ingesstina hills, south-east of the Sudan. It would then be flown to Kauda town in the Nuba Mountains in Southern Kurdufan, and from there to Rumbek capital of the Lakes State. Next was Yei town and finally from there to Juba city, where the burial would officially take place. The Sudanese leaders, led by the President of the Republic Omar Hassan Ahmad el Bashir and distinguished dignitaries of the world witnessed the burial of Dr. John at the site which is known today as the Mausoleum. Prayers were firstly conducted at the Juba All Saints Cathedral in Mobil. Speeches were delivered by the following people, Madam Rebecca de Mabior, Mabior Garang de Mabior (son of the late leader), the late long-time friend Ugandan President Yoweri Kaguta Museveni, President of the Republic of the Sudan Omar el Bashir and General Salva Kiir Mayardit, who was 1ˢᵗ Vice President of the Republic and President of the interim government of Southern Sudan. The sight was unforgettable, as fainted mourners were being rushed into ambulances, to transport them to the nearby Juba teaching hospital. Indeed, the death of Dr. John Garang de Mabior to the mourners in Juba was equated to almost being the prophesized end of the world. I can remember some heart-broken people saying they wished he had come to Juba walking on his feet, not in a coffin. Truly, his demise was of a giant, which the whole world will never forget.

Formation of the Southern Sudan Government and the appointment of the Southern Representatives in the Government of National Unity

After the ceremonial burial of Dr. John Garang de Mabior in Juba, the attention of Southern Sudanese was mainly focused on the swearing in of the new 1ˢᵗ Vice President of the republic, General Salva Kiir Mayardit, replacing the late chairman Dr. John Garang. I should mention here that Dr. John was sworn in on July 9, and died in the helicopter crash on July 30, 2005, traveling from Entebbe (Uganda) to New-Site in Southern Sudan. This was only 21 days after his assumption into office. In order for the SPLM to keep things rolling, the 1ˢᵗ Vice President General Salva Kiir Mayardit after assuming the office, began to fill the positions allocated by the CPA to the Southern Sudanese in the government of national unity. In the executive, ministers and deputy ministers were appointed. This also happened in the legislative assembly. Deputy speaker of the Sudan national legislative assembly, Ustaz Atem Garang Deng and members representing the SPLM were appointed.

This didn't bypass the administration of the Central Bank of Sudan, which also had a deputy from the SPLM, Honourable Elijah Malok Aleng. Since it was the text of the CPA agreement dictating the show, the SPLM received a larger share of the representation in the foreign service for the first time in the history of the Southern Sudanese people.

As this was happening in the Government of National Unity, the representation had to be replicated also in the interim government of Southern Sudan. The National Congress Party was to have a share in the interim government of the south. The southern loyalists who supported them during the war of liberation, were included in both the executive and legislature. Some ministers, whom I need not mention their names, were part of the executive. Meanwhile, the deputy speaker of the Southern Legislative Assembly was a man who deserted the SPLM/A in the 1990's. The text of the Comprehensive Peace Agreement was also inclusive of two other areas in the Northern Sudan. Members of those areas joined the SPLM/A and fought hard as full members of the movement to liberate themselves. These areas are Southern Kurdufan and Southern Blue Nile (Ingesstina Hills), plus the contested area of Abyei.

The head of the administration in the two areas was to be rotated between the SPLM and the National Congress Party, for a three year period. Should the SPLM start as the head of the government in Southern Kurdufan, then the leadership in Southern Blue Nile would be assumed by the National Congress Party, and after three years they would switch and change the leadership. In the case of Abyei, the leadership would solely remain in the hands of the Ngok Dinka people. The administration of the area would be chaired by the nomad Misseriya tribe, who hailed from Kurdufan State. It is worth mentioning that Nomad Misseriya originate from Northern Kurdufan, as mentioned earlier. Every year they come to the Abyei area in the dry season, in search of water and green pastures for their animals. In the end, they developed an interest in controlling the Abyei area and take the land from its owners.

The Abyei problem - in my opinion - is a social issue between the rivalling tribes of the Ngok Dinka and the nomadic Misseriya. This social issue could be addressed if the Khartoum government was fair and honest. However, political interests in the area have prevailed over the social matters and this is why Abyei is a contested area between the two tribes. Therefore the nomadic Misseriya are included in the CPA and take a share in the administration of Abyei. I will cite a Dinka proverb here which says, "Riel a wur yic". This means - might or strength, always overcomes the right. In other words, a stronger person can take and own the legal right of a weaker person, if he has the might. Abyei is a known Dinka land, but the nomads from Misseriya with the strong Khartoum government behind them, are doing all they can to forcefully seek ownership of the known Ngok Dinka land.

In the formation of the southern government, the 1st Vice President of the Republic was the head of the government, deputised by Dr. Riek Machar Teny. The president of the interim government would always shuttle between Juba and Khartoum to implement his assigned duties in both cities. In his absence, Dr. Riek would act as the head of the administration in the south. General James Wani Igga was the head (speaker) of the Southern Legislative Assembly. Meanwhile, Justice Ambrose Riiny Thiik became the head of judiciary.

As part of the executive, commissions were created to compliment the executive. The directorate of de-mining's authority, which I had been heading since 2004, was upgraded to the equivalent level of the commissions. A presidential decree was issued in June 2006, forming the de-mining authority (which was later corrected to read as the National Mine Action Authority). I was appointed Chairman of the authority with the status of the State Minister. I was deputised by Mrs.

Margaret Mathiang Deng and three members namely, Commander Makuei Philemon Majok Kuong, Mr. Egidio Taban Lupai and Mr. Luka Ngor Anau. Duties and functions of the authority were to clear landmines, cluster remnants, unexploded ordinances (UXOs) and other war remnants in every corner of South Sudan, so the land can be properly utilised by its inhabitants. Since the National Mine Action Authority did not implement mine clearance, it's role would be policy making, supervision, coordination and prioritisation of working NGOs in addition to commercial companies, in the areas to operate in. This would be in accordance with government preferences and choices.

After the establishment of National Mine Action Authority, we encountered challenges relating to the recruitment of qualified manpower to work in the authority, due to the following reasons:

1. Since de-mining is a technical field, it was not easy to find enough qualified manpower to implement mine clearance
2. It was time to establish the government system in the south. For that matter, the employers wanted the best people to successfully run their departments. The employees themselves had their preference of the best ministries and other government institutions to occupy the best future positions. Therefore it was not an attractive option to find employment with the unfavourable de-mining authority which potentially would not exist for long.
3. South Sudan was lacking the qualified manpower capable of running the system to the required standard, at that time. Given the length of the civil war, it had left behind so much debris, dangerous to the lives of people, animals and the environment.

Another challenge encountered was the training of the newly recruited staff. Although our staff were not implementers of mine clearance in the field, they needed the necessary knowledge to perform their duties at an acceptable level. Their mandate was to supervise, coordinate and monitor the implementers. As well as this, they were required to prioritise the areas to be cleared, which can't be successfully accomplished unless they are more knowledgeable than the workers. The UNDP mandated to support the National Mine Action Authority, by sending out staff to different training centres around the world. Some were trained at the James Madison University (JMU) in Virginia, United States of America (USA). Others were trained in Hashemite Kingdom of Jordan, Embakasi Military Training Centre in the Republic of Kenya and finally the People's Republic of China.

Equally, it was an obligatory right on the side of the United Nations Developmental Programme (UNDP) to supply the National Mine Action Authority with building supplies such as chairs, tables and other office equipment. Along with this, the provision of computers, printers and a photocopy machine were vital and most important was the usage of transport vehicles. As a government institution, it would not reflect well on us not to have any contribution towards its establishment. We therefore managed to acquire or complete other unprovided supplies e.g. fuel and maintenance of the vehicles when they were due for service. Without interruption, this process continued for six years until the UNDP unilaterally ceased the continuation of the support. The United Nation Mine Action Services (UNMAS) assumed this role, but could not fill the shoes of the UNDP. Support from UNMAS could not meaningfully match the provisions from UNDP.

Epilogue

Thank you for taking the time to read my story. I hope it provides some understanding and appreciation on my country's rich history.

I believe it's important to pass these stories down to future generations, who are living either at home or abroad. Listed below are some personal highlights from my career.

- I was honoured to serve as the Chairperson for the committee of refugees at the Pinyudo Refugee Camp. In 1990, I was promoted to the rank of Alternate Commander. Later I continued as a Chairman of the displaced camp in Pochalla.
- I led the SPLA forces to Kerkemoge, aiming to prevent advancing enemy forces heading towards Kapoeta Town in 1992, and later around Torit. At the beginning of 1993, I was appointed Chairman of the Ame Displaced Camp. I worked with Norwegian Peoples Aid as an Administrator in 1997. I was honoured by the SPLM leadership to represent the SPLM/A Movement in Egypt and the Middle East in 2000, after my job with the NPA came to an end.
- Given my diplomatic role in 2000, my name was placed on the army reserve list with the rank of Brigadier General.
- In August 2004, I was appointed Director of the South Sudan Mine Action Directorate in 2004 and my status was raised to the level of Chairman of the Commission.
- Since this has been written, I still hold this position and reside in South Sudan.
- Lastly, I hope this memoir serves to remember the many brave and innocent people who lost their lives during these years.

General Salva Kiir Mayardit

Francis Mading and Dr. Majak Agot Atem

Jurkuch Barach with his 2nd wife Nyibol Nathan Riak Anyuon

Dr. Garang Mabior Atem

Jurkuch with the family

Atem Deng Garang Kuek

Abuoi (Kuarang) Akoi Yaak

Jurkuch Barach with his first wife Achol Juach Diing

Jurkuch Barach's wedding anniversary with his wife Achol Juach Diing

Dr Yaak Jurkuch Barach

Jurkuch Barach Jurkuch in 1978

Dau Akoi Jurkuch

Jurkuch Barach Jurkuch

Jurkuch Barach Jurkuch

Index

Aamir 272
Aba 75
Ababa 19, 21, 26, 32-3, 76, 78, 95, 111-2, 115-6, 129, 143-5, 147-8, 151-2, 156, 169-170, 174, 177, 198, 251, 261, 297
Abasher 65
Abd 56, 58, 65, 74, 78, 221, 246, 249, 263, 267-8, 271
Abdon 264
Abel 3, 51, 297
Abit 141, 193, 217, 221, 249, 276, 278
Abobo 94-95, 157, 175-6
Abrham 3
Abui 217
Abuja 230
Abuk 217
Abul 239
Abuoi 3, 314
Abwong 10-11

Abyei 216, 271, 304-5
Achek 43
Achol 4, 90, 112, 139, 217, 250, 274
Acholi 242
Acholis 242
Achuei 217
Achuek 94, 279
Achuoth 108
Achuothdit 109
Acknowledgements 3
Acuoth 95, 217
Adam 246
Addis 19, 21, 26, 32-3, 76, 78, 95, 111-2, 115-6, 129, 143-5, 147-8, 151-2, 156, 169-170, 174, 177, 198, 251, 261, 297
Adeerdit 122-123
Adhor 123
Adit 217
Adohr 216

Adolf 60
Adong 9
Adura 17-20, 68-9, 72, 79-80
Adut 63-65, 121
Advocacy 282, 285
Afewerki 272
Africa 3, 22, 50, 54, 77, 109-110, 149, 239, 261, 266, 269, 276, 279, 291
African 11, 26, 40, 77, 95, 97, 102, 113, 167, 200, 203, 266, 272, 275, 278, 288
Africans 26, 203, 259, 267-8
Agada 118, 127, 192-3
Agareb 35
Agasio 126-127
Agaw 264
Agoot 3, 47, 151-2, 165, 175, 223, 236
Agot 310
Agoth 258
Agua 99
Aguer 12, 14, 216
Agwang 293
Ahmad 56, 58, 65, 75, 78, 245, 267-8, 271-2, 276-8, 302
Ahmer 166
Ahram 267
Ajack 244
Ajak 3, 8, 12, 14, 53, 90, 153, 170, 217, 245
Ajaman 278
Ajang 90, 95, 97, 105, 164, 172, 194, 211, 250
Ajawin 118, 133, 135, 170, 188, 194, 196, 204, 207, 248, 294, 299-300
Ajieth 99
Ajith 217
Ajuong 5, 9, 38, 89, 155
Akasha 263, 273-4
Akau 3
Akobo 16-17, 23, 53, 74, 131-5, 182, 191
Akoi 3, 7, 51, 90-1, 216, 243, 314
Akok 63-65, 121
Akol 38, 118, 126-7, 133-5, 146, 170, 174, 188, 194, 196, 198, 204-5, 207-210, 215, 244, 248-9, 294, 299-300
Akon 274
Akoon 193
Akot 135, 161, 299-300
Akou 88, 122-3, 126-7, 129, 192-3
Akuei 34, 192-3
Akuein 94, 217
Akuochpiir 127
Akuon 119, 131, 133
Akuot 24
Akur 94, 153

Alaak 90, 164, 172, 246
Alak 55, 91, 93
Alan 137-139, 141
Aleer 141, 221, 249-250, 276, 278
Alek 217
Aleng 246, 300, 304
Aleu 233, 280-1, 285-6
Ali 202, 258, 270-2
Aliei 239
Alier 51, 97, 114-6, 122, 124, 127, 129, 139, 141, 148, 160-2, 164, 172, 237, 297
Alith 246
Allah 221, 249
Almighty 61, 236, 275
Alony 44
Aloor 111
Alor 55, 95, 111-2, 145, 278
Alt 216
Aluel 99
Aluong 3, 148, 153, 179, 181, 210, 216, 237, 292-3
Alwi 241
Ambrose 305
Ame 205, 229-232, 234, 236-241, 244-7, 249, 255-6, 308
America 75, 107, 166, 262, 265, 269, 272, 276, 279, 290, 293, 307
American 93, 186, 266, 290
Americans 266-267

Amin 263, 273-4
Amir 278
Amira 90
Amisha 243
Ammunitions 128
Amsterdam 275, 290
Amum 165, 246
Anau 306
Andrew 247
Anei 90
Angola 95, 290
Angolan 95, 110
Anip 180
Ann 210
Ansar 75
Anthony 38, 143
Antonov 183-184
Anyang 144, 160, 216, 233
Anyanya 13-14, 18-21, 23, 301
Anyeth 124
Anyieth 220, 224
Anyuak 117-119, 128, 153-4, 185-8, 192-3
Anyuaks 128
Anyuat 43
Anyuon 4, 310
Aper 99, 102
Arab 26, 77, 173, 200, 202, 260-2, 267-8, 272-3, 275-8
Arabic 31, 63, 77, 259, 269

Arabicize 26
Arabis 267
Arabism 203
Arabization 76, 266
Arabs 9, 25-6, 77, 203, 205, 211, 266-7, 269
Ardeb 276-277
Arial 9
Arman 246
Arok 3, 22, 32, 38, 102-3, 122, 132, 134, 140, 210, 217, 299
Arop 145, 257
Arou 82
Aru 114, 245
Aruaal 217
Aruai 153, 237, 246
Asmaa 267
Asmara 264, 277
Asoud 115, 118-9, 127, 194
Assossa 148
Aswa 206, 234-5, 239-241, 244-6, 255-6
Ata 75
Ataba 259
Atabani 270
Atali 193
Atem 3, 7, 11, 24, 37, 47, 60, 86, 95, 97, 99, 102, 105, 113, 151, 160, 166, 172, 175, 177, 193, 211, 217, 223, 237, 246, 293, 300, 303,

310-1, 313
Atempi 206
Ateny 79
Atepi 234, 239, 241, 246
Ater 116, 144-5, 154, 216
Athor 211
Athorbei 258
Atlanta 266
Atlantic 275
Atta 263
Australia 166, 264-5
Authority 280, 286, 289, 306-7
Awad 65
Awal 114
Awan 38, 241
Awar 233
Aweer 175
Aweil 71
Awet 135, 161, 299-300
Awiir 10
Awiny 244, 247
Awuol 216
Ayany 280-281, 285
Ayen 90
Ayicho 137, 139
Ayichu 141
Ayiei 99
Ayiik 48
Ayiom 216
Ayod 7, 83, 194, 199

Ayom 160-162, 164, 217, 237
Ayuaal 5
Ayual 5
Ayuel 33, 130, 155, 170, 224, 228, 246, 250, 299
Ayuen 26, 32, 97, 115-6, 122, 124, 127, 129, 139, 141, 217
Ayur 217
Azandi 167
Azhari 75
Aziz 246
Baabanen 137
Babaanen 3
Babo 60
Baboor 250
Baguor 218
Bahr 31-32, 51, 71, 78, 173, 195, 208, 214, 235
Baidit 140-141
Bailiet 7-9, 12
Balaa 56-58, 65
Banna 51
Bany 17, 38, 78, 80, 82-4, 89, 112, 139-141, 143, 194, 210-1, 229-231, 233, 244, 246, 248, 298-9
Barach 64, 86, 158, 164, 172, 190, 237, 239, 246, 249-250, 259, 274, 310
Barchuch 137

Bari 93
Baro 18-19, 22, 30, 41-5, 60, 69, 72, 113-4, 157, 175, 177
Bashir 272, 302-3
Battalion 10, 26, 31-2, 41, 103
Battalions 72
Bentiu 162, 170
Bernard 186
Biar 37, 95, 97, 105, 113, 160, 211, 217, 228, 300
Biel 218
Biem 218
Biliu 60
Bilpam 12-15, 17-8, 23, 35-6, 40-1, 44-7, 55, 57, 59, 61-3, 67, 69, 79, 81, 83, 89, 113-4, 154, 160, 165
Biong 153
Bior 51, 90, 95, 115, 118-9, 127, 129-130, 160, 194, 211, 216, 229, 274
Biowei 91
Birr 91, 144, 172
Blue 201, 271, 304
Bol 17, 38, 40, 44-5, 48-9, 51-2, 58-9, 61-5, 68-9, 74, 78, 84, 140, 143, 146, 186, 210, 218, 231, 248, 299
Bolbek 38, 40
Bole 95, 111-2

Boma 35-36, 73-4, 79, 118, 131, 135, 191, 193-5, 219-220, 222-3, 235-6
Bonaparte 60
Bonga 22, 24-5, 27-32, 35-7, 40, 45, 55, 67, 79, 89, 91, 94-5, 99, 114-6, 119, 134, 151-5, 157, 165, 175
Bonio 221, 223, 236
Boo 235
Bor 6-7, 18, 23, 31, 49, 51-3, 74-5, 79, 82, 88, 118, 132, 140-1, 150, 162, 189-191, 194-5, 198-9, 205-6, 210-1, 218-9, 222-3, 234, 237-8, 295, 302
Boyoy 142
Brazil 107
British 77, 203, 210, 265
Brussels 275
Buffalo 53, 71
Bukteng 16, 81, 84-6, 89-90
Bul 7, 11, 90, 216-7, 246
Bullen 114, 148, 160
Buoi 217
Burbiege 17
Bussiya 250
Cairo 75, 258, 260, 263-4, 273-4, 276, 279
Canada 265, 280
Capabilities 52

Capital 211, 272
Capt 91, 93, 97, 119, 122-3, 216, 218, 247
Carpentry 284
Chaat 229, 274
Chagai 37, 113, 160, 300
Cham 118, 127, 193
Chan 216
Chang 218
Charles 218
Chath 99
Chatim 218
Cheng 3
Children 78, 162
Chiman 118, 147
China 307
Chinese 267
Chol 3, 23, 38, 41, 43-4, 49, 55, 59, 79, 84, 86-8, 90-1, 93-4, 99, 118, 129, 147, 151, 188, 196, 216-7, 237, 246, 299
Cholkeny 83
Choll 88
Cholo 128
Chot 114
Chotjak 11
Choy 256
Christian 203, 239, 242
Christians 26, 77, 268
Chuang 179

Chuei 11-13
Chukudum 221, 246-8, 255
Chung 3
Chuol 218
Chuong 153, 292-3, 296
Clement 129, 137, 144, 175
Col 299
Colin 271-272, 279
Companies 47
Congo 167
Cuba 94-97, 102-8, 110-1, 113, 115
Cuban 95-96, 98-100, 102, 104-7, 109-110
Cubans 99, 102, 107
Cush 293
Dahb 76
Dak 116, 144-5, 154
Damadollo 174
Dan 269
Daniel 38, 44, 135, 155, 161, 216-8, 258, 272, 299-300
Danish 287
Dar 266
Darfur 201
Dau 3, 9-10, 51, 90, 124, 141, 217, 221, 249-250, 276, 278, 292
David 86
Dawnhier 3
Debriziet 145

Degay 218
Dem 235
Demining 287
Democracy 197
Deng 3, 9, 37-40, 44, 55, 79, 86, 89-91, 93-5, 99, 102, 108, 111-3, 122-3, 129, 139-141, 145, 148, 153-5, 158-9, 162-3, 165, 170, 172-5, 177, 193-4, 211, 216-8, 233-4, 236-7, 243-5, 258, 278-9, 285, 292-3, 303, 306, 313
Dengjok 17
Dengtiel 26
Dengtil 32
Deu 190, 239
Dhab 74, 263
Dhaeen 78
Dhal 216
Dhieu 11-12, 18, 224, 228, 233
Dhongjol 79
Diing 122, 139, 177, 230, 246, 250, 274, 299
Dima 148, 165, 172, 178
Din 270
Dinka 10, 31, 63, 78-9, 82, 88, 105, 118, 128, 132, 188, 205-6, 210, 237, 239, 304-5
Diu 28, 79, 218
Doleb 224-225
Dot 180

Downhier 217
Drs 213
Dualdahab 15-16
Dubai 277-279
Duk 210
Dul 218
Duot 3, 60, 90, 95, 115, 129, 194, 211, 216-7, 239-240
Dut 39, 94, 211
Dutch 275
Early 57
East 5, 95, 174, 210, 257, 276, 308
Eastern 31-32, 190, 195, 201, 205, 231-2, 234-5, 247
Egidio 306
Egypt 5, 75, 148-9, 174, 257-261, 263-5, 267-9, 273-6, 279, 281, 308
Egyptian 26, 77, 258-261, 265, 267-8, 275
Egyptians 260, 269
El Mahdi 78
Eldoret 253, 255, 257, 274-5
Elijah 160-162, 172, 228, 237, 246, 300, 304
Embakasi 307
Embassy 275
Emphatically 143
English 31, 44, 66, 100, 107, 273
Entebbe 292, 295-7, 303
Equally 74, 140, 241, 307

Equatoria 31-32, 71, 74, 116, 150, 159, 166, 168-170, 190, 195, 205, 208, 219, 231-2, 234-5, 247, 289
Equatorial 32, 171, 195, 214, 229, 235, 243-4
Equatorians 31-32, 128
Ereer 137
Eretria 266, 272
Erjok 129
Europe 166, 229, 265, 279
European 239, 275-6
Farouk 263-264, 273-4
Fiil 37
Flus 133
Foxholes 81
France 276
Francis 68, 72, 310
French 186
Fur 258
Gabriel 94, 99, 108-9, 161, 172, 181, 210, 216, 246, 301
Gadhafi 262-263
Gaffer 58
Gahuth 72-73
Gai 20-21, 24, 33, 146, 153-4, 161, 165, 172, 174-5, 218
Gajaak 46, 62
Gajak 35
Gak 7, 48, 216
Gakyuom 10

Gallerio 230, 299
Gambella 46, 90-1, 94, 112, 114, 117, 141-2, 144-5, 157, 159, 168-9, 171-2, 174-6, 188, 251
Garang 3, 6, 22, 24-5, 29-30, 35, 38, 40, 44, 48, 50, 63-5, 67-8, 76, 78, 85-6, 90-1, 94-5, 102, 108-9, 113, 115-8, 121-2, 126-130, 139-142, 145, 147, 149-150, 153, 156, 158-9, 163, 166-8, 173, 177, 181, 188, 192-3, 196, 198-200, 202-8, 211-5, 217, 225, 230, 233, 246-8, 252, 259, 262-3, 270-1, 273, 276-8, 285, 291-9, 302-3, 311, 313
Garjiek 23
Gatchai 218
Gatjang 218
Gatlok 44
Gatluak 218
Gatluk 89
Gatwech 218
Gatyur 218
Gayin 120, 127, 129, 137
Gazal 31-32, 71, 78, 173, 195, 208, 214, 235
Gazi 270
Geizan 170
Geneva 290
George 211, 269, 271

Georgia 266
Geu 129, 250
Gezera 75
Gezouly 76
Gieng 218
Gienya 301
Gier 3, 153, 179, 292-3, 296
Gieth 3
Gilo 116-117, 127, 178-181, 192-3
Gismallah 21
God 41, 61, 140, 157, 160, 180, 236, 250, 267, 275, 301
Gofa 170
Gola 142
Goodness 180
Gordon 23, 84, 86-7, 188, 196, 299
Gorkur 181, 186-8
Governance 271
Gulf 173, 278
Gulu 239-241, 249
Gumuruk 129, 136, 141
Guny 60
Guot 217
Guryay 137
Hadeed 60, 68
Hadi 75
Hague 275
Hailemariam 23, 149, 156, 174, 176, 199, 215
Hakim 210, 216

Haleem 267-268
Happenings 183
Hashemite 307
Hashim 75, 263
Hassan 74-75, 263, 302
Hassen 272
Havana 96-97, 106, 110
Health 280
Heathrow 290
Hilda 272
Hilton 277
Hilu 246
Hippo 55-57, 69, 72, 82
Hippopotamus 54
Hitler 60
Holland 276
Homishkureb 201
Hon 272
Hosseini 262
Hoth 3, 102, 235
Huronyang 299
Hussein 9, 75
Husseini 267
Hussini 75
Ibrahim 276-277
Igga 118, 135, 220, 224, 230, 248, 299-300, 305
Ikotos 150
Illababur 175-176
Illubabor 19
Imatong 243
Indigenous 281
Ingasna 264
Ingelizy 224
Ingesstina 302
Inglezi 228
Instantly 123
Iputu 228-229, 231-4
Iron 35, 68-9, 72
Isaac 44, 89-90, 227-8, 231
Isaiah 237, 246, 272
Islam 269
Islamicisation 76
Islamicize 26
Islamification 266
Islamist 290
Ismael 75
Ismail 120, 131, 136, 140-3, 259
Isoke 150
Israel 268
Issa 263-264, 273-4
Italy 276
Itang 17-24, 29, 33-4, 46, 55, 72-3, 89-91, 111-4, 139, 141-5, 148, 152-4, 156, 163, 165, 171-6, 178
Itupu 229
Jaafar 263
Jaafer 5, 32-3
Jaffar 262, 264, 272
Jaffer 74-75, 199

Jahilliya 77
Jalhak 170
James 3, 9, 102, 118, 135, 216-7, 220-1, 224, 230, 235, 248, 290, 299-300, 305, 307
Jamus 10-12, 16-7, 23, 45, 55
Jashua 137
Jebel 51
Jededah 258
Jeeps 72
Jekow 218
Jeroboam 3, 216, 296-7
Jerusalem 55
Jesh 166
Jewish 268
Jiel 218
Jikeny 218
Jiol 52
Job 255
John 6, 22, 24-5, 29-30, 32, 35, 38-40, 43-4, 50-1, 67-8, 76, 78, 83, 85-6, 91, 94-5, 102-3, 108-9, 113-9, 121-2, 126-130, 135, 140, 142, 145, 149-153, 156, 158-9, 161-2, 166-170, 173-4, 181, 188, 192, 196, 198-208, 211-6, 218, 225, 230, 247-8, 252, 259, 262-3, 269-271, 273, 276-8, 285, 291-300, 302-3
Johns 276
Johnson 60, 272
Jok 99, 124, 217-8, 234, 246, 264
Jokau 18
Jokou 42-49, 52-9, 61, 65-74, 78, 90, 175, 177
Jong 218
Jongkuch 160
Jonglei 17, 32, 150, 189-190, 302
Jongroor 97, 122
Jongulei 5, 7
Jook 216
Jordan 307
Joseph 21, 33, 119-120, 131, 133, 193, 210-1
Journeying 106
Juach 4, 27, 79, 112, 139, 175, 217, 250, 274
Jual 218
Juba 7, 31, 33, 49, 51-2, 116, 143, 150, 191, 211, 223-4, 228-9, 233, 239, 244-5, 263, 286, 288-9, 302-3, 305
Jumaa 60
Jurkuch 3, 5, 7, 51, 64, 158, 163, 172, 190, 239, 243, 249-250, 259, 274, 310
Juuk 26, 32, 41, 49, 59, 61, 67, 150, 161, 189, 210-1, 224, 230, 236, 279, 299-300
Kabashi 167

Kabula 137
Kachlech 18
Kaguta 272, 295, 297, 302
Kaibui 134
Kailech 218
Kaka 60
Kakuma 160, 249-251, 253-5, 257, 274-5
Kalashnikov 62
Kampala 250, 296
Kang 210-211
Kapoeta 74, 103, 109, 132, 189-191, 193-5, 219-224, 236, 249, 288, 308
Kassella 202
Kathekiah 99
Katinya 129, 144, 175
Katiri 150
Kauda 302
Kaya 288
Kenedy 127, 129
Keneti 227
Kengen 219
Kennedy 120, 137
Kenya 157, 160, 166, 182, 185, 199, 221, 249-255, 258, 260, 266-7, 269, 271, 273, 275, 278-9, 286, 307
Kenyan 181, 223, 250, 252-4, 269, 272, 279, 286-7

Kenyans 157
Kenyi 153
Kerbino 17, 35, 38, 40, 44-5, 47-55, 57, 59-65, 68-9, 72, 74, 78, 140, 210, 248, 299
Kerewa 137
Kerjok 79
Kerkemoge 308
Kerkomoge 220
Ketinya 137
Khalid 77
Khamis 52
Khartoum 17, 24, 26, 58, 65, 70, 74-8, 84, 86-7, 136, 150, 191, 194-5, 201-3, 205-9, 212, 214, 219, 236, 244, 262-6, 270-2, 277, 295-6, 301, 305
Khawaja 239
Khor 133, 146, 224-5, 228
Khormashi 221
Khot 217
Kibaki 254, 272, 286
Kiir 22, 29, 32, 38, 44, 47-8, 67, 94, 124, 132, 134-5, 140-2, 144, 174, 176, 179-180, 184, 193-4, 219, 222, 230, 232-3, 236, 247-8, 270, 276-7, 294, 298-301, 303, 309
Kilio 228, 234-5
Kimatong 221
Kir 17, 53

Kisumu 250
Kit 245
Kitchener 137
Kitgum 241
Kiyalla 150
Knowledge 52
Koach 3, 9-10, 246
Koang 3, 39, 83, 217-8
Koat 218
Kok 153
Kon 51, 90, 129-130, 224
Konange 279
Kong 23, 84, 86-7, 121, 124, 188, 196, 231, 299
Kongor 5
Konyi 120, 131, 136-7, 140-3
Korkomege 236
Koryom 27
Kowa 33-34, 94, 118, 135, 230, 246
Kuach 81, 211
Kuai 51, 297
Kuany 216, 218
Kuanyin 17, 35, 38, 40, 44-5, 47-9, 51-2, 54, 57-65, 68-9, 74, 78, 140, 210, 248, 299
Kuanylou 16, 81, 144
Kuch 146
Kuek 3, 177, 193, 313
Kuer 216-217

Kueth 216
Kuir 247
Kuju 137-139, 141
Kulang 3, 135, 216, 218, 296, 299
Kunthuol 81
Kuochrot 233
Kuol 3, 26, 32, 37-9, 41, 49, 55, 59, 61-2, 64, 67, 95, 111-2, 145, 148, 150, 153-4, 158-9, 161, 177, 189, 210-1, 216, 218, 224, 228, 230, 233, 235-7, 247, 278-9, 299-300
Kuong 306
Kuoreng 7, 11, 90-1, 216
Kuot 218
Kur 26, 32, 41, 44, 49, 59, 160
Kurdufan 201, 302, 304
Kurenge 15
Kurmuk 170, 302
Kurumuk 170
Kushner 186
Kut 51, 297
Kwoa 299
Kwong 116, 154, 217
Labone 241-243, 255, 257
Lado 27
Lagu 21
Lam 83, 118, 133-5, 170, 174, 188, 194, 196, 198, 204-5, 207-212, 215, 218, 244, 248-9, 294, 299-300

Landcruiser 276
Landmines 287
Langabu 228-229
Lapon 231, 235
Lashor 239, 241
Lashore 240
Lastly 308
Latuka 228
Lavington 280, 287
Lawanda 95
Laying 284, 302
Lazaro 269-270
Lazim 133
Leek 123, 243
Lem 216
Leralera 227
Liberation 6-7, 25, 197-8, 271, 280, 286, 295, 302
Libya 199, 262
Libyan 75
Lietenant 87
Lifeline 255
Likuangle 138-139
Likuanglei 129-133, 135-141, 143, 147
Lion 35, 37, 44-5, 55, 57, 66, 69, 72, 82
Liriya 228
Lith 218
Lobonok 244-245

Lodwar 250-251, 253, 275
Loggichogio 181-182, 185, 190, 251, 253
Loki 137, 185, 189, 253
Lokurnyang 27, 129
Lol 71
London 130, 290
Longyiero 228
Lony 218
Lootah 277-279
Loronyo 235
Lorries 18, 20
Lou 20
Louis 217
Lts 79
Luach 11
Lual 3, 38, 94, 124, 137, 141, 177, 206, 230, 237, 279, 299
Luanda 95, 110-1
Luckily 12, 40, 111
Lueth 114, 177, 193, 217
Luka 38, 153, 306
Lul 87-88
Lupai 306
Maadi 273
Maban 170
Mabil 224, 293
Mabior 6, 22, 24, 29, 38, 40, 44, 50, 67-8, 76, 78, 86, 91, 102, 108-9, 126-7, 140, 142, 149-150, 153,

156, 166, 168, 175, 188, 192, 196, 199, 204-6, 208, 213-6, 225, 230, 247, 252, 262, 270, 273, 276-7, 285, 291-9, 302-3, 311
Mabor 42, 175, 232
Mach 148, 216, 233
Machakos 267-270
Machar 38, 78, 83, 89, 112, 135, 143, 160-1, 170, 174, 179, 188-9, 194, 196, 198, 203-210, 212, 215, 229-230, 244, 246, 248-9, 289, 294, 298-300, 305
Machec 68, 72
Machuor 3, 216, 296
Maciek 127
Macon 210
Madhier 218
Madibo 218
Mading 233, 310
Madison 290, 307
Maduk 3, 9
Madut 38, 40, 143, 160, 179
Magerus 58
Maghot 234
Magong 216
Maguet 216
Magwei 150
Magwi 229-236, 244-5
Mahdi 75, 78, 263
Mahjoub 75
Mai 3, 102, 235
Majak 3, 18, 47, 151-2, 154-5, 157, 165, 175, 180, 217, 223, 236, 310
Majier 33
Majok 79, 148, 217-8, 220, 306
Majuch 113
Majur 121
Maki 33-34, 94, 118, 135, 230, 246
Makol 37-40, 99
Makuach 18, 20, 23, 35, 37-8, 40-1, 99, 122-3
Makuei 113-114, 177, 193, 216, 306
Malak 174
Malakal 5, 7-9, 12-3, 17-8, 23, 31, 53, 69, 121, 125-6, 134, 140, 170, 194, 301
Maley 218
Malith 90
Malok 246, 300, 304
Malong 38, 124, 129
Malony 3, 88, 122-3, 126-7, 129, 192-3
Malou 12, 14, 146, 216, 236-7
Malual 43, 72-3, 90, 123
Malut 170
Mama 112
Mamur 227-229, 231
Manasseh 174
Mangistu 156, 174-6

Mangoak 53, 57, 59-61, 63-4, 69, 72
Mangok 18, 23, 41-2, 67, 69, 79, 90, 154
Mano 137
Manpower 201
Mansur 77
Manut 186
Manyang 26, 28, 32, 41, 49, 59, 61, 67, 79, 150, 161, 189, 210-1, 217, 224, 230, 236, 279, 299-300
Manyangdit 173-174
Manyiel 130, 155, 170, 216, 299
Manyirany 123-125
Manyok 3, 86, 216
Manyuon 144, 216
Margani 78
Margaret 306
Marial 19-20, 44-5, 47, 55, 60-1, 65, 67, 180
Maridi 166-167
Mario 238, 246
Marol 90
Marshall 3, 137, 139
Maspin 34
Matatu 274
Mathiang 181, 306
Matil 218
Mawar 218
Mawut 43
Mayak 257
Mayar 83
Mayardit 22, 29, 38, 44, 48, 67, 132, 140, 142, 174, 176, 180, 193-4, 230, 232-3, 236, 247-8, 270, 276, 294, 298-300, 303, 309
Maybe 103
Mayen 24, 79, 166, 193, 233, 237, 239-240, 246, 300
Mayiik 83
Mayuen 39
Mbarara 296
Mecheak 164, 172
Meki 299
Mengistu 23, 149, 199, 215
Mengistus 205
Metaphorically 3
Mete 228-229
Metu 174
Michael 37-38, 40, 114, 144, 177, 193, 216, 246
Mickael 38
Military 28-29, 42, 44, 52, 91-2, 102-3, 109, 111-2, 122, 130, 151, 165, 174, 176-7, 189, 196, 307
Minefields 288
Mirgani 263
Misseriya 304-305
Moammar 262
Mobil 302

Modi 230, 299
Mohamad 78, 199, 202, 262-3, 270, 272, 276-7
Mohamed 5, 8, 26, 32-3, 53, 58, 74-5, 77-8, 272
Mohamoud 245
Mohidin 5
Moi 272
Molana 78
Moli 256
Molugeta 146
Monyaak 145
Monytoach 145, 257
Morwel 38
Mothan 137
Mou 174
Moulana 263
Mubarak 75, 262
Mudathir 77
Mugali 241, 257
Mugeri 235
Mulla 129
Mum 240
Muor 238, 246
Murle 118, 120, 126, 128-9, 131, 136-140, 142-3, 185, 193
Murleland 140
Musa 272
Museveni 272, 295-7, 302
Muslim 265, 267

Muslims 77, 200, 267-8
Mwai 254, 272, 286
Nadipal 287
Nai 3, 79, 88, 122-3, 126-7, 129, 192
Nairobi 221, 249-250, 253-4, 256-7, 266, 270-2, 275-280, 286-8, 291
Naivasha 270-271, 276, 279, 286
Nakdiar 8, 10, 53
Nakuru 253
Nanam 133-134, 141-2
Napoleon 60
Narus 189, 195-6, 219, 221, 223, 236, 287
Nasir 8, 11, 15, 47, 55, 66, 85-7, 188, 194-7, 203-4, 206-216, 231, 233-4, 243-4, 246
Nathan 4, 172, 310
Negotiators 270
Nemeiri 75
Netherlands 275
Ngachigak 136
Ngachilok 73, 103, 109
Ngacilok 104, 132, 135-6, 299
Nganthow 137
Ngare 137
Ngatinga 293, 296
Ngiwei 90
Ngok 9, 82, 206, 304-5

Ngor 68, 72, 90, 166, 237, 306
Ngot 258
Nhial 264, 285
Nile 5, 7, 31-2, 43-4, 53, 70-1, 74, 78, 133, 135, 150-1, 155, 162, 170, 194-5, 201, 206, 208, 214, 235, 261, 267-9, 271, 304
Nilotic 80
Nimeiri 5, 26, 32-3, 75-6, 78-9, 199, 262-4, 272
Nimeiry 25, 58
Nimule 150-151, 241, 244-5, 255-7
Nonetheless 35, 115, 141
Northwest 251
Norwegian 229, 231, 239, 242, 255, 287, 308
Nowehi 26
Nuba 33-34, 180, 201, 258, 264, 271, 302
Nuer 20, 35, 45-6, 63, 66, 68-9, 72, 78-80, 83, 128, 188-190, 205, 208, 217, 237, 249
Nuers 62
Nul 51, 229, 274
Nur 271
Nuwayhi 77
Nyaang 44-46, 69
Nyachigak 73, 103-4, 109, 136, 299

Nyacigak 132, 135
Nyalma 144
Nyandeeng 109
Nyandeng 217, 294
Nyandieng 13-14, 18-9, 84
Nyang 246
Nyankiir 249-250, 274-5
Nyarkueth 15
Nyayo 272, 279
Nyibol 4, 310
Nyibuyi 144
Nyilma 129, 175
Nyok 217
Nyoplew 44-45, 47, 57, 60, 66-7
Nyuak 5
Nyuol 186
Nyuon 17, 35, 38-9, 78, 80-5, 89, 112, 140, 143, 194, 210, 217, 229-236, 244, 246, 248, 298-9
Nyuons 231
Obbo 244-245
Obote 227, 231
Oboth 121, 193
Odol 193
Oduho 33, 210-1
Ogel 244-245
Ohere 231
Ohyee 57
Okello 119-121, 193
Okeruk 231

Okich 165, 246
Omar 258, 302-3
Omega 292
Omer 272
Othman 78, 221, 249, 263, 270-2
Othoman 258
Ottawa 280, 284
Owinykibul 241, 244-5
Oyay 153, 170, 244-5
Pacts 275
Padaang 9, 14, 82
Padunyiel 181
Pagak 170
Pageri 229-231, 234, 246-7, 256, 298
Pajwok 150, 241, 244-5
Pakur 218
Palotaka 244-245
Panahoth 120-126
Panchol 114, 159
Pangak 83
Panhom 32, 216
Panwiir 5
Panyagor 210-211
Panyikwara 232
Panyuan 218
Patience 161
Paul 38, 51, 216, 229, 233, 274, 279
Paulino 89

Pawel 7
Payam 5
Peringa 221
Peter 3, 32, 127, 216, 218, 231
Philemon 306
Pibor 35, 49, 51, 74, 116-136, 138-144, 161, 191, 193-5, 199, 219, 222-3
Pieng 3, 39, 154, 158-164, 173, 233-4
Pierre 231
Pigi 206
Pinar 97, 104, 106, 108-9
Pinyudo 116-117, 144, 148, 152-4, 157-166, 168-9, 171-9, 182, 192, 236, 308
Pitia 127
Pochalla 49, 51, 74, 117-9, 174, 176-9, 181-196, 199, 223, 236, 308
Pogei 244-245
Poktap 7
Polataka 231, 241
Politico 102, 174, 176, 196
Pout 99
Pow 43
Powell 271-272, 279
Presidency 204
Puor 216
Puot 135, 218, 299

Qadeemtariq 289
Qoran 32
Rabb 242
Racal 70
Rahaman 74, 78
Rahman 58, 263
Rashid 258
Reath 218
Rebecca 109, 292-4, 302
Reech 3, 216
Rehabilitation 189, 229, 283
Rehman 65
Rejaf 244
Remsis 259
Reng 234
Renk 170
Resas 21
Resistant 243
Riak 3-4, 99, 161, 172, 216-7, 274, 296-7, 310
Richard 129
Riek 135, 153, 161, 170, 174, 188-9, 194, 196, 198, 203-212, 215, 218, 244, 247-9, 289, 294, 299-300, 305
Riiny 38, 258, 305
Rin 42, 172, 175-6, 232
Rio 97, 104, 106, 108-9
Rohaman 56
Ruei 99

Rumbek 270, 291, 293, 302
Ruon 218
Ruot 218
Russian 95
Russians 267
Rwehito 220
Sabir 5
Sadeeg 51, 78
Sadig 78
Sadiq 263
Saeed 246
Salah 270
Salva 22, 29, 32, 38, 44, 47-8, 67, 94, 132-5, 140-2, 144, 174, 176, 179-181, 184, 193-4, 219, 222, 230, 232-3, 236, 247-8, 270, 276-7, 294, 298-301, 303, 309
Samaritan 52, 88, 277-8
Sambeyweo 269-270
Samuel 20, 24, 116, 144-5, 148, 154, 167
San 96, 107, 110
Sargeant 63
Sebit 258
Secrecy 25
Secretariat 246
Sergeant 26, 48, 63-5, 243
Sharif 245
Sheikh 270-272
Shiluk 128, 249

Sitona 221, 249
Siwar 74, 76
Sobat 9-10, 15, 85
Somalia 272
Southerners 34, 198-9, 203-4
Soviet 104-105, 146
Spanish 99-100, 107
Stephen 3, 137, 139
Sudan 5-7, 13, 16, 18-20, 23-6, 29, 33-5, 50-1, 53, 55, 57, 66, 68-9, 74-7, 81, 84, 103, 109, 117, 120, 132, 140, 148-9, 167, 169-171, 177-8, 182-3, 185, 189, 192, 196-202, 204-6, 208-9, 211-4, 217, 229, 241-3, 247, 255-8, 260-272, 274, 276-281, 286-7, 291, 295, 297, 300, 302-4, 306, 308
Sudanese 6, 8, 15-6, 19, 21, 23, 25-6, 30, 34, 36, 39, 41, 44, 49-54, 56-8, 69, 75, 77, 85-7, 93, 103-4, 116, 121, 126, 142, 146-8, 153, 155-6, 161, 167, 171, 175, 177, 181, 183, 186-8, 190-3, 195, 198, 200-5, 209, 211, 225, 230, 234, 236, 241, 244, 251-9, 261-9, 271-280, 293-4, 297, 301-4
Sunday 192, 292
Swar 263
Taban 154, 165, 172, 174-5, 306
Taha 270, 272

Talanga 150
Tambura 166-167
Tang 301
Tangon 258
Tanzania 266, 295
Taposa 195, 221
Tata 111-112
Tea 111
Temesgen 255
Teny 135, 161, 170, 188, 196, 203-5, 208, 210, 248, 289, 294, 299-300, 305
Thach 218
Thanypieny 216
Thenypieny 32
Thiajak 23, 73-4, 78-9, 81
Thiik 305
Thirdly 13, 54, 222
Thon 22, 32, 38, 102-3, 132, 134, 140, 210, 218, 299
Thony 218
Thoura 5
Thuch 9
Tigrinya 199
Timothy 151
Titbaay 173-174
Toang 218
Tolor 15
Tomorrow 13
Topography 100

Torit 150, 189-191, 195, 206-7, 209, 216, 221, 223-9, 231, 234-6, 239, 288, 308
Tot 151
Toyota 42-43, 91, 276, 286
Tripoli 262
Troika 272
Tuach 218
Tueny 172
Tukul 112
Tuorkuny 218
Tut 20-21, 24
Tweny 42, 175, 232
Twic 5, 210
Twin 266
Uganda 150, 199, 238, 240-2, 247, 250, 255, 266, 272, 295-7
Ugandan 237, 241, 247, 287, 292, 295, 302
Ugandans 241
Unaccompanied 181
Undecided 231
Unionist 78, 263
Unity 247, 303-4
Ural 18, 20, 113-4, 116
Ushamlom 178
Ustaz 5, 163-4, 166, 273-4, 303
Vastness 143
Verde 110
Vert 95
Vice 51, 270, 289, 295, 297, 301, 303, 305
Virginia 290-291, 307
Waat 125-126, 133-4, 140, 150, 210
Wahid 271
Wal 177, 230, 299
Wang 218
Wangkulei 12, 51, 302
Wani 118, 135, 220-1, 224, 230, 248, 299-300, 305
Wanji 93
Warabek 228, 250
Warbek 224
Warsaw 275
Washington 290-291
Wathkei 7
Wau 195, 235
Weaponry 100
Wei 23
West 172
Wethour 218
Whilst 28-29, 43, 87, 89, 97, 169, 241, 257, 260, 275
Wieu 38
William 17, 35, 38, 78, 80-5, 89, 112, 129-130, 139-141, 143, 160, 194, 210-1, 229-236, 244, 246, 248, 298-9
Wilson 41, 44, 49, 59, 233

Wives 11
Women 16, 163
Wunthou 11
Wuor 216
Wuornyang 230
Wutlang 15
Yaak 3, 5, 7, 90, 112, 216, 250, 314
Yaat 218
Yak 206, 218
Yakatit 145, 147-9, 152
Yambio 166-167
Yang 218
Yasir 246
Yayi 144
Yei 167-168, 255, 288, 291-3, 302
Yen 99
Yoel 217
Yoweri 272, 295-7, 302
Yuot 218
Yusif 94, 135, 299
Yusuf 33-34, 118, 230, 246
Zachariah 3, 60
Zagazig 5
Zaire 199
Zalzal 122
Zenawi 272
Zendia 31-32, 71
Zinc 94, 113, 115, 142, 169
Zu 122, 125-6